©orporate cultures and global b®ands

2nd Edition

2nd Edition

MARS · COCA-COLA · KIKKOMAN · McDONALD'S · IKEA · BENETTON · BMW · NIKE · STELLANTIS
LINDT · NOKIA · SONY · VIRGIN · TOYOTA · FIAT · DAIMLER · CHRYSLER · ROVER · LEGO · DISNEY

edited by
Albrecht Rothacher

NEW JERSEY · LONDON · SINGAPORE · BEIJING · SHANGHAI · TAIPEI · CHENNAI

Published by

World Scientific Publishing Europe Ltd.
57 Shelton Street, Covent Garden, London WC2H 9HE
Head office: 5 Toh Tuck Link, Singapore 596224
USA office: 27 Warren Street, Suite 401-402, Hackensack, NJ 07601

Library of Congress Cataloging-in-Publication Data
Names: Rothacher, Albrecht editor.
Title: Corporate cultures and global brands / edited by Albrecht Rothacher.
Description: 2nd edition. | New Jersey : World Scientific, [2025] |
Includes bibliographical references.
Identifiers: LCCN 2024053267 | ISBN 9781800617117 hardcover |
ISBN 9781800616998 paperback | ISBN 9781800617001 ebook |
ISBN 9781800617018 ebook other
Subjects: LCSH: Brand name products--Management--Congresses | Branding (Marketing)--
Congresses | Corporate culture--Congresses | Corporate image--Congresses |
Competition, International--Congresses
Classification: LCC HD69.B7 C63 2025 | DDC 658.8/27--dc23/eng/20250521
LC record available at https://lccn.loc.gov/2024053267

British Library Cataloguing-in-Publication Data
A catalogue record for this book is available from the British Library.

For any available supplementary material, please visit
https://www.worldscientific.com/worldscibooks/10.1142/Q0501#t=suppl

Desk Editors: Murali Appadurai/Gabriel Rawlinson

Typeset by Stallion Press
Email: enquiries@stallionpress.com

Contents

Acknowledgements

The rise and fall of corporate empires, national companies going global, changing their governance in the process and creating products which purposefully elicit emotional consumer reactions as brands — all this is fascinating stuff not only for successful practitioners but also for readers and researchers alike. All participants of the seminar on "Comparative Business Cultures" held at the Economics Department of the National University of Singapore during 2003 shared this spirit of intellectual excitement and discovery of the most diverse corporate and marketing worlds, which are captured in the contributions of this volume. Hence, I am most obliged to my young researcher colleagues for their interesting and lively chapters. My thanks go to Asmizar bin Abu (McDonald's), Chia Peng Theng (Nokia), Melissa Chin (Disney), Chua Sin Lay (Mars), Annalisa Dass (Nike), Pauline Javani (Zubrowka Bison Vodka), Cheryl Lim (Benetton), Lim Jia Woon (Toyota), Lim Teck Nam (Virgin), Ong Wei Ling (IKEA) and Michelle Phua Yifei (Coca-Cola).

As the author of the remaining chapters, I am also deeply grateful to Jenny Tan and Zareen Tia of the Asia Europe Foundation (ASEF) for their meticulous secretarial skills when putting my scribbles into a decent typewritten draft. Last but not least, my thanks go to my long-suffering family for enduring yet another book project.

Preface to the 2nd, Updated Edition

I am very grateful to the publisher's wise suggestion to produce a second updated version of this volume of 18 corporate histories and case studies of successful global brand development. Twenty years is a long time not only in our personal lives but also in the lives of corporations, which are also unfortunately mortal and must survive in the rough and unforgiving marketplace of world competition. Strategic mistakes can quickly turn out deadly, and nobody is too big to fail. Even in successful companies, two decades usually mean at least two generations of managers at the top. And in less successful ones, they change at the frequency of soccer coaches. Yet, in quite a few of our corporations, the founder's family still retains some managerial influence, usually for the better.

When published in Singapore in 2003, the book generated a lot of reader interest — and I proudly remember a pile of copies for sale at the bookstore of Changi Airport, with a reprint in 2005. There was a legitimate translation by Longstone Publishing in Taipei as *Pinpai beihou de gushi: pinpai jingying celüe yu qiye wenhua* in 2006, which was subsequently pirated by Guanxi Normal

University Press. As the saying goes, imitation is the sincerest form of flattery (Oscar Wilde).

The book at the time resulted from a collection of research papers of highly talented graduate students, plus a few papers of my own, at a seminar on Intercultural Management at the National University of Singapore. In the meantime, my then "young researchers" as befits well-trained NUS graduates have turned into well-established mid- to senior-level professionals and executives.

As an editor, I have taken the liberty to update their contributions gently without changing the gist of their well-presented narratives and conclusions, which have withstood well the test of time. To each of the 18 corporate chapters, I have added a final subchapter on subsequent developments, for the contents and shortcomings of which I remain solely responsible.

Management decisions, as the reader will quickly note, are also affected by fashions: sometimes mega-mergers and acquisitions to achieve price leadership are the craze of the season; sometimes wide diversifications to spread risks and probe for breakthroughs; and as a reaction when many such dreams and ambitions fail (as they usually do), the decision by a new management to cut losses, disinvestment or focus on core businesses. It appears from our volume that global food and drink producers (like Mars, Lindt, Kikkoman, Coke and McDonald's), a sports supplier like Nike, a furniture dealer like IKEA and a conservative car maker like Toyota are less affected by these cycles than high-tech firms like Sony or Nokia, for whom unforeseen sudden innovations appeared as life-threatening, fearing the fate of dinosaurs within the span of a few years. Companies like Lego and Disney, after straying away from their original fold to cut losses have returned profitably to their old core competence. The same of course can be said about the two failed short-lived mega mergers covered here: DaimlerChrysler and BMW-Rover. While Rover has disappeared, Chrysler has been submerged in yet another, this time tripartite, adventure with Peugeot and Fiat, called

Stellantis, on which the jury is still out. Daimler and BMW have both rediscovered premium cars as their very core, whose brand value must not be damaged by haphazard acquisitions. Sir Richard Branson's adventurous management of Virgin obviously follows an opposite path: apart from his airline and space business, to enter into as many new business lines as possible as joint ventures in order to explore unexpected opportunities — which however usually fail as lessons with little learning effect.

Basically, it appears that companies in which the founder family still has a managerial or shareholding influence (like Mars, Toyota, Kikkoman, IKEA, Lego and Nike) by and large have followed a steadier course of internal growth compared to those run by professional managers dependent on quarterly returns for their bonuses and reappointment. Sometimes, however, these families — third generations typically — like in case of Benetton and the Agnellis (Fiat), appear to divest from their companies and rather put their wealth into diversified family holdings, thus ending an industrial era. Not all of our corporate histories are shining success stories. In the case of Seibu-Saison, for instance, both companies of the two hostile brothers, which did not survive the end of Japan's boom years, have disappeared. Yet, it is reassuring that a company like the Polish Zubrowka has survived well even the most hair-raising ownership changes, thanks to the quality of its one and only product: one of the world's best vodkas.

Did corporate cultures ("the way we do business here") survive these turbulent two or three decades? It seems that they did so best in the often family-led steady corporate environment relying on organic growth and limited targeted acquisitions, keeping their core business intact — thus aiding staff morale, recruitment, productivity, minimising internal frictions and finally profits and future growth. The opposite is true in the helter-skelter world of mega mergers, haphazard buying and selling of companies and their staff (much like in the Middle Ages, entire villages were sold), the divestment of established product lines and the wholesale shedding of traditional factory sites. Short-term gain clearly leads to long-term pain. Evidently, it is up to our esteemed readers to draw their own conclusions.

My sincere thanks go to Allard K. Winterink of WSPC for his most helpful initiative and his continued encouragement and unfailing support.

Albrecht Rothacher
Brussels and Seeboden (Carinthia)
October 2024

Corporate Identities and Successful Branding

Until recently, global brands have been seen as a licence to print money. With the right label and generous PR budget, sugary lemonades, greasy meat buns, tee-shirts or sports shoes could be sold for a multiple of their original manufacturing costs to an ever-growing number of credulous, happy and somewhat simple-minded consumers.

Yet, quite a few of the world's most celebrated brands face unforeseen difficulties, which seem unrelated to direct management mistakes or largely ineffective boycott calls: McDonald's, Coke, Disney and U.S. carmakers have all been struggling with reduced sales and slimmed margins.

The most prominent American brands stood for both fear and promise of a homogenised global way of life aligned with U.S. patterns, levelling national tastes and cultural preferences towards the smallest common denominator of humankind.

For many industrially backward, developing and former Communist countries, these brands surely offered progress in terms of reliable qualities, services and the notion of participation in the

American way of life: even the idea of consuming food, drinks, and products and enjoying them at any moment was seen as liberating.

However, once the memory of scarcities was overcome, discretionary incomes increased and a basic familiarity with the American way of life and consumption was established, the novelty value and compulsive appeal of U.S. mass brands began to decline.

Rather than striving for uniformity, consumers began to opt for greater freedom of choice and ever-greater diversity and product segmentation to express their personal likes and individuality, including a revival of national and regional brands, even in the U.S. (very visible, e.g., in Lone Star, Texas).

U.S. mass brands, that bogeyman of anti-globalisers, may have had their golden days in the 1990s, the decade following the fall of the Iron Curtain, behind them. But a much larger collection of more differentiated, well-focused and properly managed national and multinational brands is still very much alive and kicking with a great future ahead of them. Newly branded consumer sectors, such as telecoms, financial services and IT, or even in capital goods production, are being added to the classical staples.

What then are brands — that elusive buzzword of corporate visionaries, marketers, ad men, retailers, addicted teenagers and globalisation critics?

Simply put, a brand is the soul of a product. It facilitates consumer choice by representing reliable qualities, images and pricing. If properly communicated and maintained, it can also evoke powerful emotional qualities in consumers, even potentially promoting lifelong loyalty to the product.

A brand owner thus needs to maintain their focus, value their brand and avoid the pitfalls of reckless stretching, discount selling, excessive national product differentiation and abrupt modernisations.

Clearly, companies with successful brands grow quicker and are more profitable than commodity producers or companies with inconsistent and ineffective brand policies.

It remains, however, imperative that, often during rapid growth, the corporate identity remains in harmony with the brands and their professed core values. The pitfalls of corporate history are manifold. From the original larger-than-life founding fathers (typically the inventors of the brand), generational succession is rarely smooth. Bureaucratisation by professional managers in public companies, which often succeed the third- to fifth-generation founder–owner families, represents the risk of brand loyalty loss, as hired CEOs and greedy shareholders may be more loyal to themselves than to their brands. Corporate mergers and takeovers (typically by bored top management motivated by too large a war chest) usually spell more trouble than gain, as corporate cultures and, frequently, brand identities are irreparably damaged by wild diversifications that look intelligent only on paper or by mergers whose "synergies" usually destroy the acquired brands, treating them like unloved stepchildren.

The concept of corporate culture is perhaps even more elusive. According to John Middleton, it is related to the atmosphere at work: "the way we do things around here", reflecting "patterns of shared values and beliefs created over time". In organisations, corporate culture sets the norms for acceptable behaviour, change and conservatism, creativity and conformity, group orientation and individuality, customer service and in-house orientation, among other things.

Society at large and national business culture play a significant role with respect to social knowledge, rituals, ideologies and values, as they apply to hierarchy, information sharing, employee participation, negotiation and communication behaviour, gender roles, career patterns, remuneration and labour relations. There are also significant regional variations. Even within a homogenous national culture like the U.S., the Californian way of doing business varies from how it is done in Dallas, Texas, or in Atlanta, Georgia, let alone in New York City or in Detroit. These differences are even more pronounced in countries with greater historical regional differences.

Sectoral styles also play their roles: a bank has a different corporate culture from a steel plant, a trucking company or a design studio. Charles Handy differentiated four types of organisational cultures:

1. *Power Cultures*: They have one central source of power, typically exercised by a charismatic founder or their successors in a fairly authoritarian manner. The company is led in a strong, decisive and forceful way, can react quickly, and leaves little initiative to middle management. All this is good for quick growth if the decisions are vindicated by market acceptance. But it could equally be a recipe for disaster if the decisions turn out wrong. Typical examples are start-up firms in their early decades.
2. *Role Cultures*: They are practised within large bureaucratic companies with prescribed roles, procedures and delegated authority. Job descriptions and procedures count rather than personalities. The organisation becomes predictable and routine, but also inflexible and slow. Established banks, insurance companies, big conglomerates (such as the Japanese keiretsu), public companies and firms with high capital intensity are classic examples.
3. *Task Cultures*: They represent small work groups that get their jobs done through networking and human interactions. Individuals have a high level of control over their work. Hierarchies are flat, and the work style is informal. This is typical of PR agencies, real estate agents and marketing firms.
4. *Person Cultures*: Here, individual operations dominate; personal values and professionalism count. Institutional loyalties are weak. This applies to consultancies, law firms, academia, research and journalism.

More than any meaningless mission statement, a robust corporate culture is an asset. It guarantees the long-term performance of an organisation, as it has been carefully built up and evolved in line with the business environment and in harmony with the national culture of its home country. Oral corporate history, including gossip, heroic myths and corporate philosophy, plays a role, as does personnel policy, i.e., "Who gets in, who gets fired and who gets promoted?", and preferred management behaviour, which could oscillate between authoritarian, *laissez faire* and participative styles and between formality and informality in procedures. For long-term employees, this leads to a sense of belonging and motivation beyond their job description and allows the formation of important communication networks for action and quick information.

Corporate cultures are put at risk by reckless downsizing and outsourcing and by mergers and takeovers. Ultimately, in the view of Terrence Deal and Allan Kennedy, it is the bottom-line orientation of fund managers, who overemphasise short-term shareholder value and thus destroy the social fabric essential to a company's long-term organisational health and prosperity.

As employment becomes increasingly insecure and "me first" emerges as the only rational strategy for survival, corporate loyalty is the first casualty. Downsizing and outsourcing betray the trust of employees. In-house skills and corporate memory are lost. Outsourced contract workers feel alienated, doing the same job for lower wages. Those who survive feel guilty and operate with lower morale, higher absenteeism, low profile and greater outward conformity. Product and service quality, as well as customer relations, suffer. The same applies to corporate takeovers, in which the losing side's corporate culture is forced out, as fund managers expect rapidly reduced payrolls as evidence of promised "synergies" (which in reality hardly ever materialise).

For brand management, corporate identity is of key importance: in order to be successful as a credible brand, both must remain in harmony: Disney's family values must be practised in corporate behaviour; Virgin's studied youthfulness must be reflected in corporate informality; the approachable PR of IKEA and Lego must be practised in actual customer relations; and a bank must be seen as a respectable and formal organisation. Thus, when Dresdner Bank, a solid institution of reserved German bankers, was taken over by the brash insurance salesmen of Allianz, not only did their corporate culture go down the drain, but so did their customers' confidence, their volume of deposits and their bottom line.

National business cultures play an important role in corporate identities and brand images. German and Japanese products stand for engineering prowess and reliability, and their business organisations are known for participative bureaucracies ("role cultures").

French and Italian products are reputed for their design, flair and creativity, and their business organisations are typically power cultures with great authoritarian distance and an alienated workforce. While the designs are brilliant, problems in manufacturing quality, delivery and after-sales service can be expected.

There is nothing wrong with either national style — but what happens if you blend them? The chemical and pharmaceutical companies Hoechst and Rhône-Poulenc merged to form a hybrid synthetic entity called Aventis. Two established, well-branded companies disappeared to form a faceless and flavourless neuter: a company without an identity. Its product sales, regardless of their individual qualities, were anticipated to suffer, and so they promptly did. Having become a target for takeovers, in 2004, Aventis was swallowed up by the much smaller Sanofi with French government support.

We have assembled 18 case studies in seven core consumer sectors (foodstuffs, drinks, distribution, apparel, electronics, transportation and entertainment) to demonstrate the close interconnection between corporate growth, corporate identity and brand development. Stories of qualified success are matched with those of failure, dented prospects and still unfulfilled expectations.

Some features are unique to the brand or the corporate history in question. But there are also common trends, which, with all due caution, could be distilled into more universal observations.

Mars, the company and its products (confectionery and pet food), was created by Forrest Mars, the founder's son. It still remains a well-focused family-owned company. The same applies to Sprüngli-Lindt as the only surviving independent Swiss-quality chocolate dynasty. It overcame its fifth-generation crisis and manages a smooth, focused global quality positioning for its Lindt brands.

Kikkoman is a few centuries older. During the past decades, the Mori clan succeeded in making soy sauce a worldwide condiment. With only moderate and a fairly focused diversification, the traditional family-owned company has remained on track. It survived a wine scandal in time to re-establish sound management prior to Japan's wild binge of capital misallocation and destruction in the 1980s, thus escaping unhurt from the bubble burst of 1992 and beyond.

Coca-Cola is certainly the world's best-known contemporary brand. After the original inventors were bought out, it was systematically built up by Robert Woodruff, yet it remained quintessentially a very Southern product of the U.S. As Coke seems to have reached its growth limits, the company has diversified into a multitude of juices and drinks, including very local brands such as Almdudler, an archetypical Austrian herbal lemonade, which nobody would ever associate with the Atlanta giant.

In Eastern Europe, only very few brands survived Communist mismanagement. One of the best with global potential is Poland's Vodka Zubrowka. Unfortunately political hiccups during Poland's privatisation and a certain reticence by the new brand owner Pernod Ricard, which has many promising drinks on its shelves, have thus so far prevented the effective utilisation of this potential.

McDonald's is surely an unlikely global success story of the U.S. management style. Its emphasis on automation, standardised qualities, cleanliness and quick service represented progress in most of the world's fast-food industry. After having bought out the

McDonald's brothers, Ray Kroc ensured the success of McDonald's through strong image creation and strict guidance and control over franchises and employees. It is only recently that people in more affluent markets have lost their appetite for fatty hamburger buns. McDonald's responded with a more varied menu, but primarily with reduced prices.

In distribution, IKEA is the product of Ingvar Kamprad's marketing ingenuity: the relentless global expansion of a low-cost furniture retailer offering knockdown sets and a highly spartan service. The company cultivates the Swedishness of its origins in both marketing and management styles. Informality, frugality and approachability rule — and these have proven successful worldwide.

The Seibu-Saison chain of Seiji Tsutsumi did it the other way round: it started out as an increasingly avant-garde, trendy upmarket department store and supermarket chain. Highly successful during Japan's asset inflation period, Seiji led the company on a mad credit-financed diversification drive into overpriced real estate development and went global with the Intercontinental chain. In the end, Seibu collapsed spectacularly. Seiji's brother Tsutomu Tsutsumi, who in his heyday bought the Nagano Winter Olympics of 1998, was saved only narrowly by marginally sounder finance due to the bigger capital base of his inherited hotel and railway businesses.

One of Italy's post-war textile successes was set up by Luciano Benetton and his siblings. He subcontracted production, delegated sales to exclusive franchises and focused on design and image creation by stirring public controversies. Benetton's messages of multiculturalism and a cosmopolitan lifestyle are, however, not matched by his autocratic, traditional family-oriented corporate culture and Italian-dominated personnel and marketing policies. Yet, he has managed to succeed with these inconsistencies, perhaps not by accident *à l'Italiana*.

Nike is an even younger company founded by running academics in Oregon in the 1960s. It has similarly outsourced all production and concentrates on R&D and brand management only. It maintains a forever youthful and informal corporate style and, with a huge marketing budget, pushes for an unapologetically American, masculine "can do" spirit in its corporate image.

Nokia, the Finnish forestry processor turned electronics makers since its re-focusing effort in the mid-1970s, has cultivated an entrepreneurial management style with a strong customer, design and R&D focus and continuous product innovation. Although claiming to be cosmopolitan with a high-tech commitment, with its hardworking and egalitarian management style and business ethics, it remains distinctly Finnish.

Sony, which also claims to be cosmopolitan, is similarly unmistakably Japanese. Built up by Akio Morita as one of Japan's post-war miracle companies, it diversified from being a successful electronics manufacturer into electronic entertainment through ill-fated U.S. acquisitions. Although still marginally profitable, since Morita's death, Sony has lost its way and is in search of focus.

Sir Richard Branson's Virgin Group is purposefully anti-establishment and anti-textbook. In line with its rebellious non-conformist image, it happily overstretches its low-budget brand with three airlines, soft drinks ("Virgin Cola"), cosmetics and record "Megastores", often with very mixed results. It operates on free press publicity generated by its flamboyant founder and finds acceptance notably by British and Australian underclass feelings of solidarity and their strange sense of fun. Virgin companies are bought on credit and later sold to get out of financial predicaments to no apparent purpose. Yet, against all odds, Virgin survives under Sir Richard's somewhat autocratic, spontaneous and fun-loving leadership.

Toyota was built up by Kiichiro Toyoda, who had inherited Toyoda Automated Loom Works, into the world's largest car manufacturer. Differently from Nissan, its less successful competitor, it entered overseas production reluctantly and very much remained a traditional conformist Japanese family-controlled company.

Fiat, Italy's foremost carmaker, remains under the control of the Agnelli family after a hundred years of turbulent corporate history. Under the family's autocratic management, it faced more than its fair share of labour troubles and, as a single-model company, went through pronounced cycles of boom and bust. Unfortunately, funds generated during the good years were spent on unfocused diversification to create an unwieldy conglomerate. Attempts to establish lasting footholds outside the Italian market equally came to naught. Yet, the jury is still out on the success of its tripartite adventure of the 2021 Stellantis merger with Chrysler and Peugeot.

The merger mania hit two German premium carmarkers, BMW and Daimler-Benz, in the mid-1990s. The two entered into unhappy marriages of convenience with Rover and Chrysler, respectively. Daimler had just divested itself of its earlier wild, loss-making diversification, which was aimed at creating a high-tech conglomerate. On paper, the synergies of both mergers looked wonderful: permitting access to new markets with an attractive portfolio of mass-market cars. Yet, cultural management and brand incompatibilities caused both deals to go sour very quickly. BMW opted for a quick divorce and remains a happy single ever after, with an expanded albeit focused premium car strategy, while Daimler Chrysler remains locked in its unhappy loss-inducing marriage, losing brand focus and national corporate identity as a result. Neither German engineering prowess nor U.S. patriotic corporate citizenship remain very credible for either.

Lego remained a family-owned quality toy maker, faithful to its philosophy of creative play, very Danish in its informal and participative leadership style and adherence to its corporate values, although a new generation of children and middle-class parents seems to have abandoned them. In the early 2000s, Lego became disoriented, chasing trends, before refocusing on its creative and educational toy business.

Disney did it the other way round. It also had its "family values" but aimed at the lowest common denominator in a melting pot society. Built up by the Disney brothers, it expanded into a comprehensive entertainment, media and merchandising empire under the autocratic rule of long-term CEO, Michael Eisner. In the fickle and rough entertainment business, however, Disney seems to find it very difficult to keep on smiling like its childish cartoon characters of origin. Intellectual brand consistency thus remains a persistent problem, notably when violent movies and tough corporate lawyers promise instant profits or when a politically correct missionary spirit invades its screenplays.

In order to generate a global brand, a middle-of-the-road consensual approach of common wisdom has never worked. At the beginning, there is always (or nearly always) a founding father, a marketing and production genius, who pushed things through and persisted against all odds. In our sample, these were men like Forrest Mars, Ingvar Kamprad (IKEA), the Tsutsumi brothers (Seibu), Luciano Benetton, Phil Knight (Nike), Akio Morita (Sony), Sir Richard Branson (Virgin), Giovanni Agnelli (Fiat), Kiichiro Toyoda, the Christiansen family (Lego) and the Disney brothers.

There were also those playing a similar role, who bought out the original innovator, perfected a struggling infant brand and built up and harnessed its potential. These were people like Ray Kroc (McDonalds) and Robert Woodruff (Coca-Cola).

Clearly, the brand owner-founders management style is regularly characterised as autocratic, often as idiosyncratic as well. It usually took the form of classical authoritarianism, regardless of whether in the U.S. (Mars, Disney/Eisner, McDonald's/Kroc and Coke/Woodruff), in Europe (Agnelli, Sprüngli and Benetton) or in Japan (Morita, Toyoda and Seibu/Tsutsumi). Even when informality and flat hierarchies were instructed, there was still a charismatic boss, like Kamprad (IKEA), Branson (Virgin), Knight (Nike), and

Christiansen (Lego), who discouraged middle-management bureaucrats and insisted on their perception of a consistent corporate and brand culture.

While they were irreplaceable in the takeoff stage, the second high-stakes question always refers to corporate succession. Owner-founders typically prefer dynastic succession. Their sons (daughters usually don't enter the picture) suffer from a double handicap: the larger-than-life successful fathers in their patriarchal-authoritarian ways typically overshadowed the sons (or grandsons). Often enough, they were polygamous and treated family members, including their sons, badly, or set the stage for paralysing succession struggles between their sons, who on occasion appeared as spoilt, overcharged, overeducated or simply disinterested in management. Fiat and Sony are examples. Occasionally, the inevitable strikes at a later generation.

Yet, almost all of our successful brands remain in family control: Mars, Benetton, Lego, Sony, IKEA, Sprüngli, Kikkoman, Fiat, Toyota and Virgin. Brand management by committee-like Pernod Ricard for Zubrovka Vodka or by managerial consensus appears much less effective.

Obviously, one-man decisions are high-risk decisions: they carry the prospect of a stroke of genius but with at least an equal probability of utter failure. The diversification strategies of Seibu, Sony and Fiat are examples of the latter, as were the takeover decisions of Daimler and BMW. Sir Richard's Virgin Group represents an institutionalised permanent risk. Yet, without the vision and drive of the founding fathers and their successes, Sony would still be a radio repair shop in Osaka, Lego doing carpentry work in Billund, Seibu selling obento travel provisions at Ikebukuro station, Benetton knitting home-made sweaters and Nike organising cross-country runs in Oregon forests. In fact, without its founding fathers, most companies, including Coke, Disney and McDonald's, would surely have gone out of business long ago.

As brands succeed, corporations grow, and the founder hero inevitably fades from the scene. Then, bureaucratisation sets in. Some, like Nokia, Sprüngli and Nike, managed to achieve the rare feat of establishing an entrepreneurial corporate culture. Mostly, however, hired hands take over as CEOs, whose fate through share options is increasingly decided by fund managers, who care about quarterly bottom lines and little else. All the founding fathers knew that short-termism and profitable fire sales spell the death of any brand. It therefore should come as little surprise that many global brands, especially those of U.S. origin, are in trouble today. They also knew that corporate bureaucratisation and committee decisions for brand definitions usually imply dilution: in the spirit of compromise, they typically end up meaning too many different things to too many people.

A case in point is the pronounced national identities of most successful brands. The American dream and the U.S. way of life are part and parcel of Disney, Coca-Cola, Nike, Mars and McDonald's. Kikkoman, Toyota, Seibu and Sony are clearly Japanese. IKEA is Swedish, Lego Danish, Nokia Finnish, Benetton and Fiat Italian, Virgin British, Zubrowka Polish, and BMW and Daimler German. National brand origins reflect distinct corporate national identities and brand images, firmly held by consumers. Dilution by mergers and misguided globalist corporate mission statements and PR efforts (practised by Sony, Benetton, Nokia, Mars, Coca-Cola, Disney, DaimlerChrysler and now Stellantis) only risks hurting the brand's integrity.

Claims of newly created artificial corporate identities may flatter the vanity of senior management. They do not, however, reflect the expectations and daily experiences of their customers and employees. Managerial delusions of global grandeur created by hired PR hands may be rectified at relatively little cost. More dangerous are well-filled war chests which allow takeovers and diversifications, appearing as a seductively easy shortcut to empire-building for bored senior managers. Brand management is patient work involving incremental, subtle innovation and modernisation, not the stuff to generate managerial glory in business magazines and corporate case studies, let alone to excite fund managers insistent on quick bottom-line results. Fiat, Daimler, BMW, Sony and Seibu all fell victim to this most frequent case of managerial hubris, which never generated the profits promised but only served to threaten their core brands and their companies' survival.

As global markets for uniform products did not really emerge, global operators returned to the time-proven model of international operations, where local management was again encouraged to modify products, marketing and management accordingly to local preferences.

There remains an intrinsic need for consistency between corporate cultures and their brand images. A caring family-value company like Disney cannot produce violent films or go aggressively after copyright violators. Fiat should not permit its Iveco subsidiary to produce trucks for mobile executions in China (*The Straits Times*, 13 March 2003). Charges of child labour in Third World countries follow all sportswear makers, including Nike, who have outsourced their manufacturing. McDonald's, which wants to be a family restaurant, is haunted by lawsuits of fattened teenagers, generating the worst possible publicity for a restaurant chain.

Globalisation critics since decades have levelled an earful of complaints against global brands, accusing Nestlé's infant formula of killing babies, multinationals of destroying nature and exploiting their oilfields for little local benefit with the help of corrupt dictatorships, Chiquita bananas (United Fruits) of instigating wars in Central America, pharmaceutical companies of using slum dwellers as guinea pigs, and apparel makers of exploiting child labour. Naomi Klein's *No Logo* (2000) has become the slogan of anti-globalists.

Yet, politically inspired boycotts so far have failed to make a dent. Companies like Coca-Cola, McDonald's and Nike generate

50% of their turnover in Europe, Asia, and the Middle East. Yet, even at the height of the highly unpopular U.S. war against Iraq, there was no visible impact on sales outside the Middle East. Similarly, fears of effective boycott calls against German and French brand producers in the U.S. did not materialise in 2003. Possibly, giant Stars and Stripes at German car dealerships and plants helped placate hurt nationalist feelings.

Forty years ago, Theodore Levitt in the *Harvard Business Review* famously predicted the globalisation of markets: mass transportation and communication would make distinct national tastes and cultural preferences disappear. There would be global markets for standardised consumer products.

Today, we know that with increased income levels and varied personal experiences in mature markets, the opposite happens: consumers reject standard fare and opt for wider choice and their national, regional and personal preferences instead.

This does not automatically mean: big brand, big trouble. Rather, there remains a bright future for well-managed, well-focused brands, as we have seen.

In fact, in the field of consumer products and services, the existence of well-established national brands with an international reputation is a considerable asset in terms of international competitiveness. Other things being equal, a country with strong brands across the board will perform better in international trade compared to one which produces faceless commodities.

Apart from Japan, which still has strong, if not longer overly exciting, brands, most of Asia has a problem, as Asian brand owners typically care very little for intangibles like product or corporate image, especially when it comes at a cost. Lee Kuan Yew put this perceptively: East Asia needs "maverick generals" to generate sustainable brands (*The Straits Times,* 6 June 2003). In his view, it is handicapped by its Confucian heritage, which, with its conformist discipline, worked well organising large regiments for reliable mass production, but not suited for encouraging the stubborn creativity of individuals. The subsequent case studies offer plenty of evidence on how to do this, as well as pitfalls to avoid.

Bibliography

Batey, I. *Asian Branding*. Singapore: Prentice Hall, 2002.

Blasberg, J. and Vishnamath, V. "Making Cool Brands Hot", *Harvard Business Review*, pp. 20–22, June 2003.

Deal, T. and Kennedy, A. *The New Corporate Cultures*. London: Texere Publishing, 2000.

"Fast Food in America", *The Economist*, 7 December 2002.

Fuyuno, I. "Japan's McTrouble", *Far Eastern Economic Review*, 12 September 2002.

Handy, C. *Understanding Organizations*. Harmondsworth: Penguin.

Hofstede, G. *Culture and Organizations*. London: McGraw-Hill, 1997.

Keller, K. L. *et al.* "Three Questions You Need to Ask about Your Brand", *Harvard Business Review*, pp. 81–86, September 2002.

Lewis, R. D. *When Cultures Collide: Managing Successfully across Cultures*. London: Nicholas Brealy, 1999.

"Marken — Image, Produkte, Unternehmen", Verlagsbeilage, *Frankfurter Allgemeine*, 25 June 2003.

Middleton, J. *Culture*. Oxford: Capstone Publishing, 2002.

Shah, R. "Summer School: Branding", *Financial Times*, p. 7, 21 August 2002.

Temporal, P. *Branding in Asia*. Singapore: John Wiley, 2000.

Tomkins, R. "When a Big Mac Is No Longer Good Enough", *Financial Times*, 21 December 2002.

Tomkins, R. "As Hostility towards America Grows, Will the World Lose Its Appetite for Coca-Cola, McDonald's and Nike?", *Financial Times*, 27 March 2003.

Werner, K. and Weiss, H. *Schwarzbuch Markenfirmen*. Vienna: Deuticke.

Mars Inc.: More Than Candies and Cat Food

Mars Inc. started out as a candy factory but is today a company with offices and factories worldwide. They make and market a variety of products, ranging from candies to pet food to processed rice. Their products are marketed globally and consumed in more than 100 countries. Mars Inc., despite being a multi-national company, continues to be family-owned and, until 2001, was managed by third-generation descendants, John, Forrest Jr. and Jacqueline Mars. The company was listed as the third-largest private company in America in 2002 by *Forbes*, while the family was ranked 21st on the list of the world's richest, with a net worth of $10 billion.[1]

The company's business interests include snack foods (M&Ms, Snickers, Mars, Milky Way, Dove Chocolate, Skittles, Combos, etc.), main meals (Uncle Ben's rice, pasta and sauces), pet care (Whiskas, Pedigree and Cesar), drinks (vending machines: Flava and Klix), electronics (automated payment systems) and information technology.

[1] http://www.forbes.com/2003/02/26/billionaireland.html

The company is highly private. It does not grant many interviews to the media and is also reluctant to release its financial reports, even to its banks. It should also be noted that Mars Inc. is one of the world's largest private companies, and a big spender in the realm of global advertising to market its products.

History

According to the Mars website, the company's history has two main themes: innovation and the transfer of successful innovations around the world. These two themes have defined the nature of the company's operations to this day.

The company was founded by Frank Mars in 1923, his first success after a series of failures. It was then known as the Mar-O-Bar Co. In the beginning, he manufactured an item with the same name at the factory, which was a combination of caramel, nuts, chocolate and a buttercream concoction known as Victorian buttercream. In 1924, Frank Mars ran into his son Forrest, whom he had not seen since his divorce from his first wife Ethel. Forrest Mars claimed to have suggested the idea of a portable version of the chocolate malt drink, which turned into the Milky Way bar. This new chocolate creation was a stunning new debut in the candy market at that time. The chocolate coating kept the candy bar fresh in an era when candies did not keep well for long periods of time. Also, the bar did not cost much to produce but tasted as good as chocolate. The bar provided the company with the start it needed.

By 1927, the company was renamed Mars Inc., and the factory relocated to Chicago's west side, where the freight charge was half of that in Minneapolis. The factory was built on a former golf course, and Frank Mars turned the factory into a showplace, blending well with the rich suburban neighbourhood. It gave no hints of being a factory. It was automated with what was considered state-of-the-art at that time. In 1930, Frank Mars invented the Snickers bar, and in 1932, he introduced the 3 Musketeers bar, which gave Mars Inc. the reputation of being the second-largest candy maker in America after Hershey (Brenner, 2000).

Frank Mars was content with the success of his company, perhaps due to his string of failures, but Forrest was bent on expansion and constantly pushed his father to grow the business. However, Forrest's meddling attitude in the company and constant push for expansion into Canada caused Frank to throw him out of the business. Frank Mars died fifteen months later, and the company went into the hands of his second wife (another Ethel) and daughter.

With $50,000 and the foreign rights of Milky Way given by his father, Forrest went to Europe to try his luck. His interest in the chocolate business prompted him to study with many masters in Europe, such as Jean Tobler and Henri Nestlé, by working in their factories. Later in 1933, he went to England to launch the Milky Way bar. However, the market was dominated by Cadbury Brothers Ltd. and Rowntree & Co. This prompted him to scale down his plans for a large factory and start a smaller one instead. He devoted all his money and attention into the company, so much so that his father-in-law had to bring his wife and son back to America to support them. He adjusted the taste of the Milky Way bar to suit British tastes and even marketed it egoistically as the Mars bar. Sales of the Mars bar took offs and even though Forrest Mars' attempts to introduce new candy bars failed, the company in England was nevertheless a success (Brenner, 2000).

With the success of the Mars Bar, Forrest Mars turned his attention to other things. In 1934, he bought Chappel Bros., a British company that canned meat by-products for dogs. At that time, there were no specialised foods for pet dogs and cats; they simply ate scraps from the dinner table. Forrest Mars saw an opportunity and marketed Chappie's canned food as being more nutritious. Without any competitors, he easily dominated the market.

By 1939, Mars Ltd. was the third-largest candy manufacturer in Britain, and Forrest had also set up a factory in Brussels to sell Mars bars across Europe. However, with the onset of the Second World War, he had to leave his successes because the British government started taxing foreigners. By then, he had an idea that would later become M&Ms, and when he returned to America, he looked to Hershey's for a joint venture.

Forrest Mars convinced the then right-hand man of Milton Hershey, William Murrie, about the possibilities of making a chocolate that does not melt. He had seen these candies in Spain during the civil war and was very impressed by them. Mars put up 80% of the investment, while Murrie provided the other 20% and the chocolate for the venture. Murrie's son Bruce was sent to work with Mars on this venture. The product that was launched in 1941 was M&Ms, which stood for "Mars and Murrie". However, the venture soon turned sour as Bruce Murrie found Forrest Mars a difficult person to work with and soon sold his shares to Forrest. The information on the Mars and M&Ms websites today makes no mention of Hershey's help in creating M&Ms.[2]

The candies first appealed to American soldiers because of their ability to withstand temperatures without melting. While it was a good idea, M&Ms did not sell very well initially. It made money, but it did not match up to Snickers. Therefore, in 1950, Forrest Mars hired the advertising firm Ted Bates & Co. to conduct a detailed study of the sales of M&Ms. Forrest was an innovator in using research as a marketing tool. He was the first in the candy business to do so, and it paid off. The study found that M&Ms were appealing to children, but children did not have the money. Thus, the company changed its pitch to attract parents. The agency came up with the famous tagline of M&Ms, "Melts in your mouth, not in your hands". This appealed to parents, as they saw M&M candies

[2] https://www.mms.com/en-us/explore/about-us

as clean and non-messy. With advertising slots on TV during popular shows such as the Mickey Mouse Club, M&M became the most popular candy in 1956.

With M&Ms gaining success, Forrest Mars ventured into another business, as he saw potential in a new method of processing rice. The owner of a rice mill discovered parboiling, a process that resulted in a more nutritious grain. Forrest saw potential in branding and selling the rice at a premium, which was a radical idea at that time. Nevertheless, he went forward with his plans and went off to learn about rice-making. He finally named the product Uncle Ben's Rice, after the owner of the mill. It contributed around $400 million to Mars' revenue as of 1999 (Brenner, 2000).

While Forrest Mars had been successful thus far with his company, he viewed his father's company as the ultimate challenge. He saw the company as rightfully his, since he inspired the Milky Way bar and had encouraged his father to build the Chicago factory. Under the control of Frank Mars' second wife, Ethel, and daughter, Patricia, Mars Inc. was slow to innovate (Brenner, 2000). After the death of Ethel Mars, half of her share in the company passed over to Forrest, and with this inheritance, he went to war for control against William "Slip" Kruppenbacher, Ethel Mars' half-brother. Forrest Mars fought to modernise the technology of the factory, introducing a mechanised candy production process in 1953. By 1959, Mars Inc. was the largest producer of candy-coated bars in the world, thanks to the new technology brought in by Forrest Mars. However, Forrest still wanted complete control over the company.

With the retirement of Kruppenbacher in 1959, James Fleming, Patricia Mars' husband, was appointed president and chief executive officer. Quality suffered under his management as he skimmed on expensive ingredients, such as peanuts and chocolate, and profits thinned (Brenner, 2000). Forrest Mars finally convinced Patricia to sell her shares to him, thus obtaining 80% of the company shares in exchange for placing his own companies under the Mars Inc.

umbrella. Subsequently, he convinced the rest of the shareholders to sell their shares and gained complete control over Mars Inc. In December 1964, Forrest Mars became the chairman, president and chief executive officer of Mars Inc.

Upon taking control, Forrest Mars made radical changes to the company structure according to his management style. He took away all the frivolous aspects of the company: the executive dining hall, the French chef, the oak panelling, the art collection, rugs, stained glass and the corporate helicopter. He increased salaries by 30%, replaced annual compensation with incentive pay and gave each employee a time card. There were sweeping changes made to the company that miffed some employees. Quality control was improved, undoing the cost-cutting measures implemented by James Fleming. Forrest Mars next sought to achieve self-sufficiency by producing its own chocolate. He believed in controlling all aspects of the production of his products, and even today, Mars Inc. does not contract out any aspect of its production.

Forrest Mars made many radical changes to the company after acquiring it, but he only held power for a relatively short period of nine years. In 1973, at the age of 69, he retired and turned over the reins of the company to his sons, Forrest Jr. and John Mars and his daughter, Jacqueline. It was through the efforts of these two men that the company was made a truly global company. Despite handing power over to his children, Forrest Mars continually criticised the performance of his sons and kept tight tabs on the company. As a result, the brothers appear to have held a tighter grip over the company than Forrest Mars ever did.

Forrest Mars the Man

Much of Mars Inc.'s success is directly attributed to Forrest Mars, his insights and his management style. He built the company into the second-largest candy-producing company in America and had visions of a global corporation. He had a peculiar style of managing people, which perhaps stemmed from his drive for success. As a young man, he showed signs of entrepreneurship when he sold meat that he bought at discounts to the school cafeteria at the University of Berkeley for a profit. He made so much profit that he cancelled his business classes. He later transferred to Yale University to study economics, and once again, on the side, he ran a small business. This time, he sold neckties that were meant to be discarded to students, even setting up a booth in the students' union.

Forrest Mars was also an early fan of management guides, as he read books on famous entrepreneurs, such as Ford, and was fascinated by their principles of doing business, paying particular attention to tiny and obscure details (Brenner, 2000). In his business attempts, from the Mars bar in Europe to dog food, Forrest Mars was always more interested in starting up than managing the business. As he was often quoted saying, "I'm not a candy maker, I'm empire-minded". He had thoughts of global expansion as early as in the 1920s, when he failed to convince his father to expand the business into Canada.

In his company, Forrest Mars was known for his high demands on workers and his obsession with quality. Many associates of the company who were interviewed by Brenner for her book provided anecdotes of Mars' demanding nature. His demand for perfection was so extreme that he once called up an associate in the middle of the night, requesting that a batch of M&Ms be taken off the shelves because he found a packet of M&Ms missing the legs of the "M" (Brenner, 2000).

He was also ahead of his time in empowering his employees, long before such practices became widely adopted by corporations worldwide. He paid high salaries to his employees and made each associate feel important. In a sense, each associate was like a mini engineer in their own right, as they were given complete power over their workspace, even those on the factory lines. Each associate knew how to maintain their machines, and if there was a question of quality, it was the responsibility of the employee to halt the production line.

Forrest Mars has always been an entrepreneur, and even after handing the company over to his children in 1973, he continued to dabble in businesses. In 1980, he set up another candy business, specialising in liqueur-filled chocolates. He named the company after his mother, Ethel M. This venture was successful, like most of Forrest Mars' ventures, and he managed it as he did with Mars Inc. The company today falls under the umbrella of Mars Inc.

However, despite having management ideas that were ahead of his time and having built a multi-national corporation, Forrest Mars remained relatively unknown. He and his family were strictly private, few knew about Forrest Mars the man until his death in 1999, and that was the way he wanted it.

The Five Principles

Forrest Mars' management style forms the cornerstone of the company. Today, his ideas have been written into the management philosophy of the company and are known as the five principles of Mars. They take the form of a brochure, which is available in all Mars offices and has also been translated into many different languages for the company's overseas offices and factories. These five principles are Quality, Responsibility, Mutuality, Efficiency and Freedom.

The first principle is probably the most important out of the five. It states, "the consumer is our boss, quality is our work and value for money is our goal". Quality control has always been important to the company. Forrest Mars conducted regular checks at his factories and offices, as he believed that a neat and clean environment is important for efficiency. Also, employees are expected to maintain a high level of cleanliness. For example, at the M&Ms factory in Hackettstown, New Jersey, the floors are scrubbed every 45 minutes. Another example is that of having exactly 15 peanuts on top of each Snickers bar, and maintaining a smooth surface on the chocolate coating. Mars Inc. was also the first confectionery manufacturer to date their products and seized them from distributors if they remained unsold by their expiry date, thus maintaining the freshness of the product. Also, every grain of Uncle Ben's rice is inspected by laser beams. All this is motivated by the belief that "quality means guaranteeing consumers that our brands will live up to their expectations — time after time, without deviation".

The entire operation of Mars is centred on the concept of quality, as they view that quality results from "unremitting attention to detail at every stage [of production]". Mars takes the quality of its raw material seriously. It even has a division (called the Information Services) that monitors the potential harvest of each crop, be it cocoa or peanuts, and advises the company on its long-term supply strategy. In fact, Mars engineers discovered a method of predicting the harvest of an entire crop, and today, the division even rents satellite time to monitor weather patterns and hires the best statisticians to calculate their effects on crops. All this is done to maintain the quality of Mars' products and also to benefit the company and its consumers, a principle known as "mutuality".

The second principle states that "As individuals, we demand total responsibility from ourselves; as associates, we support the responsibility of others". This principle manifests itself in the nature of the corporate structure, as all employees are seen as individuals, and each employee is considered an associate. There are no fancy titles for senior management, and the owners of the company today still continue to punch their timecards when they arrive at work. In this company, employees have equal status and address each other on a first-name basis, meetings are held only "as needed", and fancy presentations are seen as a waste of time. Also, there are no secretaries or big offices for the management; each person takes their own phone calls, makes their own photocopies and uses a coach when needed. To further emphasise the idea of responsibility, each associate has a personal responsibility in the company, as the salaries are tied to the performance of the products. If profits go up, salaries go up, but if the profits decline, so do the salaries.

The third principle refers to mutuality, which is defined as "a mutual benefit is a shared benefit; a shared benefit will endure". This is described on the Mars website as "the standard to which everyone… aspires in all our business relationships". Mars believes in benefiting everyone they deal with, be it associates, consumers or the community at large. For example, they provided refrigerated candy bar display cases for merchants in Kuwait, which allow the merchants to display Mars products prominently without fear of the chocolate melting, while candy bars from competing companies had to remain inside the freezer. This would benefit both the merchant and Mars, as both are able to profit from this. Mutuality also speaks for itself in the quality control exercised by the company. Consumers are assured of the quality of Mars' products, and Mars continues to have loyal customers. In addition, Mars has built several information portals that provide information for pet owners, such as My Pet Stop, which provides general pet care guidance. The community also benefits, as Mars also sponsors fund-raising initiatives on its fund-raising site.

The fourth principle advocates efficiency: "We use resources to the full, waste nothing and do only what we can do best". In Mars, much of the efficiency comes from the fact that the company is very much self-sufficient in terms of production and having control over all its resources. Moreover, machines at the factories operate continuously, 24 hours a day, and the products that do not pass the quality checks are put back into the mix, such that nothing is wasted. A very clear example of how Forrest Mars promoted efficiency was how he managed to introduce efficiency in every aspect of the production of Uncle Ben's Rice. The hulls of the unprocessed rice were burnt to generate part of the electricity for the plant, and he even managed to sell the ash to power plants and steel industries. According to information on Uncle Ben's Rice, the factory even recycles 53% of the water in processing rice. Associates' desks also had to be kept clean, as he believed it was the only way to work efficiently.

The final principle is that of freedom. Mars believes that "we need freedom to shape our future; we need profit to remain free". This is reflected in how it regards its employees. Employees at Mars Inc. are given much liberty, and separate divisions of the company are usually given free rein over their decisions. There is only intervention by top management when something is very wrong with the division. In fact, Forrest Mars often left his employees to do their work, *laissez-faire* style, as he was more concerned with empire-building than with actual management. In the larger sense, the private nature of the company also allows the company to have freedom, as it is not answerable to any shareholders. This also allows for investments that generate long-term yield rather than profits dictating the growth of the company. Perhaps that is the reason why Mars Inc. has never been in debt.

These five principles constitute the underlying philosophy that guides the actions of the company and its employees. They continue to be in use, assuring consumers of quality and teaching associates how to behave.

The Corporate Structure

The corporate structure of Mars Inc. is an open management style, which Forrest Mars implemented when he took over control of his father's company in 1964. He defined the structure of the company by a string of actions that eliminated all aspects of status distinctions between white-collar and blue-collar workers, such as office partitions and the executive dining area. Today, the company views every employee as an associate, regardless of their status within the company. There is no differentiation of status and each associate, including the members of the Mars family, has to use timecards. Each associate is given a 10% bonus for punctuality. Also, formality is discouraged, and everyone is on a first-name basis.

There is virtually no bureaucracy existing in the company. Meetings and memos are discouraged, and the arrangement of the furniture in offices emphasises a non-bureaucratic environment. Mars managers are seated in a wagon-wheel fashion and surrounded by subordinates to encourage communication. Employees simply had to approach their managers when they needed something, reducing the need for bureaucracy. Forrest Mars believed in openness, and he believed that with such an arrangement, everyone knew what everyone else was doing, thus increasing efficiency.

Another aspect of the corporate structure is the flat organisation of the company. There are only six rungs on the corporate ladder, with the top three occupied by the family, the executives and senior managers. There appears to be only a relatively small number of people in these top three rungs, which is surprising for a global organisation. The rungs correspond to the pay scale and are made public, such that the associates know exactly where they stand. It is also intended as a motivation for advancement.

The six-rung corporate ladder also allows for easy transfer of managers from one division to another, for example from M&Ms to Pedigree. Managers are also transferred to and from overseas divisions. This practice allows for crossbreeding of ideas and also familiarises the manager with all aspects of Mars' operations. This practice of transferring people around is made possible with the salaries being pegged to the six rungs of the corporate ladder.

The company is also divided into seven distinct and universal functions, which were originally manufacturing, marketing, sales, research and development, goods and services, finance (accounting) and personnel. These departments are now known as commercial, engineering, finance, information technology (IT), logistics, manufacturing, marketing, personnel, research and development and sales. These departments are also situated next to each other, so that each is informed of what the other is doing. This flat and simple organisational structure thus helps to produce more efficient communication lines.

With such a vast organisation, coupled with the freedom given to it, it would appear to be difficult to keep tabs on the organisation. However, Forrest Mars had a central committee to oversee the operations of the company and its diverse divisions.

The remuneration of the employees of Mars Inc. is competitive and aims to inspire loyalty. The salary is also tied to the profits of the company in order to instil a sense of personal responsibility in the associates. This came from Forrest Mars' belief that "to get the best, you had to pay the best" (Brenner, 2000). As a result, a job interview at Mars is highly coveted, and many Mars managers are said to have retired as millionaires. The system of high pay also meant that many managers stayed with Mars Inc. until their retirement.

While the corporate structure of the company appears to be good for the employees, there were nevertheless problems. Despite the high pay and freedom given to the managers, many of them found it difficult to advance to higher ranks. The family management tends to trust only a select few, and with Forrest Mars' children at the helm of the company until 2001, they were unwilling to delegate and clung to corporate power. As a result, many ambitious and outstanding executives became frustrated and moved to other companies, despite having to take a pay cut (Brenner, 2000).

Expansion Globally

Mars Inc. in the early 2000s was a multi-national corporation, with offices in 47 countries and worldwide product marketing. The idea of global expansion started as early as in the 1920s, when Forrest Mars failed to convince his father to expand operations to Canada. Today, Mars Inc. produces a myriad of products worldwide, with products to suit the palate and demands of various countries.

When bringing their products into other countries, Mars Inc. likes to be the first to arrive before its competitors. When the Soviet Union opened up, Mars was there first to generate publicity for its products such that they had a consumer base before they even set up a factory there. In fact, when Mars plans to establish an overseas division, they will send a senior manager over to "scout" the area for advertising potential and recruit people. In many cases, this person stays with the new establishment for only a short period of time, essentially to pass on American corporate culture and leave. Effectively, there is no on-site American overseer. In theory, the foreign establishment is supposed to follow the American corporate culture of Mars, but in practice, there are nuances in the foreign corporate cultures.

It appears that the corporate culture of the company has largely remained unchanged since the time of Forrest Mars, but it is the foreign establishments that have been allowed to deviate somewhat from the framework of the American corporate culture. The fact that these overseas divisions are left largely under the charge of a foreign counterpart allows the foreign manager to promote their own culture in this company, while the basic management principles are similar. The overseas division does not promote the fact that it is an American company, and they hire mainly locals. In fact, the French division of the company tends to act as if Mars Inc. were a French company. Moreover, there is typically no U.S. overseer, except the family, which tours around the world to inspect the different divisions overseas. Besides these visits, the overseas divisions are largely left to their own to innovate and run their business. Such attitudes held by the Mars brothers have allowed the growth of foreign corporate cultures. It shows the extent to which the corporate cultures in Mars' foreign divisions have deviated from the American style and adapted various styles of their own.

The five principles are also used in other countries, where they are translated and adhered to by the overseas associates. Overseas divisions also maintain a flat hierarchical structure that mirrors the management style of Mars. The management philosophy does not change much, as it adopts a task-oriented culture in all its divisions. In fact, the foreign offices even have a similar office layout.

Thus, in an attempt to achieve global reach for its products, Mars has set up foreign establishments, all of which follow the Mars management culture, but with slight cultural variations. Therefore, it is evident that the corporate culture has only changed culturally, in line with foreign norms, but the bulk of it remains close to the American model. Today, Mars Inc. has overseas divisions in Europe, the former Soviet Union, China, Poland and Australia.

The extent of Mars Inc.'s global reach is evident in the popularity of its products worldwide. Being the first American confectionery maker to arrive in Russia has its benefits, as Snickers is now a recognised word in the Russian dictionary, while its American competitor Hershey's is nowhere to be seen (Brenner, 2000). Mars Inc. also has successful international marketing in pushing its products. Their advertising strategy is generally similar worldwide, making use of identical themes for its products. One particular example is the use of the M&Ms "spokescandy" to advertise its products. The M&Ms television advertisements are also similar around the world, with the "spokescandies" speaking in the different languages of each country. To cater to global consumers, websites have been created for different countries in their native languages.

The company also uses advertising at global events to make the brand known. The Snickers bar was the official candy for the 1994 and 1998 World Cups. Mars Inc. also supposedly paid $5 million for the Snickers bar and M&M to be the official snack foods of the 1984 Olympics games. They also sponsored the Olympics in 1988 and 1992. Such advertising makes the brand known globally and helps when entering new markets. Mars also integrated its advertising with partner websites, such as Warner Home Video and Flipside network. Even though it did not sell anything online, it nevertheless raised awareness of its products. Moreover, Mars Inc. ran a highly successful internet campaign for the introduction of a new colour in its M&Ms mix, which resulted in a 145% increase in traffic on the M&Ms website. For this campaign, surfers were alerted by the Mars Inc. Masterfoods website about the poll, and there was also a significant budget allocated for this advertising effort. This increased brand awareness by raising impressions by 170%. The questions were asked in 15 different languages.

The company also achieved its global reach by adopting the same standards for its brands worldwide. Previously, Mars products were marketed differently and went by different names in different countries. For example, the Snickers bar was known as Marathon in the U.K. This made global advertising campaigns difficult. The process of standardising the diverse brands came about after the sponsorship of the 1984 Olympics. Subsequently, names and packaging have been standardised, as have advertisements. Mars even took on a project to "teach" consumers the correct pronunciation of its candies. All these were part of a global strategy that made Mars products recognisable worldwide.

Another means of its global expansion strategy was to introduce products which were successful in one country to other markets, though this did not always work out. For example, Suzie Wan, a series of Asian foods popular in Australia and New Zealand, was subsequently launched in America, but it did not enjoy the same success. Managers in Mars are asked why a product should *not* be launched in another country, rather than why it should. This is due to the company's belief in "the transfer of best practice", which is the simple belief that what works well in one country will also work well in another (Brenner, 2000). Today, the company has several best-selling brands, most of which are sold worldwide.

With an arsenal of best-selling worldwide brands, Mars Inc. is surely successful, especially since its brands are genuine global brands put forth by a "truly international company managed by international people".[3]

Prospects in the Early 2000s

Mars Inc., in 2003, continued to be a private company. It was listed by *Forbes* as the largest American food-related company, ahead of other companies such as Wrigley's and Nabisco.[4] It was also ranked third on the list, with an estimated annual revenue of $1.75 billion. Yet it remained a family business. However, there seemed to be no one in the third generation really interested in the business. There was a problem of leadership handover, as Forrest Mars' children were ageing and there was no designated successor (Brenner, 2000). In April 1999, Forrest Mars, Jr. quietly retired. His brother John Mars was then still the chairman, president and CEO of the company.

It appears also that the old man Forrest Mars had little hope in the company. It was speculated that he was so concerned about

[3] Quote given by Phil Forster, the overseer of the company's confectionery brands worldwide, in Brenner, 2000, p. 289.

[4] http://www.forbes.com

the sharing of ownership and control over his ten children that he approached the chairman of Nestlé to discuss a buyout in 1992 at the age of 88.[5]

The company has been steadily losing ground, as it has been unwilling to acquire smaller companies for fear of clashes between corporate cultures. As the senior executives of the company continually affirm, the company "[does] not buy and sell, [it] builds".[6] The reluctance to buy smaller firms has resulted in the growth of Hershey's in the U.S. Hershey's has bought up many smaller family-owned confectionery firms, such as Leaf North America, Henry Heide Inc. and Friendly Ice Cream Corp. Hershey's Food Corp. has also acquired stakes in foreign candy companies for overseas joint ventures in Mexico and Sweden. As a result, Hershey's has surpassed Mars Inc. as the top candy producer in America. The only acquisitions made by Mars in the late 1990s were DoveBar International Inc. and 56.4 percent of the French animal food company, Royal Canin SA. The acquisition of Royal Canin SA proved beneficial to the company, as it added $360 million to the company's annual sales. But these acquisitions appear to be few and far between. The most recent was probably that of the formation of a partnership between Effem Mexico SA de CV, a Mars company, and Mexico's Grupo Matre, focused on producing candy for Hispanic markets. While its competitors have expanded aggressively, Mars has been left in the dust.

Moreover, the Mars family's personal preferences dictate to a certain extent the introduction of new products. For example, the family, having grown up in England, does not like peanut butter. Therefore, there are few peanut butter products in the Mars line of products, with the only prominent one being the Peanut

[5] Brenner, Joel Glenn, "A Candy King Bar None; Forrest Mars Sr.", *The Washington Post*, July 6, 1999.

[6] Quote from Phil Forster in Brenner, 2000, p. 292.

Butter M&Ms; however, insiders claim that the Mars brothers are extremely critical of its sales. In contrast, the family enjoys hazelnuts and has tried to introduce many hazelnut products, but these do not appeal to the American palate. This is detrimental in a climate of product innovations pushed by Mars' competitors. By holding certain products back, the family has, to an extent, undermined the competitiveness of the company.

In addition, the conservative and reactive nature of the brothers has caused some marketing *faux pas*. For example, in 1976, the brothers withdrew the red-coloured M&Ms from the mix because of a controversy over the discovery of carcinogens in certain red food colourings. The colourings in question were not used by the company, but the brothers nevertheless withdrew the red M&Ms, a move which many saw as wrong and also failed to reassure consumers. It took 10 years for the red candies to return to the mix (Brenner, 2000).

The use of global advertising and astute marketing techniques has made Mars Inc. a multi-national company today, one of the biggest players in the confectionery industry. Coming from humble beginnings, this family-owned company has managed to survive for two generations, and its results speak for themselves.

The Next Two Decades

Since 2001, Mars, under non-family management, has continued its time-proven path of acquisition-led growth in its core segments of pet food, animal health, snacks and foodstuff. Since the purchase of Chappy (U.K.) in 1935 almost all important pet food makers have been added: KitKat, Shiba, Whiskas, Frolic, Caesar, Royal Canin and Trill. Its impressive range of unhealthy snacks — Ballisto, Bounty, Dove, M&M, Mars, Milky Way, Snickers and Twix — was complemented by the purchase of Wrigley chewing gums in 2008 (for $23 billion) and Kellanova, the maker of Pringles (for $36 billion), in August 2024. Kellanova had been part of Kellogg's, whose breakfast cereal business however had earlier separated and remained with W.K. Kellogg. In consequence, only Pringles chips, Cheez-Its and Rice Crispies went to Mars, joining the salty with the sweet. From Wrigleys came delicacies such as Airwaves, Hubba Bubba, Spearmint, Juicy Fruit, Doublemint, Extra, Orbit and Eclipse. To the food section came Dolmio, Suzi Wan and Ben's Original (until 2021, politically less correctly known and liked as Uncle Ben's). The pasta and pasta sauce maker Miracoli was added in 2012 from Kraft Foods. Interestingly, these acquisitions happened during a period in which the great U.S. food conglomerates such as Kraft Heinz, Mondolez and Hershey all suffered from stagnation.

Also, the veterinary clinic business was expanded: in 2017, the Veterinary Centers of America (VCA) were bought for $9.1 billion; in 2018, the European chain AmiCura, and in 2023, Heska, a maker of veterinary diagnostics and animal care products, were acquired. In 2007, the pet food ("Effem") and snack and food ("Masterfoods") strands were united under one corporate roof as "Mars Inc.", and with its 150,000 worldwide employees ("associates" in Mars-speak) centrally managed from a joint HQ in McLean, Virginia. This is now being renovated to make it fully climate-, eco-, associate- and pet-friendly, following the Mars mottos: "Better Cities for Pets" and "Create a better world for people, pets and the planet". Most of the company's turnover is generated by "quality snacking": Mars products at the tune of $18 billion and those of Kellanova at $13 billion out of a total of $63 billion in 2023. Management wants to double these sales to $36 billion within a decade, taking advantage of the Millennials' and Generation Z's habit of preferring to snack instead of eating full-course warm meals. Mars websites consequently abound in pious wishes for sugarless snacks and healthy fast food. Equally, Mars holds quality controls supreme, although it had its share of expensive recalls for ice cream, chocolate bars and even pet food during 2016–2021.

Its corporate PR similarly exhibits an overdose of political correctness, pledging to reduce its CO_2 emissions by 50% by 2030 and to go net-zero by 2050 — no doubt its associates and managers will reach McLean then on horseback or by bicycle with their pets! Equally, Mars is vocal about inclusion and diversity, wishing to promote female leaders and representation of racial minorities in its management, as well as the empowerment of women and girls in the cocoa supply chain. Unfortunately, there are still persistent, perhaps dubious allegations of child labour in its cocoa plantations in Ghana and the Ivory Coast. Perhaps a case of girls' "empowerment" gone too far?

And now, the good news: although no longer in any management role, the fifth Mars generation with a combined wealth of $142 billion is now ranked the fourth-richest family in the world (*Bloomberg*, 16 January 2024), ahead even of the Saudis and Al-Thanis. After 100 years in the candy and pet food business, this is by no means a small achievement.

Bibliography

Note: Any links to online sources were valid as of the publication of the first edition, in October 2004. Many of the pages have since been taken down.

Barnes, B. "Master Candymaker Forrest Mars Sr. Dies; Imperious Leader Built Secretive Family's McLean-Based Company", *The Washington Post*, 3 July 1999.

Blank, C. "Advertisers Back New Push for Brand Awareness", Dynamic Logic in *iMarketing News*. http://www.dynamiclogic.com/press_coverage_imark041202.php

Blank, C. "M&M Web Site Skyrockets 145 Percent as Surfers Vote for New Candy Color, according to Nielsen/Netratings". http://newsroom.ribbitt.com/pdf/mm.pdf

Blank, C. "Listing of Private Companies", *The Washington Post*, 29 April 2002.

Bredemeier, K. "Mars Buys French Pet-Food Maker", *The Washington Post*, 11 July 2001.

Brenner, J. G. "Appreciation; A Candy King Bar None; Forrest Mars Sr", *The Washington Post*, 6 July 1999.

Brenner, J. G. *The Chocolate Wars: Inside the Secret Worlds of Mars and Hershey*. New York: HarperBusiness, 2000.

New Literature, 2nd Edition

Dengel, B. "Familie Mars – die Kalorienbomber", *Financial Times Deutschland*, 28 April 2008.

Hand, A. "Mars Strategy Aims to Double Snacking Revenue", *ProFoodWorld*, 4 January 2024.

Lindner, R. and Schwarz, F. "Mars übernimmt Pringles Hersteller Kellanova", *Frankfurter Allgemeine*, 14 August 2024.

Mighty Earth. "Chocolates Dark Secret", 6 September 2019.

Mistrati, M. "Schmutzige Schokolade", 5 March 2016.

Neuper, M. "Klebrig, süß und salzig – alle unter einem Dach", *Kleine Zeitung*, 25 August 2024.

The Bitter Sweet Chocolates of Sprüngli-Lindt

Sprüngli-Lindt, as a sixth-generation Swiss chocolate maker, has weathered extraordinary turbulence in its corporate past and yet miraculously managed to survive as the only family-controlled Swiss chocolate maker from among a unique group of 19th-century quality chocolate innovators such as Cailler, Peter, Suchard and Tobler. Profitable for more than 100 years, in 2002 it enjoyed global sales of 1.7 billion CHF with 6,000 employees in Europe, Asia and the Americas.

Its brand names include Caffarel, Fioretto, Ghirardelli, Lindor, Lindt, Nouvelle Confiserie and Swiss Tradition. Products cover a full range of chocolates, including pralines, liquor bonbons, chocolate bars and wafers, Easter eggs and bunnies.

The company started in Zürich as an artisanal sugar bakery in 1845, catering to the sweet tooth of local citizenry. In 1892, it transformed itself into an innovative industrial chocolate maker, with marketing forays into France, Germany and Italy in the 1920s. In the 1960s , these European ventures were revived and consolidated. In 1992, its three main markets, Switzerland, Germany and France, still accounted for 80% of its turnover. It has since expanded into a truly global operator, with markets outside its core marketing region achieving more than 55% of sales. The combined U.S. and Canadian market alone accounted for 24%, with exclusive sales outlets ("Lindt Boutique") achieving double-digit growth rates.

Lindt's premium branding strategy, which uses only first-grade materials and focuses on purity, freshness and flavours, worked miracles in the globally stagnant chocolate market. In general, the market had been hurt by excessive cocoa prices following the turmoil and civil war in the Ivory Coast, a major commodity-producing country. Further, producers began damaging their brands by resorting to widespread discount sales.

With almost "refreshing boredom", as Switzerland's leading daily *Neue Zürcher Zeitung* put it, Lindt managed to achieve increased profits and dividends in an ever-tougher environment for the past three decades.

This positive development was by no means assured. Since its humble beginnings, "Lindt & Sprüngli" was frequently rocked by turmoil. Yet, in the Darwinian struggle of modern capitalism, it ultimately survived, expanded and prospered.

The Lindt & Sprüngli story started when, in 1819, David Sprüngli, then a poor journeyman baker, joined a well-established local sugar bakery in Zürich. When his principal died in 1836, Sprüngli, at the mature age of 60, bought out the widow and himself became a locally respected "*confiseur*" and an honourable member of Zurich's then small-town bourgeoisie. The story might have ended here if it had not been for his son, Rudolf, who, in 1845, began experiments to improve chocolate production. At the time, this was a trading secret of North Italian "*Cioccolattieri*", who, however, produced too limited an amount of inconsistent quality to satisfy the fashionable craze among women for sipping hot chocolate. Then, this was the only acceptable activity for a lady of good standing to do when in a coffeehouse alone or without related male company. The challenge was to mechanise production: how to crush and mill roasted cocoa beans, mix the bitter paste with sugar and aromatic condiments (vanilla notably) and create brown chocolate paste in a mechanised process with the help of water power?

Rudolf Sprüngli was one of a handful of Swiss inventors and tinkerers actively innovating chocolate production. Others included Francois-Louis Cailler in Vevey, Philippe Suchard in Neuchatel (who in 1879 set up his first foreign production in Lörrach, Southwest Germany, had his trademark registered and started modern marketing by inserting collectable pictures in his chocolate packs), and Henri Nestlé, who invented milk powder ("*farine lactée*") in 1867, which made milk durable. Daniel Peter then managed to combine milk with chocolate despite their incompatible fats. He solved this challenge by withdrawing fats from cocoa, adding milk powder and sugar while heating it up, and then putting the cocoa butter back in. Thus, in 1825, "*chocolate au lait*" was born. Most of these inventors lived in Suisse Romande, French-speaking Switzerland. There were workaholic pioneers imbued with the Calvinist ethic, who, in a curious apparent contradiction, devoted themselves to an indulgent luxury product — one of the few sins upon which puritan Calvinism did not frown upon.

Increased production and reduced retail prices allowed Swiss chocolate makers in the 1880s to justify their mass production of the newly found "people's food". They presented it as a nutritious wholesome food supplement contributing to the health of an undernourished population.

Given their disagreements over production styles, marketing outlook and capital needs, in 1892, Rudolf Sprüngli's sons split into the "confiserie line" (which still operates a high-class, top-quality coffee house at Zürich's Paradeplatz) and the "factory line". The latter, in order to finance the new industrial facility with its expensive, new machinery and refrigeration in rural Kilchberg near Zürich, was turned into a shareholding company in 1898, with most shares of the new "Chocolat Sprüngli AG" being held by family members, senior managers and friends. (Henceforth, in good Swiss tradition, the supervisory board continues to be packed with family and corporate friends, and shareholder assemblies are kept happy with regular dividends and sweet gift packs.)

In 1899, Sprüngli undertook a fateful merger with the chocolate maker Rodolphe Lindt of Berne. In return for a sizable amount of cash and Sprüngli shares, Lindt promised to share his elusive top-quality production secret, his customer base and production facilities. A creative but irascible and unpredictable character, Lindt had invented a special blend of his liquid chocolate paste, which was not only exquisitely tasteful but also melted when consumed like a "chocolate fondant" (and did not have to be bitten off and chewed like traditional chocolate). As a somewhat erratic "gentleman producer" uninterested in sales and systematic commercial exploitation of his invention, Lindt soon clashed with the Sprüngli people. He began ignoring his merger obligations and resumed producing his own chocolates on his own account. After a decade-long legal battle, in 1927, Sprüngli's terms of this ultimately unfriendly takeover were upheld. In 1930, the resulting company was named "Chocolatefabriken Lindt & Sprüngli AG". In the meantime, however, Lindt & Sprüngli and the Swiss chocolate industry had to survive the First World War, the loss of the Russian market due to revolution and the German market due to hyper-inflation and the 1929 world economic crisis. All Swiss chocolate makers had used the inter-war years to expand rapidly abroad. Yet, in the aftermath of Black Friday, Peter and Cailler were swallowed up by Nestlé. Suchard and Tobler ended up in today's Philip Morris (recently renamed Altria) portfolio.

Lindt & Sprüngli which had only cautiously entered a joint venture with Rowntree in Berlin (1928) and later (1932) in the U.K., was the only Swiss chocolate maker to survive independently.

The Second World War again led to the loss of most export markets and the disruption of supplies for landlocked Switzerland.

War rationing limited sales to one bar per person per month. Yet, Lindt & Sprüngli managed to remain profitable as a medium-sized regional producer. The company would have remained in that position had not Rudolph Sprüngli emerged victorious in a fifth-generation power struggle in 1962. He had written his PhD thesis on the financial and strategic recklessness of their failed Tobler competitors and embarked on a cautious course of European market expansion. Having married the heiress of a cash-rich construction company, he was able to buy out dissenting family members and minority shareholders, which suited his autocratic and increasingly egocentric management style. He strengthened his control through the quick turnover of hired managers.

Twenty years later, Lindt & Sprüngli had acquired Chocolate Gison AG in Chur, Chocoladefabrik Gubor in Langenthal and Nago Nährmittel AG in Olten (all in Switzerland). It maintained its joint venture with Rowntree ("Lindt England Ltd") in the U.K. and started production in France through its "Consortium Français de Confiserie". In Italy, it held an 11% share in Bulgheroni SpA in Varese. Following a political bribery scandal in Italy, Sprüngli bought out the remaining 89% of the discredited Bulgheroni management. In 1993, the plant was renamed "Sprüngli & Lindt SpA". Their German licence producer, Leonard Monhard in Aachen, owned by Peter Ludwig a famous contemporary art collector, He faced bankruptcy in 1986, probably because he cared more about his paintings than about the profitability of his chocolates.

Hence, Lindt & Sprüngli bought him out for DM120 million in 1987. They subsequently had to invest DM220 million for new production sites to replace the old, obsolete post-war facilities.

In 1989, in Stratham, New Hampshire, production and distribution facilities for the U.S. East Coast were set up, as was a distribution company in Hong Kong to service the Far East.

By the late 1980s, troubles set in for Lindt & Sprüngli at both corporate and private levels. Branding was inconsistent in the then four core markets: the Lindt premium branding in Germany and Italy, frequent rebates in France and "anything goes" in Switzerland.

The "group council" of Swiss and foreign managers found foreign operations to be profitable, but the traditional Kilchberg manufacturing centre turned out to be an inefficient loss-maker. This was anathema to the traditionalist Rudolph Sprüngli. The ageing autocrat had come under the influence of an attractive faith-healer with a past of ill repute, a certain Heidi Gantenbein. He divorced his long-term wife, married Ms Gantenbein and subsequently fired scores of managers based on the spiritual guidance of his new wife. The new management was forced to attend spiritual sessions with Ms Gantenbein. Witnessing the culinary bastion of corporate Switzerland in the hands of a faith-healing former striptease dancer sent shock waves around Lake Zurich. In 1993, Dr Rudolph Sprüngli retired as an honorary chairman. A no-nonsense new CEO, Ernst Tanner, was appointed, and Rudolph's son, Rudolf Konrad Spruengli, who had also fallen into disfavour with both Ms Gantenbein and his father, was reinstated as a board director. Proper euro-branding was now underway, reticent joint venture partners were turned into subsidiaries, and cost-effective reforms were undertaken at the Kilchberg site.

With a decade of sustained solid improvements, consistent production, marketing investments and innovations, the efforts of Ernst Tanner led to a steady stream of results, thus effectively defending Lindt & Sprüngli's independence, which had already been traded as a takeover candidate during the scandalous years of the early 1990s.

The Next Two Decades

Under Ernst Tanner's energetic tenure as CEO from 1993 to 2016, when he was still chairman of the supervisory board, turnover quadrupled and profits rose tenfold. In 2021, a turnover of 4.6 billion

Swiss francs (CHF) produced net profits of 490 million CHF. It takes a marketing genius to motivate customers to pay such premium prices for a commodity like chocolate, which supermarkets try to sell at discounted prices. Besides the intrinsic qualities of the chocolates and pralines sold, their meticulous packaging and marketing, the up-market takeovers had to be right: Caffarel in Turin, Monheim in Aachen, Ghirardelli in San Francisco and, finally in July 2014 for $1.4 billion, Russell Stover Candies Inc. in Kansas City, the leading traditional American praline maker with a market share of 60%. Lindt could now cover the entire U.S. market; yet, it became very dependent on seasonal sales, such as Christmas, Easter and Valentine's Day. For year-round sales, a global network of upmarket speciality Lindt shops was established, including online orders, and Roger Federer, the Swiss world tennis champion, was hired as a brand ambassador. This upmarket speciality marketing effort makes perfect sense. As a gift item, you usually don't impress your date or fiancée or honour your mother-in-law or an esteemed retiring colleague by offering her discount chocolates in a paper bag. Twelve global production sites with 15,000 employees, from its traditional Kilchberg plant above Zürich to Stratham in New Hampshire, ensure that the products remain reasonably fresh. They remain focused on the premium chocolate sector proper, pralines, chocolate Santa Clauses, Easter bunnies and chocolate and hazelnut spreads. As imitation was rife, a series of trademark disputes were settled with mixed results. Like most chocolate makers around the globe, Lindt could not escape the usual allegations of using child labour in its cocoa chain during harvest time in West Africa. Like others, it responded by setting up a foundation for sustainable agriculture to train local farmers, which of course failed to satisfy its merciless critics.

After Mars, Mondelez, Ferrero, Hershey and Nestlé, Lindt today is the world's sixth-largest chocolate maker. But it also boasts the second-most expensive share price, after Warren Buffet's Berkshire Hathaway ($600,000) — at 100,000 CHF. The dividend is partly delivered in kind: a suitcase with 5 kg of premium chocolates.

Following the Kremlin's attack on Ukraine in February 2022, Lindt, like many other non-military suppliers, decided to close its eight shops in Russia in order to avoid public criticism. Yet, chocolate-crazed Russians don't need to starve. Parallel imports still continue via Serbia, Turkey, Azerbaijan, Kazakhstan and China, albeit at a premium price above the premium.

Bibliography

Note: Any links to online sources were valid as of the publication of the first edition, in October 2004. Many of the pages have since been taken down.

"Lindt & Sprüngli — ein mastiges Praliné", *Neue Zürcher Zeitung*, 2 April 2003.

"Lindt & Sprüngli — Group Structure". http://www.lindt.com/international/aboutus/group.asp

"Lindt & Sprüngli liefet erneut Resultat von der Schokoladenseite", *eBand aktuell*, 1 April 2003.

"Lindt & Sprüngli steigert Umsatz 2002", *Basler Zeitung*, 29 April 2003.

Lindt of Switzerland. http://company.monster.com.Lindt/

Lüchinger, R. *Kampf um Sprüngli*. Frankfurt/Main: Verlag Ullstein, 1995.

New Literature, 2nd Edition

Bonazzi, M. "Lindt & Sprüngli: Diese Aktie ist ein teurer Spaß", *Wirtschaftswoche*, 11 March 2024.

Gehringer, R. "In Schweizer Schoggi steckt Kinderarbeit", *Rundschau*, 10 January 2024.

Kikkoman: Far Travelled Sauces

Kikkoman, by 2003, was a two-billion-dollar company, the world's largest soy sauce producer with 4,000 employees worldwide and sales in nearly 100 countries. It is the only Japanese company which has managed to expand in the drinks and seasonings sector internationally. In fact, Kikkoman has succeeded in making its soy sauce variants globally recognised condiments beyond the traditional confines of Japanese and Chinese cuisine.

The founding myth has it that Kikkoman soy branding started in Noda along the Edo River near Tokyo after Shige Maki, the clan's tough and resourceful ancestral mother, made a narrow escape from the besieged Osaka Castle during the 17th century civil wars. In any event, it is well documented that, in 1661, the Mogi-Takanashi clan began brewing shoyu (natural soy sauce) in Noda, a small town in Chiba Prefecture. It was one of the typical rural industries developing in Tokugawa Japan, when urbanisation created increasing demand for rurally produced textiles, pottery and processed foods. (One should recall that in the 18th century, Tokyo had become the world's largest city.) Yet, production patterns were distinctively premodern. Until the Meiji era (beginning 1868), the Mogi as owners hardly exercised any managerial functions. Toji (foremen) were in charge of the (decentralised) production, oyakata (labour recruiters) hired and paid the fluctuating day labourers, and a separate front office staff did clerical and sales work. This semi-autonomous and loosely coordinated production structure lasted well into the 20th century.

A first step towards a more consolidated owner-management system was taken in 1887, when a local cartel, the Noda Shoyu Brewers' Association, was formed in response to the oversupply and excessive competition in the Kanto shoyu market, where the Noda producers jointly held a share of 5–10%. The cartel lasted 30 years and set common purchasing, price, wage and shipping arrangements to Tokyo, their major market outlet. In 1911, the cartel built a railroad link to Noda, thus expanding the brewers' regional marketing to a national scale.

Yet, the requirements of modern fermentation technology, enabling more economic high-volume, low-cost production required ever-closer cooperation for the needed capital-intensive investments. At this point in 1917, the nine Mogi-Takanashi clan families decided to bolt the cartel to form their own "Noda Shoyu Corporation", putting up as its flagship brand "Kikkoman", the most successful among the various family brands. The merger created by far the largest Japanese soy sauce producer at the time. Its stocks and directorships were divided and exclusively held among the principal families of the clan, all related by century-old descent and intermarriage.

By 1925, the Toji-directed work groups were abolished and replaced by formal production structures supervised by recently recruited managers, who introduced rigid work supervision and discipline. This period of organisational transformation coincided with the emergence of union activities, which found the all-male labour force in the food industry (Japan's second-largest industrial sector then, after the textile industry, which employed largely dormitory-locked country girls) more congenial. Resenting the aggressive modernisation, Noda workers in 1923 — under Sodomei, a reformist union's leadership — went on a month-long strike over work conditions. The strike was settled by Chiba's prefectural governor with a face-saving compromise for both sides. Four years later, the Great Noda Strike was to make social history in Japan. The Sodomei union branch, having recruited 1,500 out of 2,000 employees and accumulated a considerable war chest, felt challenged by more radical unionists and by wage cuts ordered by the Mogi management. The strike lasted 218 days and ended in total failure. The union ran out of money, while Noda Shoyu, through non-unionised plants and by hiring new labour, managed to keep its output unaffected throughout. The pay claims had to be abandoned, the union disintegrated and most fired workers were not reinstated.

Only after this strike — coinciding with the nationalist appeals of the new right-wing government of General Tanaka — did the Mogi clan adopt a conscious "corporate family" ideology, introducing in the 1930s the usual paternalist, symbolic and material fringe benefits for regular employees and a seniority-based payments system. By that time, Noda Shoyu Corporation had well developed into a rural *zaibatsu*, directed by a clan-owned holding company, comprising a local bank, a transport company, a railroad and production facilities in Korea and Manchuria, exporting to Hawaii and the U.S. West Coast and dominating Noda, its corporate town of 20,000 inhabitants.

During the war years, the company continued to produce and was even able to pay dividends to its clan owners.

After the war, the U.S. occupation's anti-*zaibatsu* drive forced the holding company's assets to be sold, stripped the clan family heads off their formal power to enforce the family codes and brought a new union to the Noda Shoyu Co. Yet, the corporation found its way around some of the new rules. Found guilty of price fixing and as a "price leader" by the recently founded anti-trust "Fair Trade

Commission", the company responded by acquiring its own fully owned distribution network. Top management positions — unaffected by the 1964 renaming to "Kikkoman Shoyu" (and later in 1980 to "The Kikkoman Corporation") — continued to be (and still are) exclusively held by the members of the Mogi clan. The Mogi/Takanashi families still hold 25% of Kikkoman's shares, while "friendly enterprises" such as Nihon Seimei Insurance and Mitsubishi Bank control another 20%. Only the relationship with the company union seems to have reversed. Contrary to what we know about Japan's labour history, the Noda Shoyu union started as a management-run union in 1946, but turned socialist in 1949 and has remained so. In the early 1960s, the union and the allied Socialist Party took over the Noda mayoralty and the majority of the municipal assembly; thereafter, they started to dissociate the corporate town from the ruling clan and its enterprise.

With the Westernisation of Japan's diet, the need for shoyu flavouring declined, and so did its per capita consumption in Japan. Until 1962, the clan management responded by buying up the market shares of traditional competitors in this contracting market. Then, adopted sons took over the presidency and pursued more innovative strategies for corporate survival: promoting overseas sales of soy sauce to non-Japanese consumers as an "all-purpose, international seasoning" and securing their U.S. market share by opening a plant in Wisconsin in 1972. The new Kikkoman management further diversified in both traditional products, such as sake, shochu (a vodka-like liquor), plum wines and other seasonings and in imported brand ketchups, juices, soups, wines and brandies. With 60% of sales in the early 1980s still accruing from soy sauce (and holding a 40% share of its Japanese market), Kikkoman at a sales volume of $600 million was, at the time, one of the few internationally competitive Japanese food processors. They are usually handicapped by the country's high level of agricultural protection, pushing up input prices.

In 1969, JFC International Inc. was acquired. It produces some 8,500 oriental foodstuffs, mostly under the brand name Dynasty, but also Nishiki Premium Grade Rice and Ozeki Sake. In 1990, Kikkoman strengthened its partnership with Del Monte (for whom it has acted as an importing agent in Japan since 1963). It acquired permanent marketing rights for the Asia-Pacific region (except for the Philippines) for all Del Monte products, which are notably fruit juices, canned pineapple and peaches, tomato ketchup and dried raisins.

Different from many Japanese companies, Kikkoman's diversification remained focused on the food sector proper. Its international drive also proceeded cautiously over the decades, thus avoiding the pitfalls of many other Japanese companies during the pre-1992 boom years.

When the Japanese bubble finally burst, Kikkoman survived, as it recognised an early warning signal to which it responded well. In the mid-1980s, Kikkoman's attempt at internationalising almost proved its undoing. It sold its Mann's wine as a premium high-quality wine in Japan, trusting that its customers' connoisseurship did not go very far. Unfortunately, at the time, glycol anti-freeze was found in diluted Austrian wines. Promptly, traces were also found in Mann's wine, proving that the claimed high-quality vintage brands were rather cheap blends of bulk wines bought haphazardly from dubious traders.

Stringent quality controls, the reliance on quality wine imports and the resignation of a series of Mogi clan managers in atonement (which facilitated generational succession) helped Kikkoman rebuild its Mann's brand as a decent table wine over the years.

According to Kikkoman's honorary CEO, Yuzaburo Mogi, "Our new, vigorous management team is working to enhance our worldwide expansion through the establishment of new plants that will enable us to move our products more efficiently while seeking strategically located promising markets".

Kikkoman's approach was to actively seek expansion through recipe contests, cooking classes and editorial PR in food journals — the use of its sauces in non-traditional Western dishes, such as hamburgers, stews and salads. This strategy was risky, given the innate conservatism of culinary tastes, but it paid off.

Today, the growth of demand for Kikkoman soy sauces and teriyaki sauces is exclusively outside Japan (where competition is tougher and the population is stagnating), particularly in North America, Europe and South-East Asia. Hence, Kikkoman, at the time, increased the output of its Wisconsin plant by 40% to some 130,000 kilolitres of soy sauce and teriyaki sauce and of its Singapore and North Holland plants by 20%, each to 12,000 and 9,000 kilolitres, respectively.

In the field of seasonings, and supplies for fine dining globally and for decent wines and effective biotechnology in Japan, Kikkoman is thus well positioned.

The successful family management of the Mogis over 10 generations is certainly a remarkable achievement over all human and historical odds.

Kikkoman follows the slogan "Flavors That Bring People Together", and the company is devoted to promoting international cultural exchange. It does so through involvement in educational and student exchange programmes, such as Youth for Understanding for high school students and AIESEC, a work/study programme for university students. It also organises many cooking classes worldwide.

The Next Two Decades

Kikkoman's international expansion continued relentlessly during the following two decades. By 2023, 75% of sales were overseas, and only 25% in Japan proper. Even more pronounced, 75% of profits were generated in North America, 11% in Europe and only

9% in Oceania and Asia. In the meantime, Kikkoman has repositioned itself through its "JFC International Foods" subsidiary as the major wholesaler and distributor of Asian food and beverages for hotels, restaurants, caterers, wholesalers and retailers on the North American market. Thus, they supply the whole range of Asian foods, in total more than 10,000 items, from Nishiki rice grown in California, noodles, beverages, seafood, snacks, confectionary to kitchenware and chopsticks — in short, anything you would expect in any decently stocked Asia shop, far beyond its own Kikkoman produce. These wholesaling and distribution operations accounted for 73% of its turnover, while its own production and manufacturing contributed only 31% (allowing for some uncertainties in counting) of sales. It was a role Kikkoman, or any other food manufacturer in Japan, could never have dared to exercise domestically given the cartelised strength of the domestic traditional wholesale and retail systems. Abroad it was different, and exotic imported foods offered more attractive margins.

Yet, it continued its own export and marketing drive relentlessly. Its core Kikkoman natural soy sauce exports went up from an index of 100 (1974) to 2,900 (2023), representing a global production of 400 million litres per year. In fact, in the U.S., "Kikkoman" has become a byword for any quality soy sauce without additives, preservatives or colourants (which has become a problem in some Chinese restaurants where Kikkoman bottles are refilled with chemical concoctions). The other product ranges were maintained and expanded: ketchup, Teriyaki sauces for meat, condiments, Manjo mirin (sweet sake for cooking), fruit spirits, sake, Mann's wines (for domestic consumption), lemonade, juices, food supplements, enzymes and health foods, and in 2008, with Kikkoman Soyfoods Co., it moved into soymilk production as Japan's largest maker of Kibun soy milk.

Yuzaburo Mogi, honorary CEO and chairman of Kikkoman's board of directors, who in 1960 had studied at Columbia's Business

School, explained *ex post* the difficult strategy of creating demand in the U.S. and Europe for a product where there had been none. So, they started very modestly in 1957 with a small sales office in San Francisco to cultivate the West Coast's Asian community and military returnees from Japan and Korea. Weeklong cooking demonstration were held in supermarkets, showing the use and taste in meat preparations (like in Australia later). In 1961, the East Coast was handled from New York, in 1965 the mid-West from Chicago and finally the South from Atlanta. Local production was started in rural southern Wisconsin, where wheat and soy beans were in abundance. The location was close to Chicago and hence central in the U.S. The workforce was motivated and crime rates were low, Mogi observed. The "sushi boom" of the 1980es and the popularisation of Japan's food culture further helped sales, with a steady growth of 5% per year. In June 2024, the existing plant in Walworth was expanded, and a new $800 million plant in Jefferson County was inaugurated by Mogi — to which U.S. tax credits of $15.5 million also contributed.

In Taiwan, Kikkoman had entered into a joint venture with Uni-President Enterprises Group, the nation's largest food producer, back in 1990. Together, they ventured into the mainland and set up a plant in Shanghai in 2002 and then two more near Beijing and Tianjin in 2009. In 2014, Kikkoman however set up its own fully owned sales company in China. Marketing in Brazil started in earnest with a plant in Sao Paulo in 2021, whilst in India beginnings are still very modest, starting with the usual cooking competitions and seminars for chefs, covering, *inter alia*, the use of soy sauce with pineapples and watermelons…

Bibliography

Note: Any links to online sources were valid as of the publication of the first edition, in October 2004. Many of the pages have since been taken down.

Dow Jones. "DJO Japan's Kikkoman to Boost Overseas Soy Sauce Output", 18 April 2003.

Fruin, M. W. *Kikkoman: Company, Clan and Community*. Cambridge, Mass: Harvard University Press, 1993.

Ketchum. "Case Study: Kikkoman International Inc.". http://www.ketchum.com/displaywebpage/0,1003,797,00.html

NFIA. "Company Profiles: Kikkoman Corporation". http://www.nfia/html/company/c_kikkoman.hmtl

The World of Kikkoman. http://www.kikkoman.com/contents/company/comoverview.html

Yates, R. E. *The Kikkoman Chronicles: A Global Company with a Japanese Soul*. New York: McGraw Hill, 1998.

New Literature, 2nd Edition

Mogi, Y. "Emblematic of Abenomics, Kikkoman is a case study of global success", *The Worldfolio*, 8 June 2015.

Rothacher, A. *Die Rückkehr der Samurai. Japans Wirtschaft nach der Krise*. Heidelberg: Springer, 2007, pp. 218–222.

Who Loves McDonald's?

The mere mention of hamburgers will naturally bring an immediate association with the leading brand, McDonald's. Even though McDonald's is not the creator of the hamburger, nor is it the pioneer of fast-food restaurants, its revolutionary approach to franchising fast-food outlets and its successful corporate strategy enabled it to become a fast-food juggernaut that is recognisable throughout the entire planet. Perhaps that is not a hyperbole, and in fact, McDonald's Corporation could be forgiven for boasting in 2003 that "it is the world's leading food service retailer with more than 30,000 restaurants in 118 countries serving 46 million customers each day". Its success was further symbolised by the fact that "the corporation generates more than $40 billion in annual systemwide sales".

In order to understand the success of McDonald's, it is imperative to look back at the background of this fast-food restaurant. Over the years, there has been a popular debate over who the real founders of McDonald's are: Is it the McDonald brothers, or is it Ray Kroc? A satisfactory answer would be that, while the McDonald brothers, Richard and Maurice, were the founders of the first McDonald's restaurant in San Bernardino, Ray Kroc was the man who took the concept of the McDonald's fast-food restaurant, franchised it and turned it into the money-spinning juggernaut it is right now. The McDonald brothers may have been portrayed as easily contented non-entrepreneurs by Ray Kroc in his semi-autobiography, *Grinding It Out*, but the fact that they were quick to capitalise on the success of drive-in restaurants in California in the 1940s showed their entrepreneurial skills, which would be embodied in the McDonald's *esprit de corps*. Concerned with the negative image of female car-hops driving business away, the brothers revolutionised the concept of fast food. The menu was cut down to only nine items so that food could be produced in an assembly-line-like manner. Hamburgers were priced at 15 cents, and the relatively low price attracted customers in droves. At the same time, despite producing food *en masse* and in quick time, the quality of the food served was among the best in the area; nobody fried French fries as crispy and delicious as the McDonald's restaurant in San Bernardino.

The success of the McDonald's restaurant in San Bernardino caught the attention of a Multimixer salesman, Ray Kroc, in 1954. Kroc was intrigued with the large amount of purchases made by the McDonalds of his Multimixers, which were used to make milkshakes. When he drove down to the desert town of San Bernardino, he was impressed by the restaurant. He felt that such a concept could generate a lot of attention if it were to be expanded nationwide. However, Kroc was surprised that the McDonalds would rather stay behind in San Bernardino than participate in the joint venture that he had proposed to them. Nevertheless, without the founders, Kroc's entrepreneurial spirit drove him to create McDonald's Corporation in 1955. He would lease out franchising licences to operators who wanted to start a McDonald's of their own. Kroc himself was the first franchisee, with his store in Des Plaines, Illinois, and the success of that restaurant served as a model for other franchisees and a showcase for future operators.

At this point in time, it is important to note that when Kroc decided to enter the fray of fast-food restaurant operations, he thought less about the amount of money it would make but more about making McDonald's a household name across the U.S. He dreamt of seeing McDonald's restaurants in every city and suburb across America, and it was his nature to go all out and win at all costs in his bid to make McDonald's a successful entity. In this endeavour, he was willing to be "ruthless" towards the brothers by buying the rights to the name McDonald's, even denying them the right to use their own name McDonald's for their original store in San Bernardino. At times, he appeared highly authoritarian.

Perhaps the early success of McDonald's from 1955 onwards until the end of that decade could be due to Kroc's single-handed, authoritarian-like management. This was made possible since the McDonald's corporation started out in 1955 as a small company, with only Kroc's secretary at Prince Castle, June Martino, and the grillmen at the Des Plaines store on his company's payroll. Kroc himself was still drawing a salary from his job at Prince Castle, which also supplied McDonald's with its Multimixers. In 1956, Harry Sonneborn was appointed by Kroc as the financial wizard of McDonald's and joined the company. While Kroc may have been authoritarian in terms of setting the rules and regimentation that every McDonald's franchise, restaurant and employee must follow to the letter, he gave Sonneborn full autonomy over the company's financial management since Kroc himself admitted that he was not a "money person". The McDonald's mechanism was not only fuelled by Kroc's vision, desire and meticulous planning but also by Sonneborn's pragmatism to keep McDonald's financially afloat. These two contrasting personalities might be bound to clash every now and then, and Kroc himself admitted that he would often argue with Sonneborn over the future direction of McDonald's. It was up to June Martino, who was no longer a mere secretary to Kroc but a person directly influential in the development of McDonald's as a corporation, to mediate with empathy, as she herself was the embodiment of the human element in the McDonald's corporate management mechanism. Martino was seen by Kroc as the person who gelled and synergised the different personalities together to work for the betterment of McDonald's Corporation. She would also, in countless number of times, act as the mediator between Kroc and Sonneborn. Eventually, Martino was to become the matriarch of McDonald's Corporation.

By 1960, McDonald's had already grown into a corporation that adopted an almost family-like structure at the top. Kroc was the father. He was the patriarch who set out the tasks for his employees and franchisees, his "children", to follow. As a "father" to the company, Kroc was very charismatic, and he inspired his employees to strive hard so that in the end, they could feel like a winner if McDonald's emerged triumphant in terms of meeting the objectives he had set. When Kroc promoted his McDonald's concept to potential franchisees, he would meticulously lay out plans and would be honest in informing them how much profit they could stand to make from their venture with McDonald's. Kroc believed that McDonald's Corporation must not profit at the expense of its franchisees but that it must give full support to enable its franchisees to succeed. Full support came, and still comes, in the form of providing high-quality food and equipment supplies at discounted rates, as well as providing thorough employee training to those working at the counters and kitchens, since quality food is vital to a McDonald's restaurant's success.

Only when its franchisees reaped profits from their venture could McDonald's achieve any success from the joint venture.

Kroc was a strict conformist and would not tolerate any nonsense and deviation from the plans he had drawn out for a standard McDonald's franchise. Kroc himself set equally demanding standards and work ethic for his employees at the McDonald's Corporation headquarters. However, to dub Kroc a dictator may be missing the mark since he was very open to ideas from anyone, be it a high-ranking executive at the McDonald's HQ or even the counterman at a McDonald's restaurant. This openness was vital to the eventual success of McDonald's. The most popular item on McDonald's menu was soon no longer the fifteen-cent hamburger that had been the trademark of the McDonald brothers since the 1950s, but new items like the Big Mac, the Filet-O-Fish and the Egg McMuffin. If Kroc had really insisted all franchises to sell hamburgers at 15 cents per piece and to adhere strictly to his menu list, the franchises would have folded. Kroc allowed his franchisees to be creative so that they could serve their purposes well and, in turn, serve the corporation's interests well too. This enabled Lou Groen, a franchisee in Cincinnati, to introduce the Filet-O-Fish, which helped his restaurant rack up more sales. Herb Peterson would introduce the Egg McMuffin for the breakfast menu so that his McDonald's in Santa Barbara could open in the mornings to boost sales, while Jim Delligatti introduced the Big Mac, which would become the mandatory and most coveted item on every McDonald's menu list. In terms of marketing the McDonald's name, Kroc also allowed the franchisees to use their creativity, and the operators of the franchise in Washington, DC, John Gibson and Oscar Goldstein, scored big with the creation of Ronald McDonald to promote McDonald's among the young population.

Kroc emphasised commitment to McDonald's in each of his employees. In fact, Kroc himself embodied the spirit of commitment. It was a common sight to see Kroc working in his Chicago headquarters until late evening, and when he finished, would have to rush all the way to the subway station to catch the last train. This leading-by-example personality developed a strong loyalty among executives not only towards Kroc but also towards McDonald's Corporation. This spirit is clearly shown in John F. Love's corporate biography, *McDonald's: Behind the Arches*, where he relates the story of a senior executive, Donald Smith, who left McDonald's after being promoted as its vice president, to become the president of its arch-rival Burger King. Even though Smith would later return to Chicago as an executive in a different company, the other McDonald's executives did "not associate with him", for they would never forget nor forgive his betrayal.

During its early days in the 1950s, McDonald's would promote itself by serving an "All-American Meal". Eventually, it would be exporting Americana and its "All-American Meal" to other parts of the world. The first international expansion began just across the border in British Columbia, Canada, where the first franchise was opened in 1967. The McDonald's International Division was created in 1969, and its first restaurant overseas was opened in the Netherlands. The franchise in the Netherlands followed the successful formula of McDonald's in the U.S. too closely that it did not take into account several crucial local factors that almost turned the venture into a disaster.

While the success of McDonald's in the U.S. came largely from the suburbs, which were developing as more nuclear families set homes up there, the suburbs in the Netherlands were sparsely populated, as its population remained more concentrated in the cities. Nevertheless, always eager to learn from mistakes, in 1971, McDonald's opened up its first franchise in Asia, with Japan as its chosen site. For this venture, McDonald's Corporation allowed the Japanese franchisee, Den Fujita, to experiment by introducing locally favoured items on the McDonald's menu. However, Fujita also realised that McDonald's could never compete with the established sushi and family restaurants in Japan that served traditional dishes, so he decided to change the eating habits of the Japanese population. Hence, in order to achieve this aim, Japanese children were often the target of promotions and advertisements, whereby they would pressure their parents to eat at McDonald's. This "Americanisation" strategy worked not only in

Japan but also in various other countries in Asia, including notably in Singapore. In Singapore, almost every McDonald's advertisement features the whole family, children included of course, dining out at McDonald's. McDonald's International has certainly made McDonald's an important feature of an Asian family's regular dining-out-together experience.

Americanisation does not stop at "McDonaldising" the family eating habits but also in terms of corporate management. Since the success of McDonald's in the U.S. is due to its American corporate culture, where the low power distance between employers and employees enabled free exchange of ideas and creativity, McDonald's corporate structure in Asian countries would naturally adopt the American corporate culture. Instead of adhering to the characteristically high power distance of the Asian corporate culture, which may stifle creativity and the free exchange of ideas, the American corporate culture helps instil creativity among the junior-level employees and also ensures that the senior executives would not rest on their laurels and be free from criticism.

As long as people around the world are eating hamburgers and as long as hamburgers are associated with McDonald's, the future of the corporation looks bright. Despite the billions of dollars' worth of profits made by McDonald's Corporation, the company makes a strong effort to portray itself not as an evil multi-national corporation but as a company that contributes a lot to the welfare of the community, as shown by its Ronald McDonald Houses community program. The human element of a corporation is vital to the success of McDonald's, and thus the Hamburger University was set up to provide training and career advancement to its employees. Thus, it is not an exaggeration to say that the success of McDonald's does not depend solely on profit maximisation but also on the desire of its executives to make McDonald's part of the family and the community at large.

The Next Two Decades

McDonald's continued to grow incrementally and has remained by far the world's largest fast-food operator and franchisor in 120 countries. Its annual turnover reached $23.2 billion in 2022, with profits standing at a healthy $6.2 billion. Other statistics are more elusive. Are there really 1.8 million global employees or a mere 200,000, depending on sources? One figure includes all franchisees and their staff, part-timers, delivery boys and students jobbing on vacation; the other includes only full-timers at McDonald's proper. The same with the number of "restaurants", which vary between 37,000 (6,000 fully owned and 31,000 franchisees) and 41,800 also for the same year (2022). The explanation: there are huge variations in sizes, given management's endless appetite for national and regional experiments, ranging from the classical stand-alone family restaurant to McDrives, McCafes, McWalks, McHomes, McDeliverys and in-house facilities on ferries and trains and in railway stations and petrol stations, without any seating facilities. Where does a "restaurant" start? There is even a – probably short-lived – novelty called CosMc's, which, as a Starbucks imitation, offers soft drinks, tea and cold coffee. The idea to compete in the crowded pizza market with a "Donato Pizza" chain already flopped. Searching for ever-elusive higher growth figures, fearing that burgers could go out of fashion and under permanent public criticism as suppliers of addictive junk food, management equally and endlessly tinkered with the menu card, sometimes with outstanding success; for instance, under Jim Cantaloupe's long reign as CEO (from 1991 until his death in April 2004), McDonald's introduced salads and offered breakfasts and thus utilised longer opening hours. Since 2015, the Veggie Burger and synthetic Plant Burgers and McPlant Nuggets (from Beyond Meat) have been on offer, although regulars continue to prefer Big Macs or Chicken McNuggets nonetheless. Now, you can of course expand a menu card endlessly, but then you are turning slow food and increasing inventory costs.

As a global mass operator, McDonald's obviously had to take care of religious prescripts, notably over meat consumption. Hence, in heavily Catholic areas on Fridays, there are FishMacs on offer. Among Israel's 183 restaurants (as of 2020), 50 are kosher and close on Saturdays owing to the Sabath. In the Islamic world, there is only halal meat on offer, and the rules of Ramadan are respected. In India, there is neither beef nor pork on offer, but burgers are made of poultry and lamb meat ("McMaharaja" — note that some maharajas have fallen on hard times). There are also non-religious national variations. In Japan, the "Teriyaki Burger" and "Chicken Tatsuta" with adopted dressings are most popular, and in the Netherlands, it is the "McKroket".

In Latin America, it is not advisable to advertise Yankeedom too obviously. So, a subsidiary called "Arcos Dorados" with 2,300 restaurants in 20 countries, 95,000 employees and a turnover of $3.3 billion (2023) runs the show nonetheless. In China, the opposite is the case. With 5,000 restaurants (2022), it has become McDonald's second-largest national market after the U.S. proper, with expansion plans to reach 10,000 by 2028. It stands for prestige, hygiene and reliable food qualities. Whoever has ever visited and eaten at a Chinese food court understands why. The beginnings were slow: in Taipei, Taiwan in 1984 and then in Shenzhen on the mainland in 1990. But in 1992, in Beijing, by far the world's largest McDonald's was inaugurated. On opening day, 40,000 customers were served by 1,000 employees.

With 10% of China's population, Russia had been a similar success story — until March 2022. McDonald's opening in January 1990 in the decaying Soviet Union at Moscow's Pushkin Square was attended by none other than President Boris Yeltsin. Despite 20 counters, queues stretching half a kilometre formed throughout the day. People who in their lifetime had experienced nothing but drab counters, unfriendly service and bad food in public eateries felt that they were suddenly in an American movie. Following Putin's war against the Ukraine, HQ in Oak Brook, like many producers of highly visible consumer items, did not want to be singled out for criticism — although hamburgers can hardly be identified as dual-use weapons! After a successful presence of 30 years in the country, an admired American icon capitulated without a fight: 850 restaurants with 82,000 employees closed at the cost of \$1.2–1.4 billion. The loss of the Russian market amounted to a turnover loss of 9% at the tune of \$2 billion per year. The new Russian owner, who could purchase for an undisclosed bargain price, resumed operations in June 2022 as "Vkusmo i Tochka" ("Delicious, full stop"). Although cheaper, immediately visible was the decline in quality, cleanliness and service.

The management practices at McDonald's offer a curious spectacle from afar. Obviously, running a manufacturing firm or a five-star hotel seems to be intellectually more stimulating than negotiating with local suppliers, controlling franchisees, tinkering with restaurant design (green roofs instead of red ones) and dreaming up marketing gimmicks or a new burger dressing. Yet, all of current and previous top management have spent decades at McDonald's often being shifted around ruthlessly from continent to continent. Only those who met the turnover, profit and expansion targets (which, during the BSE and COVID-19 crises, were often beyond their control) — which seem to be fairly mechanically set between 2% and 5% per year with several hundred new openings — survived headquarters' scrutiny in Illinois and were promoted. Europe, for instance, is divided into four supervisory districts to avoid managers "going native": West (including Germany and Austria), North, South and East. If the hated competition of Burger King, Wendy's or KFC does better in a given market, management heads do roll.

This also applies to the top. In 2014, Don Thompson was fired as CEO after a quarterly fall in turnover of −7% was recorded.

His successor, Steve Easterbrook, had to go four years later, after the divorcee had a romantic affair with a colleague, falling foul of American puritanism.

This is not to say that McDonald's is considered a paragon of civic virtue. Rather the opposite. I spare the reader the generally well-rehearsed criticisms of being the origin of most obesity, diabetes and heart diseases, as well as contributing to mountains of unrecycled plastic and wrapping garbage, and being a global shirker of corporate taxes. But this is not to say that all facile criticism levelled at this most visible representative of the American way of life is fair or justified. Thus, it is the object of campaigns against all meat consumption proper. With or without vegan burgers, McDonald's does not make a difference. Then, it is argued "McJobs" were representative and role models for precarious underpaid youth employment. In fact, these jobs were and are often the entry ticket into the job market for otherwise poorly qualified youths. Finally, there is this cultural reproach of "McDonaldisation" as an assumed streamlined, standardised and globalised way of life. First, consumption is never compulsory. Second, those who were forcefully starved from it in Eastern Europe, Russia and China embraced it with enthusiasm and with a vengeance — for a while, with good measure — while retaining their national cultures. So, all is not wrong with the giant from Oak Brook, Illinois.

Bibliography

Kroc, R. *Grinding It Out: The Making of McDonald's*. New York: St. Martin's Press, 1987.

Love, J. F. *McDonald's: Behind the Arches*. New York: Bantam Books, 1995.

Watson, J. L. (ed.) *Golden Arches East: McDonald's In East Asia*. Stanford, California: Stanford University Press, 1997.

Wawro, T. *Radicals and Visionaries*. Irvine, California: Entrepreneur Press, 2000.

"Welcome to McDonald's". http://www.mcdonalds.com

New Literature, 2nd Edition

"50.000 McDonald's Filialen bis 2027", *Tagesschau*, 7 December 2023.

Jewers, C. "McDonald's to exit Russia after 30 years", *Daily Mail*, 16 May 2022.

"Konkurrenz nagt an McDonald's", *Handelsblatt*, 25 October 2013.

"McDonald's Chef muß gehen", *Die Zeit*, 29 January 2015.

"McDonald's entläßt Chef wegen Beziehung mit Mitarbeiterin", *Der Spiegel*, 4 November 2019.

"Supersparmenu", *Manager Magazin*, 11 April 2003.

For God, America and the Real Thing: The Coke Story

A billion hours ago, human life appeared on earth. A billion minutes ago, Christianity emerged. A billion seconds ago, the Beatles changed music. A billion Coca-Colas ago was yesterday morning.

— Robert Goizueta
the late CEO of Coca-Cola, explaining in April 1997
that one billion Cokes are sold every two days worldwide[1]

Originally designed as a cure for the flu in 1886, Coca-Cola has turned into the world's largest manufacturer, marketer and distributor of non-alcoholic beverages. And in the process, it has indeed become an icon of globalisation. Back in 1989, the Company sold $8.6 billion worth of beverages, and by 1999, its sales had more than doubled to $19.8 billion, for an annualised growth of 8.67% (*Motley Fool*). To date, The Coca-Cola Company has diversified

[1] For more on Goizueta's leadership role in The Coca-Cola Company, refer to "Goizueta and Juan Antonio Samaranch", in David Greising's *I'd Like the World to Buy a Coke: The Life and Leadership of Roberto Goizueta.* NY: John Wiley, 1998, pp. 251–257.

its products to more than 300 brands whilst operating in over 200 countries worldwide.[2]

The "Good Ole" Days

In 1885, John Pemberton,[3] an Atlanta pharmacist, registered a trademark for "French Wine Cola — Ideal Nerve and Tonic Stimulant", a brew he had developed in a three-legged pot, which he apparently stirred with an oar. The name was appropriate since the stimulant is said to have contained cocaine, along with wine and a few other ingredients. After about a year, Pemberton decided to change the formula; he removed the wine and added caffeine and, for flavour, extract of kola nut.[4] At that point, his partner and bookkeeper, Frank Robinson, changed the name to Coca-Cola because he thought the two Cs, written in the Spencerian script, which was quite popular at that time, would look good in advertising. Coca-Cola, which joined the ranks of the many mysterious potions being peddled by travelling salesmen, was thus sold as a cure for both hangovers and headaches.

In a twist of events, Georgia businessman Asa Candler[5] bought the sole rights to Coca-Cola from John Pemberton in 1889. To expand the business, Candler began to sell Coca-Cola syrup to wholesalers, who in turn sold it to drugstores. In 1889, Benjamin F. Thomas and Joseph P. Whitehead of Tennessee approached Candler with a proposition to bottle Coca-Cola. They promptly sold regional bottling rights to other businessmen in the South and later to the rest of America, thus creating a network of independent bottlers

[2] Obtain latest press releases and financial statements of the Company vis-à-vis the Coca-Cola website. http://www2.coca-cola.com/ourcompany/ourheritage.html

[3] "Dr. John S. Pemberton: Originator of Coca-Cola", *Pharmacy in History*, vol. 29 (1987), no. 2, pp. 85–89: Allen, *Secret Formula*, pp. 18–22.

[4] See "Use of the coca plant": in "Wonderful Coca", AC, June 21, 1985.

[5] Refer to Asa Candler, "Confidence in your Product", *1916 Bottlers Convention Booklet*, p. 76.

numbering about 1,000 by 1930. Each bottler had an exclusive right in perpetuity to bottle Coke in their area, and no one else except the soda fountains could sell Coke in the market. The bottlers[6] actually owned the Coca-Cola trademark in their territories, and the company could not then refuse to sell them syrup (Oliver, 1986). This simple contract was to revolutionise the Coca-Cola business, giving birth to one of the world's most innovative and dynamic franchising systems in the world (Pendergrast, 2000).

Robert W. Woodruff, "The Boss"

In 1919, Candler sold the company to Ernest Woodruff for a hefty $25 million. Subsequently, in April 1923, Woodruff 's son, Robert, became president of Coca-Cola. "The boss", as he came to be called, would soon make the name Coke virtually synonymous with America around the world. Yet, this dominant figure worked behind the scenes in relative anonymity. He had even hired public relations personnel to keep his name out of the newspapers and told the publisher of *The Atlanta Constitution* that he did not want to see his name in that paper again unless he was convicted of rape. Interestingly, a plaque on his desk read, "There is no limit to what a man can do or where he can go if he doesn't mind who gets the credit", a saying that perhaps no other corporate president before or since has endorsed. With his fedora and a cigar permanently jutting from his teeth, he led the company through the strength of his personality.[7]

Even to his closest associates, Robert Woodruff remained much of an enigma. Standing at an even six foot, his commanding

[6] Ralph B. Beach, "History of the Coca-Cola Bottler's Association", CC Bottler, April 1959, pp. 99–106.

[7] Woodruff prescribed a rigid Ichauway itinerary for his guests. "When you are with Bob Woodruff ", remarked Freeman Gosden, the white actor who played Amos in *Amos and Andy*, "you are going to have a good time all right, but you are going to have it his way" (Elliot, *Mr. Anonymous*, p. 55).

presence made him seem much larger than life as he chewed on his ever-present cigar whilst silently assessing a room he had just entered. Without a doubt, Robert Woodruff had an indescribable presence and magnetism. For this reason, Coca-Cola men would do seemingly almost anything to win his favour and have since demonstrated fanatical loyalty over the years. Yet, on the surface, Woodruff was a singularly uninteresting man. Simply put, he didn't read.[8] Several of his intimates swore that he never finished a book in his life, and he refused to look at any correspondence that went beyond a single page, relying on aides to digest the material for him. He was also reputed to be unappreciative of culture, history or art. When stuck in traffic only minutes from St. Peter's in Rome, he impatiently ordered his driver to turn around. "But Mr. Woodruff, we're only five minutes away!" his secretary exclaimed. "That's close enough", Woodruff snapped.

It is essential to note however that Robert Woodruff aptly inherited the corporate culture of Coca-Cola, a drink that already acquired a semi-mystical aura. In addition, he understood how to manipulate corporate structure in order to maximise profits, privacy and control while minimising taxes and governmental scrutiny. In 1923, Robert Woodruff expanded the former Information Department into the Statistical Department, which soon performed what would now be called the department for pioneering market research. During the decade's last three years, this department frenetically laid the foundations crucial for an enhanced scientific approach to selling more Coca-Cola (Pendergrast, 2000, p. 161).

Also, Woodruff embarked on an important mission to standardise the quality and output of Coca-Cola around the world. He did this by relating the message of a reward system to the bottlers: for if you abided by his rules, you were rewarded with

[8] It has been speculated by certain scholars the possibility of Woodruff being dyslexic, amongst others such as George Patton, Woodrow Wilson, Thomas Edison and Nelson Rockefeller.

more advertising support, more encouragement and more perks; if you choose otherwise, you would consequently find yourself with virtually no support and possibly becoming ostracised by the many other members of the "Coca-Cola family". Woodruff found another solution for failing bottlers during the 1920s: simply buying them out of their crisis, which proved to be an effective economic move.

In addition, Woodruff also pioneered the Seeds of Foreign Conquest, applying his energy and organisational skills to birthing overseas markets. In 1922, with an expenditure of some $3 million, bottling franchises were started all over Europe, largely funded by Coca-Cola and run by locals in those selected regions (Pendergrast, 2000, pp. 164–166). In terms of advertising and publicity, the company has always believed in marketing its products well through aggressive advertising and the like, spending more than $4 billion annually on advertising and marketing worldwide. During the Second World War, a different sort of advert rendered Coca-Cola's brand name famous worldwide. Coke supplied to the American GIs fighting overseas, which served as a powerful message and became iconic of American presence abroad. According to a returning war veteran, "Personally, I think that The Coca-Cola Company's cooperation with the Army in getting Coca-Cola to the men in the field is the best advertisement that Coca-Cola has ever had". Writing to his company boss, he explained that, "The things that are happening to these men now will stick with them for the rest of their life".[9]

[9] In a poll of veterans in 1948 conducted by the *American Legion Magazine*, 63.67% specified Coca-Cola as their favourite soft drink, with Pepsi gaining only 7.78% of the total vote. In the same year, Coke's gross profit on sales reached a staggering $126 million, as compared to Pepsi's $25 million. As the Coca-Cola Company's unpublished history stated, the wartime advertisement "made friends and customers for home consumption of 11,000,000 GIs [and] did [a] sampling and expansion job abroad which would otherwise have taken 25 years and millions of dollars". See Pendergrast, *For God, Country and Coca-Cola,* London: The Orion Publishing Group, 2000, p. 212.

And in the 1980s, in an attempt to compete with the preferred taste of Pepsi-Cola, Coke revamped its original recipe to one that boasts of superior taste to that of Pepsi and even the original Coke flavour. However, that proved to be a marketing disaster, as people were outraged with the insertion of a "new" coke. As a result of the New Coke disaster, the original Coca-Cola garnered much more than $4 billion worth of publicity, rendering the Company's horrendous advertising irrelevant. The venerable cola roared back to claim its lead as the premier American soft drink. Unintentionally, Goizueta and Keough had converted the gigantic marketing blunder into a commercial coup (Allen, 1994).

Roberto Goizueta,[10] who became Woodruff 's successor, had always said that Coke products should be more popular than water. In terms of marketing Coke, the most powerful Coca-Cola, appeal has not ultimately been sexual or physiological but communal: if you drink Coke, the ads suggest, you will belong to a warm, loving, accepting family, singing in perfect harmony.

Coke Nation Embodying Corporate Culture

At The Coca-Cola Company, employees are fervently attached to their employer. "Everyone is very loyal to the company, they are very proud of all of the accomplishments achieved there. There is a certain amount of pride many of us take knowing that we have helped get us to this point", according to one employee in a conducted research poll. Indeed, Coke is the very lifeblood of the company, and its employees shunned the sainted liquid at their peril. One former financial auditor describes the company's culture as quite strong. where people are expected to drink Coke.

[10] Goizueta left an astonishing legacy; see Patricia Sellers, "Where Coke Goes from Here", *Fortune,* 13 October 1997, p. 88.

The intense loyalty meshes with what is invariably described as a "conservative" atmosphere, an ambience linked to the sheer size of the company. Coke has a very conservative corporate culture; however, it is a large company with a seemingly diverse corporate culture. The company is very proud of its heritage and integrity. Coke people tend to be professional in dress and nature and are geared towards conservative behaviour. This is not to say that enthusiasm is not appreciated. In many cases, it is often required.

The headquarters of The Coca-Cola Company is located in downtown Atlanta, Georgia. According to an insider of the corporate headquarters, "there is extreme security before you even gain access into the Coke nation, and it continues throughout the complex". The company actually has a Health Management Department staffed with health and fitness specialists whose job is to reduce healthcare costs and encourage healthy habits in the company. The company also subsidises all of the services at its Coca-Cola's home campus, which include fitness centres and other amenities.

The Coca-Cola Company likes to propagandise that "Coca-Cola" is the second-best known expression in the world, next to "Ok". It is thus no wonder that The Coca-Cola Company credentials apparently stands out on a resume. With the ubiquity of the product and the outstanding performance of its stock in the past few decades, the brand and business success culminate in a proverbial recipe for super-high prestige — especially in areas such as finance and marketing. It is reported that Coke has a great reputation everywhere in almost every area they are in. They like to believe that there is quality in everything they do, and they work very hard at maintaining that quality.

Insiders describe Coke's benefits package in glowing terms. Besides the benefits of the corporate campus, employees have the option to finance their car with the help of the company, have several healthcare plans to choose from, can reimburse their tuition, have a stock-purchase option and can enjoy a 401(k) plan, which has made many a Coke employee's retirement a golden one. There are also days off at Six Flags Atlanta, free ice-skating, Thanksgiving Dinners and concert tickets available in the Coca-Cola section reserved in the front at almost any major venue in the country. And of course, there is the "all-you-can-drink" aspect of working at Coke, reportedly distributed through coolers, fountains and vending machines set up specifically for employees. So, all you have to do is push the button, and the Coke can drops.

Coke is not known for its outstanding record on diversity efforts, but if employees in Atlanta are to be believed, corporate headquarters is teaching the world to sing in perfect harmony, making Coca-Cola a truly international company by hiring people of all races, religions and cultures. The diversity may be also drawn from the mixed backgrounds of management people and those working under them. Coke's revered former CEO, Roberto Goizueta, was a Cuban immigrant himself, personifying the very aura of the Coca-Cola establishment as a self-made man, a perfect symbol of the American dream rising to the pinnacle of success.

Criticism of Coca-Cola's Culture

It is not surprising that Coca-Cola finds itself in deep trouble in Europe. And this has to do with the company's corporate culture. If you think about it, Coca-Cola sells sugared water. That's all. Just sugared water. Yet, it has managed to do it so skilfully for so long that it has taken on an almost mystical aura, even for its employees. Its success is due to a corporate culture that combines superior marketing with aggressive legal enforcement. Coca-Cola lawyers are among the most aggressive in the world, enforcing the company's rules on how and where Coca-Cola is sold.

This combination of marketing and legal muscle has made the company extraordinarily successful, and perhaps left it feeling a tad omnipotent. However, entering the dust-up in Belgium and France over supposedly contaminated Coca-Cola products, we see that the company's culture didn't allow it to respond as quickly as it should have, and the result was a costly crisis. The culture is determined by how the CEO wants the company to run. Doug Ivester, Coca-Cola's CEO during the period 1997–2000, was a good numbers man but unimpressive in public relations, thus resulting in this *mea culpa*.

The incident happened on 8 June 1999, when 33 students in Bornem, Belgium, collecting bottle caps for a contest, complained of nausea and headaches and attributed it to the Cokes consumed. Clearly, the Coke brass was caught off-guard by how rapidly the crisis escalated. On 16 June, two days after the Belgian government had placed a ban on all Coke products, Doug Ivester issued his first public statement, a bland bit of bureaucratese, saying that the company was "taking all necessary steps" to ensure and safeguard its beverages' quality. But the following day, Ivester flew to Europe to exercise personal damage control. Penning an apology that ran in full-page ads in European newspapers, he appeared in a 90-second TV spot and offered to buy every Belgian, 10 million of them, a free coke! Finally, by 24 June, both Belgium and France had rescinded their bans, although Coke still had to destroy its remaining stock before it could rejuvenate production. The massive recall cost the company and its major bottler over $100 million, but more damaging was its severely tarnished image, broadcasted over Europe extensively (Pendergrast, 2000).

Another obstacle to Coca-Cola's image and sales, particularly in Europe, is a general feeling of anti-Americanism. "There are many Europeans", commented one journalist, "who genuinely believed that the object held aloft by the Statue of Liberty is a Coke bottle".[11] Other criticisms include occasional concerns expressed over the alleged inclusion of cocaine in the Cola. However, cocaine is documented to have been removed from its formula since 1903. Of late, controversial debates of the drink being a health hazard in relation to its caffeine and phosphoric acid content have also risen sharply (Allen, 1994; Oliver, 1986).

Turning to the World (Global Strategy)

By the early 1970s, investments in Japan had blossomed into the largest Coke market outside the U.S. In 1973, Japan contributed 18% of Coca-Cola's entire corporate profit, despite an increasingly militant consumer movement and various administrative import barriers. In 1972, Jimmy Carter revealed that he had ambitions beyond Georgia, asking Paul Austin for Coca-Cola's support if he ran for President. Austin agreed without contemplating that the nationally unknown Carter would actually succeed. Nonetheless, when the Georgian governor groomed himself by travelling overseas to Tokyo and Brussels, ostensibly to boost the nation's trade but also garnering considerable international experience and exposure, Coca-Cola employees there squired him around the country, providing background information on local politics, culture and economy.

With Austin's sponsorship, Carter successfully joined the prestigious Trilateral Commission set up by David Rockefeller and the East Coast establishment as a fellow member.

In 1977, Paul Austin quietly flew to Cuba, where he held closed-door secret meetings with Fidel Castro, presumably to negotiate the

[11] See Richard Kuisel, *Seducing the French: The dilemma of Americanization*, Berkeley: University of California Press, 1993. Referring specifically to "Yankee Go home" which documents the Left, Coca-Cola, and the Cold War, pp. 37–69.

company's return to the country, even though Coca-Cola officially held a $27.5 million claim against Cuba for confiscating its plants in 1961. His mission proved unsuccessful, except for some Havana cigars, which Castro had sent to Robert Woodruff through Austin. Having promised President Carter that he would report on his trip to Cuba, Austin then met with him briefly in the White House. When acid-penned columnist William Safire learnt of the episode, he concluded that it was a nefarious scheme to obtain Cuban cane. "The Carter-Coke-Castro sugar diplomacy is not merely a potential conflict of interest," wrote Safire. "It's the real thing."

Austin was more successful in negotiating for Coca-Cola's entry into Portugal, Egypt, Yemen, Sudan, the Soviet Union and China. Though none of these coups could be attributed directly to Carter's intervention, the American President's well-publicised bias towards the soft drink undoubtedly provided essential leverage for its success. For instance, the long-awaited Portuguese permission coincided uncannily with the U.S. Treasury Department's approval of a badly needed $300 million loan.

Thus, with the implicit Carter clout behind them, the Coca-Cola men triumphed in country after country — with the exception of India, where Coke departed in 1977 rather than reveal its formula to the government.[12] Their achievements, however, came only after years of patient negotiations that predated any presidential aid, as with Bob Broadwater's efforts in Moscow. Although Pepsi had an exclusive Soviet cola contract running through to 1984, Kosygin's men decided Coca-Cola could be served at special events. In 1978,

[12] In 1977, the nationalistic Indian government demanded that all of the soft drink be manufactured inside India, which meant revealing its secret formula. Coke refused, and the Company reluctantly withdrew, abandoning 22 bottling plants. "India may swallow Coke", *Time*, August 22, 1977, p. 44.

Broadwater signed a contract to supply Coca-Cola to the Spartakiada, the East Block sports festival during the following year. That would serve as a warm-up for the 1980 Moscow Olympics, where Coke paid $10 million for exclusive rights to the event. Fanta Orange would successfully fizz not only during the sporting events but also on a long-term basis throughout the Soviet Union (Pendergrast, 2000).

The real Austin plum, however, fell into his lap late in 1978, when Coke's executive Ian Wilson, holed up in a Beijing suite, hammered out an arrangement with the Chinese Communists only days before the U.S. State Department normalised relations. Now, despite Mao Tse-tung's pronouncement in his *Little Red Book* that Coca-Cola was "the opiate of the running dogs of revanchist capitalism", the highly popularised beverage has found its home on the Chinese mainland. And around the world, Coke pumped money into newly designated "anchor bottlers" — Coca-Cola Enterprises in the U.S., Australia's Coca-Cola Amatil, Mexico's FEMSA, Mexico's PANAMCO, South Africa's SABCO and Malaysia's Fraser & Neave — which have since executed Coke strategy across geographical borders. That had to be its ultimate global networking strategy, a game plan consolidating its strongholds all over the world effectively.

Coca-Cola's Asian Strategy

Strategic moves made in Asia by The Coca-Cola Company have been driven by two key elements of its global strategy. These include implementing a worldwide "anchor bottler" system and, secondly, developing under-served markets wherever they are found around the world. One of the main driving forces of Coca-Cola's global strategy has been to realign and strengthen its worldwide bottling system. The goal is to generate extensive increases in unit case volume, net revenues and profits at the bottler level, thereby generating increased shipments of Coca-Cola concentrate.

Traditionally, Coca-Cola often starts the process of strengthening its bottling system in a given region or country by buying out local bottlers and subsequently enhancing their production, distribution and marketing capabilities. Coca-Cola then sells off the local bottler to one of its "anchor bottlers", which becomes solely responsible to the Coca-Cola Company for the management of the bottling and distribution operation.

Anchor bottlers are essentially large and well-capitalised firms that share Coca-Cola's commitment to growth and have demonstrated to Coca-Cola that they have a strong management team and the capability to manage bottling operations in more than one country. The strategic alliance between Coca-Cola and the anchor bottler is structured to provide benefits for both partners. Coca-Cola provides the capital for financing the growth of the anchor bottler by taking equity in the firm. In return, Coca-Cola obtains membership on the board and the opportunity to participate in the strategic directions undertaken by the anchor bottler (Robert, 1998 and London: *Financial Times*, 1998).

Over the past three decades, Coca-Cola has established anchor bottlers in North and South Americas, Europe and Asia. In 1997, the company completed bottler transactions worth more than $8 billion, and it now has equity positions in bottlers responsible for more than 60% of its worldwide case volume production. Coca-Cola's anchor bottler system has been one of the main reasons for its widening global scheme, giving it a competitive edge over Pepsi-Cola. The system gives Coca-Cola more direct control of its global business and enables it to deal with its worldwide operations regionally rather than on a more fragmented and less efficient country-by-country basis.

The Asian anchor bottlers of Coca-Cola and achieved 20 years ago were as follows:

◊ Coca-Cola Amatil (CCA), based in Sydney, which controls bottling and distribution in Indonesia, the Philippines and South

Korea, and also has been one of Coca-Cola's European anchor bottlers;

- ◊ Fraser & Neave Coca-Cola of Singapore (F&N), which has Coca-Cola bottling operations in seven smaller countries in the region (Malaysia, Brunei, Cambodia, Nepal, Pakistan, Sri Lanka and Vietnam);
- ◊ Swire Beverages, which operates in Hong Kong, Taiwan and China, and Kerry Beverages, which shares bottling responsibilities with Swire in China.

Asia still accounts for only a relatively small percentage of Coca-Cola's global business. The region thus still offers opportunities for growth that far exceed prospects in its domestic market. From a global perspective of Coca-Cola, Asian markets are under-served and represent prime targets for development. As demonstrated in calculated statistics, Coca-Cola sees significant opportunities in South Korea and China, where the population consumes much less of Coca-Cola products than in some other Asian countries. For example, India, where 950 million people drink an average of only four servings of industrial soft drinks each year, is seen as yet another vital market (Robert, 1998).

Global Culture

In the case of Coca-Cola, its corporate headquarters are based in Atlanta with a very dominant, task-oriented role culture. After the death of the powerful and charismatic leader Robert Woodruff, the company lost some appeal of the power culture environment. Notably, the culture within is extremely strong with ties and loyalty to the product and company vision fervently attached. The goal of reaching the masses and making Coke more popular than water is a dream that is fast becoming commonplace. In light of its move to globalise, what the company did was to successfully invest heavily in research and development to mee the needs of its customers worldwide.

With 80% of Coke's profits coming from sales outside the U.S., Goizueta officially recognised the importance of the global nature of the business by reorganising the company's management structure. Previously, there had been two primary units, namely classified under "North America" and "International". Now, he simply divided the world into five major groups, with North America being one of those partitions. "We not only *see* our business as global", he wrote, "but we *manage* it that way … We understand that, as a practical matter, our universe is *infinite*, and that we, ourselves, are the key variable in just how much of it we can capture". (Pendergrast, 2000, p. 448.)

Thus, he went by the dogma of "think globally, but act locally". This catchphrase probably originated with Goizueta, though other CEOs snapped it up in the trendy 1980s and used it as their own mandate. Regardless of its provenance, Coca-Cola has demonstrated its wisdom, dipping into its own history for much guidance. In China and Indonesia, for instance, the first task involved building a strong infrastructure comprising concentrate factories, glass manufacturers, bottling plants, trucks and point-of-purchase signage — in American terms, this is time-warping back to 1905. On the other hand, in the former West Germany and Japan, the company already had a well-established business, but similar to the U.S. of the 1970s, there exist too many bottlers vying in small territories, rendering the task there of consolidation (Pendergrast, 2000, p. 468).

In terms of a "globalised" common corporate culture, the Coke team remains largely American in running its businesses, aggressive in negotiating deals, tough in lawyering and engaging in powerful lawsuits for survival and self-protection. Based firmly on American philosophy, the company has even been accused of cultural imperialism, particularly by the French. In Europe, Coca-Cola managers also try to keep its outlook and image American although shifty at times, thus resulting in the *mea culpa* such as the Belgium and French dust-up, where the company was allegedly selling contaminated Coke. Failure to respond quickly and efficiently whilst adhering to the needs of the particular culture cost Coke millions of dollars, and even more damaging was its loss of image and credibility.

In Asia, bottlers are given independence in managing the operations and their execution, although the parent firm is the overall in charge of other marketing strategies and details. Depending heavily on advertising, the Coca-Cola Company sells Coke synonymously with America, thus branding them as largely American exports deemed to conquer the global markets. With regards to product diversification and variety, Coke tries to remain streamlined and has not since come up with an exceptional amount of localised versions after the failure of the "new Coke blunder" in the 1980s.

The way they allowed for change and flexibility probably lies in the fact that they allocate bottler rights and autonomy to run the factories, provided that the quality and services are deemed satisfactory by Coke personnel from its HQ. There is no direct localisation of products to gain global reach, unlike in the case of McDonald's and its franchises worldwide. There, autonomy is given with respect to product diversification, and menus unique to locations are distinguished. For Coke, differentiation occurs in the event that firms operating in Indonesia probably have a bottler adapting to a culture quite different from one based in America.

The Pepsi Challenge

While Coca-Cola grabbed headlines around the world, the business back home was stagnating. Pepsi made inroads on the valuable take-home market, scooping Coke with one-and-a-half- and two-litre plastic bottles. As a symbol of Coke's loss of direction, *1600 Pennsylvania Avenue*, the Broadway production, which had cost the company $800,000, folded after seven performances, as *The New York Times* critic Clive Barnes pronounced it as simply being "tedious and simplistic". Thus, while Coca-Cola switched to the lacklustre "Coke Adds Life" campaign in 1976, Pepsi bounced back with its new invocation to "Have a Pepsi Day". As usual, Coca-Cola undoubtedly maintained a product focus while its rival concentrated on lifestyles.

Seemingly almost by accident, Pepsi launched a simultaneous strategy in direct contrast to its traditional approach. Pepsi man Dick Alven had been sent to Dallas with the almost hopeless mission of injecting life into the business there, where Pepsi claimed a miserable 4% of the soft drinks market. Alven convinced his boss that they needed drastic measures, so they petitioned Pepsi headquarters to allow them to use the local Stanford Agency instead of BBDO. Bob Stanford, who had discovered that Pepsi had beaten Coke in taste tests while promoting a 7-Eleven generic cola, boldly suggested a daring assault on competitor Coca-Cola. In 1975, Dallas TV stations aired commercials urging viewers to "Take the Pepsi Challenge", showing candid shots of die-hard Coke consumers astonished to discover that they preferred Pepsi in such blind taste tests. It seems that Pepsi had stooped to such an outrageous, virtually taboo approach, since comparative ads were considered unsports-manlike. Nonetheless, the results were indisputable, as within two years, Pepsi's Dallas market share jumped by 14%.[13]

While Coca-Cola's domestic market share remained relatively flat, Pepsi's steadily rose throughout the 1970s. In 1977, Pepsi's advertising budget had actually surpassed Coca-Cola's for the first time, with each firm spending just over $24 million a year on their

[13] See Timothy J. Muris, David T. Scheffman, and Pablo T. Spiller, *Strategy, Structure and Antitrust in the Carbonated Soft-Drink Industry,* Westport: Quorum Books, 1993.

main brands. By the following summer, Nielsen market figures demonstrated that Pepsi had finally overtaken Coke in super-market sales, dubbed the "free choice" arena. Defensive Coke men asserted that their drink still held an edge in the total retail outlets. In response, "they must use some strange numbers", speculated John Sculley, the combative young Pepsi-Cola president.

The world's most far-flung or globalised corporate empire was also poised for a world of trouble, rippling out from Asia. In Indonesia, the rupiah went into free fall in January 1998, and as unemployment soared, Coke sales plummeted. In counteracting this crisis, Doug Ivester urged managers to fight back rather than "to simply hunker down and ride out the storm". He reminded them that they're investing for long-term gains, thus building along the way new capabilities to deal with *any* type of uncertainty. In obedience, Asian Coke managers tossed out their carefully articulated annual marketing plans and adjusted to new conditions, creating "market impact teams" to work at the street level, getting product to vendors as quickly and cheaply as possible.

To make matters worse for Coke, Roger Enrico was then leading a recharged PepsiCo. In October 1997, Enrico successfully spun off Pepsi's restaurants, including Taco Bell, Kentucky Fried Chicken and Pizza Hut, as Tricon Global Restaurants, allowing Pepsi to focus only on soft drinks and snack foods. Until then, Coke fountain salesmen could stymie Pepsi sales by dominating fast food chains. However, Pepsi soon struck new deals with Pizza Inn, Hard Rock Café, Planet Hollywood and Warner Brothers theatres. Nonetheless, Coke owned 65% of the U.S. fountain business, compared with Pepsi's 22%. Coke countered by cementing a multi-year contract with Burger King and Wendy's adding to its other outlets (Pendergrast, 2000, p. 427).

In frustration and retaliating, Pepsi then sued Coke in 1998, alleging that Coca-Cola violated the Sherman Anti-Trust Act by threatening to cut off supplies to food-service distributors if they carried Pepsi, too.[14] Coke freely admitted dumping distributors that carried Pepsi. Indeed, its contracts specified that offering Pepsi was a "conflict of interest". But Coke asserted that its rival could always sell its soda directly to customers and that its distributors were fundamentally "an extension of Coca-Cola". The complex lawsuit would probably remain unresolved for years to come (Muris, 1993).

In 1998, as it celebrated its centennial, Pepsi also moved aggressively to offer and acquire new drinks. When acesulfame potassium, trade-named Sunett, a new sugar-free sweetener with alonger shelf-life than aspartame, was approved by the FDA, Pepsi came out with Pepsi One, a new one-calorie diet drink.[15] Pepsi's Mountain Dew continued to grab large segments of market share especially with teenagers. To counter Coke's highly successful Sprite, Pepsi now introduced Storm, its own caffeinated lemon-lime concoction. Finally, Pepsi bought over Tropicana for $3.3 billion, giving it the market-leading premium orange juice to aggressively counter Coke's Minute Maid.[16]

A World Without End for Coca-Cola?

Despite Pepsi's new feistiness, Coke still continued to dominate Pepsi outside the U.S. by a 3.6-to-1 margin. Although it would take a miracle for Coke to reach its goal of garnering 50% of the U.S. market share by the year 2001, by 1999 it had snared 45% as com-

[14] Larry Light, "Litigation: The choice of a new generation", *Business Week*, May 25, 1998, p. 42.

[15] Diet Coke was introduced way back in 1982, proving a huge hit with its consumers.

[16] "Pepsico buys Tropicana", *Advertising Age*, July 20, 1998, p. 25. "Beverage Wars intensify as PepsiCo Acquires Tropicana", *Chain Drug Review*, Aug. 10, 1998, p. 6.

pared to Pepsi's 31%. The Big Red Machine may have been slowed by global economic woes, but it still appeared unstoppable in the long run. Roberto Goizueta had always said that Coke products should be more popular than water. Was it then a "World without End" for the age-old soft drink company?

> *You can run from it, but you can't hide. Sooner or later, no matter how far you think you've ventured from the comforts and conveniences of the modern world, Coke will find you. Go to the foothills of the Himalayas, the hurricane pounded fishing islands off the coast of Nicaragua — go to the birthplace of civilization, if you like. Coca-Cola will be waiting for you.*
>
> — *The New York Times* editorial, 1991

As the world shrank to a global village,[17] the appeal of Coke and Big Macs as "luxury" items increased, and some nutritionists expressed concern that these would soon gradually displace cheaper, traditional, healthier cuisine.

"When advertised in a culturally appropriate way with appealing symbols", wrote an anthropologist, "the public consumption of such foods and soft drinks turns out to be a principal form of identification with Western lifestyles and power. Their long-term negative consequences are not fully assessed, but it is highly probable that they will progressively undermine the older [core diet] of poor agrarian societies" (Pendergrast, 2000, p. 445).

[17] See "Americanization of the Global Village" in Roger Rollin's *The Americanization of the Global Village: Essays in comparative popular culture,* Bowling Green, Ohio: Bowling Green State University Popular Press, 1989. Also, Jon Roper, "Encountering America: Altered States", in *Americanisation and the Transformation of World Cultures*, eds. Phil Melling and Jon Roper, Lewiston: Edwin Mellen Press, 1996, p. 1.

Similarly, although French critics initially called Euro Disneyland "a terrifying giant step toward world homogenization" and "a cultural Chernobyl", another Frenchman pointed out: "If French culture can be squashed by Mickey Mouse ... it would have to be disturbingly fragile" (Storti, 2001, p. 112). Nonetheless, Coke is now widely available in French cafes, but it is served almost as if it were an aperitif rather than a soft drink. "One might want to consider the 'Frenchification' of America", wrote Richard Kuisel in *Seducing the French*, "as well as the Americanization of France. If anything, we have learned that modern culture is eclectic and porous". In other words, we might regard the current cross-pollination of cultures as a kind of evolution rather than homogenization (Pells, 1997). "The differences among races, nations, cultures and their various histories are at least as profound and as durable as the similarities", wrote Australian essayist Robert Hughes, who predicted that the future belongs to "people who can think and act with informed grace across ethnic, cultural, linguistic lines", a seemingly perfect description of today's top Coca-Cola managers.

For a second year in a row, *Fortune* named The Coca-Cola Company the most admired American company. Its prospects seem bright despite caution from various economic gurus. With greater product diversification, innovations and acquisitions, Coca-Cola looks set to widen and deepen its markets worldwide. The overwhelmingly question remained, however: "What must we do to make a billion Coca-Colas ago be this morning?" This adept question brings to mind Coca-Cola's business strategies and philosophy. As Goizueta himself observed, "Working for The Coca-Cola Company is a calling. It's not a way to make a living. It's a religion" (Greising, 1998). Thus the global prospects of its legacy live on despite bleak economic downturns and hard knocks from its competitors as long as converts around the world believably remain loyal to the cult of Coca-Cola.

The Next Two Decades

Under the able chairmanship of Roberto Goizueta (from 1980 until his death in 1997), with the invention of Diet Coke, and his immediate successors, the Coca-Cola Corporation could further expand and enjoy its status as the world's largest drinks producer, selling 4,000 products in 200 countries, in fact in all of them except for Cuba and North Korea. Its annual report stated proudly that 1.3 billion drinks were sold daily by Coke or its affiliates, and 55% had a Coke or Coca-Cola trademark on them.

With a revenue of $46 billion (2023), net profits at $10.7 billion and a stock exchange valuation of $261 billion, it was easily the world's third most valuable brand, which funds like Berkshire Hathaway (9.25%), Vanguard Group (8.6%) and Black Rock (5.5%) were happy to co-own. While Coke stuck to its core soft drink business, arch-rival PepsiCo was diversifying away into snacks and Quaker Oats.

What had been predicted time and again did happen late in 2016: Coke and Diet Coke sales began to suffer both on the U.S. and global markets. Consumer concerns over the sugar content and health risks of artificial sweeteners had begun to take their toll. First, a very moderate cost-cutting programme was announced to satisfy shareholders: cutting 1,200 jobs (out of more than 100,000 worldwide) and reducing costs by $800 million. More importantly, James Quincy, the new CEO (2017–), embarked on a two-pronged strategy: first, to consolidate and control Coke's associated bottling operations worldwide and secondly, to engage in a global acquisition spree to pick up almost any more or less "healthy" soft drink maker he could lay his hands on.

Coke's bottling and retail role used to be very straightforward: they did not do it. They would ship only the syrup concentrate and other beverage bases, such as coffee beans, tea leaves and juice concentrates, to their trusted licensed bottlers, let them do the bottling with filtered water and sweetener added and do the marketing to retailers, restaurants, caterers and vending machines within their established exclusive territories. Historically, these low-margin yet capital-intensive operations were done by fairly small regional companies. Over time, Coke insisted on larger operations, squeezing out the smaller ones and buying shares in large "anchor bottlers". Quincy then undertook a massive global consolidation of his bottling partners. He sorted them into nine multinational headquarters, located in the U.K., Switzerland, Turkey, Mexico, Chile, Hong Kong, China and Japan, with often very curious regional competences, diverse lead partners and capital participations, plus four in the U.S., located in North Carolina, New Hampshire and Florida. In 2016, he had already purchased the majority holding of Coca-Cola Beverages Africa for $3.15 billion from the Belgo-Brazilian beer giant AB In-Bev (formerly SAB Miller), with a seat in Port Elizabeth (South Africa). These 14 global bottling groups he tried to consolidate with the help of a "Bottling Investment Group" (BIG), set up as early as in 2006, which is to tighten the screws and control their management in a process charitably called "refranchising". You either play along or you bottle for someone else.

Acquisitions were and are done in a fairly haphazard way of companies, both big and medium, accepting minority participations and long-term partnership agreements covering marketing and productions and product line swaps between a giant and the dwarfs.

In 2005, a Russian drinks producer was bought, covering 25% of the Russian fruit juice market. In 2007, it was Fuze Beverages, a maker of vitamin- and mineral-enhanced juices. In 2011, it was Honest Tea, a bottled tea maker. ZICO followed in 2013, producing coconut water. In 2014, 17% of Monster Beverage was bought for $2.15 billion. In 2015, again a minority stake in Suja Life, making cold-pressed juices. In 2017, Topo Chico, producing sparkling water in Mexico, was purchased, and in 2018, it was Mojo Kombucha in Australia, Moxie, a soda maker in Maine, and the sports drink Body Armor. The latter was seen as a counterstrike against market leader Gatorade, owned by Pepsi and the attempt to get a foothold in the global sports drinks market valued at $27 billion.

Also, in 2018, Coke bought Costa Coffee, the world's second-largest coffee chain after Starbucks with 4,000 shops (mostly in the U.K.), from Whitbread hotels for $51 billion. Coke wanted to benefit finally from the global trend towards more expensive coffee consumption. So far, its only brand, Georgia, has been bestselling only in Japan (more so than Coke proper). Now, it had acquired global reach. But how all those widely diverse brands and business cultures will be united under the gospel from Atlanta still remains a mystery.

Attempts to buy the leading Chinese Huiyan Juice group (with a 40% market share) in 2009 for the generous sum of $2.4 billion led to naught, as the Ministry of Commerce vetoed the deal, pretending anti-monopoly concerns, a fairly novel notion in Chinese industrial policy. This would have been the largest friendly industrial takeover in the modern Chinese economy in a fairly non-strategic sector. But it was not to be, with lessons to be drawn for Chinese takeovers elsewhere.

Like all U.S. multinationals, Coca-Cola remains in the firing line for all sorts of environmental and political evils, real or imagined. Foremost, and most seriously, is the production of plastic bottles. There are unsurprisingly pious pledges to recycle 100% of them by 2030. Boycott calls by half-baked student assemblies have little novelty value nor impact. Current issues range from the alleged support for the dictatorial king of Swaziland, death squads in Columbia or Israel's policy in Gaza — all presented on the internet without a shred of evidence. This show will no doubt go on, soon be forgotten and replaced by something else.

Bibliography

Allen, F. *Secret Formula: How Brilliant Marketing and Relentless Salesmanship Made Coca-Cola the Best known Product in the World.* New York: HarperCollins Publishers, 1994.

Brown, R. and Washton, R. *Leading Drinks Manufacturers in Asia: Corporate Strategies in the Face of Crisis.* London: *Financial Times*, 1998.

Graham, E. C. and Roberts, R. *The Real Ones: Four Generations of the First Family of Coca-Cola*. NJ: Barricade Books, Inc., 1992.

Greising, D. *I'd Like to Buy the World a Coke*. NY: John Wiley, 1998.

Kuisel, R. *Seducing the French: The Dilemma of Americanization*. Berkeley: University of California Press, 1993.

Melling, P. and Roper, J. (eds) *Americanisation and the Transformation of World Cultures: Melting Pot or Cultural Chernobyl?*. Lewiston, NY: Edwin Mellen Press, 1996.

Muris, T. J., Scheffman, D. T. and Spiller, P. T. *Strategy, Structure and Antitrust in the Carbonated Soft-Drink Industry*. Westport: Quorum Books, 1993.

Oliver, T. *The Real Coke, the Real Story*. London: The Chaucer Press, 1986.

Pells, R. *Not Like Us: How Europeans have Loved, Hated, and Transformed American Culture since World War II*. New York, NY: Basic Books, 1997.

Pendergrast, M. *For God, Country and Coca-Cola*. London: The Orion Publishing Group, 2000.

Pitts, R. *Strategic Management: Building and Sustaining Competitive Advantage*. Cincinnati: South-Western College Publishers, 2000.

Rollin, R. *The Americanization of the Global Village: Essays in Comparative Popular Culture*. Bowling Green, Ohio: Bowling Green State University Popular Press, 1989.

Storti, C. *Old World/New World*. Yarmouth, Maine: Intercultural Press, Inc., 2001.

New Literature, 2nd Edition

"Beverage giant Coca-Cola acquires 16,7 pc stake in Monster for $ 2,15 bn", *Pittsburgh News*, 16 August 2014.

"Coca-Cola kauft 2.größte Kaffeekette der Welt", *Manager Magazin*, 31 August 2018.

"Coke's China juice move collapses", *BBC News*, 18 March 2009.

Geller, M. "Coke buys remaining stake in Honest Tea", *Reuters*, 1 March 2011.

La Monica, P. "Coca-Cola to cut 1200 jobs as sales slump", *CNN*, 25 April 2017.

Tucker, S. "China blocks Coca-Cola bid for Huiyuan", *Financial Times*, 18 March 2009.

Zubrowka Bison Vodka: The High is the Limit

Screwdriver, Cosmopolitan, Black Russian and Bloody Mary… what do these cocktails all have in common? Why, vodka, of course! Indeed, vodka is the focus of this chapter, which takes a look at the history and production of this world-famous spirit. More than just looking at its history, though, this chapter also intends to examine the Polish vodka industry, paying particular attention to efforts to privatise the industry while assessing the potential of the up-and-coming Zubrowka Bison Brand Vodka.

History of Vodka

Vodka, as we all know it, is a clear and potent drink, often used as a base for numerous long drinks and cocktails, and is typically associated with the Russians (think Stolichnaya). However, one should be wary of accrediting the Russians with the discovery of the drink in the presence of the Poles, especially since the latter claim that it was their discovery and not their eastern neighbour's. Regardless of who discovered this world-famous drink, it is certain that there are at least four predominant players in the vodka industry: Russia,

Finland, Sweden and Poland. However, as earlier mentioned, it is the last one that takes centre stage in this chapter.

The term "vodka", derived from "Zhiznennia voda" in Russian or "aqua vitae" in Latin, meaning water of life in English, is very much a part of the Polish culture and lifestyle. In Poland, vodka means "little water" (Eisenberg), but we all know how misleading that term is. Strong alcohol was first discovered in Poland in the 8th century and initially used only for medicinal purposes. The Russians seemed to have used certain methods of distilling vodka back in the 12th century, but according to Polish historians, vodka was discovered in Poland in 1405, only later reaching Russia ("History of Vodka"). The origins of this spirit remain somewhat elusive, but suffice to say that in both countries, vodka is very much embedded into the people's lifestyles. In the 16th century, the production and sale of alcohol were permitted by the King of Poland, but such sales were restricted to the gentry, from which a 10% tax was extracted. With the establishment of a vodka industry of sorts, the concept of vodka as a national drink was introduced in the 17th century. It was also during this time that Poland began to export its vodka to the northern European countries. By the 18th century, their distilling techniques had greatly improved, and the triple distillation had been developed.

How Vodka is Produced

According to Gary Eisenberg, vodka is simple to make, and the ingredients involved consist of almost anything that is fermentable. Often, vodka is produced from rye grain, wheat, barley, oats or potatoes, although the derivation of vodka from sugar cane and sugar beets is not unheard of.

The production of vodka has been refined over the centuries, with producers constantly looking for new ways to improve the quality of their vodka in order to give their products an edge in terms of flavour. The process of vodka production is not complicated. Simply put, the fermented product (i.e., rye, potatoes, wheat, etc.) is distilled and then filtered several times through charcoal (preferably birch charcoal) to get rid of impurities until a smooth, clear and odourless liquid is obtained (Tyler). Voila! Vodka is born!

The delicious experience of smooth Polish vodka is a result of strict standards imposed on producers, who must at least triple-distil their vodkas. Some vodkas are filtered four times, and often at least two of those are through charcoal. This filtration process removes impurities, which can contribute towards some harshness in the vodka (Channels).

Vodka in Poland

In Poland, the Polish word for vodka is "wodki", which refers to any kind of drink that has more than 20% alcohol content. The vodka that we refer to here, however, pertains to the clear vodka that is popular in the West and which is referred to in Poland as "czysta wodka" ("History of Vodka").

Poland is home to more than 20 different brands of vodka and produces a multitude of vodka varieties. Fortunately, Polish vodka can be divided into three general categories. These are "unflavoured vodkas", "flavoured vodkas" and "real traditional flavoured vodkas" (Deibel).

"Unflavoured vodkas" are generally believed to be pure vodkas, extremely clear and therefore of superior quality. This is a result of multiple filtrations that the vodka undergoes, removing impurities and resulting in an exquisite-tasting spirit.

Impeccable in quality, these vodkas are often meant for mixing or drinking ice-cold.

The second category comprising "flavoured vodkas" includes those easily found in convenience store coolers. They are considered extensions of already existing brands and are often flavoured peach, melon, cherry or a variety of other fruity flavours. These "flavoured vodkas" are produced in order to satisfy the consumption preferences of the masses. That means they probably do not pack as much punch as the pure stuff. This is because the dominant character of the drink is the fruity flavouring, while the vodka plays a secondary function of providing the alcohol content (Deibel).

The third type of vodka is one that is unique and rather interesting. Referred to as the "real traditional flavoured vodkas", these vodkas are special, as they are created from time-honoured recipes, which call for all-natural ingredients to enhance the flavour of the brew. Using herbs, spices and other more unusual ingredients such as bison grass to flavour their vodka, brands such as Wisent, Krupnik and Zubrowka have found a place for themselves in this fascinating niche market. What makes these traditionally flavoured vodkas so special is that their recipes have been passed down over generations and represent a means for Poland to make a mark on the international vodka market with an innovative and distinct flavour, enjoyed thus far only by connoisseurs and locals in Poland (Deibel).

Zubrowka Bison Brand Vodka

One of the leaders in the latter category is a brand of traditionally flavoured vodka, called "Zubrowka Bison Brand Vodka". A rye grain vodka unusually flavoured with bison grass, Zubrowka has an original, one-of-a-kind flavour native to Poland. Attractively packaged, each bottle contains a blade of bison grass. As the Polish name for bison is "zubr", the vodka is aptly called "Zubrowka". The vodka has a faint green tinge, unlike other vodkas, and has a 40% alcohol content. This greenish tinge can be attributed to the fact that bison grass is infused into the vodka.

So, what is this "bison grass"? Well, it is a sweet grass found abundantly in the Polish Bialowieska Forest, which is eaten by the European bison. The bison is looked upon as a regal creature, great in size and majestic in appearance ("Zubrowka"). Perhaps it is these qualities that we are encouraged to associate Zubrowka with. Indeed, while some consider it a royal drink, others find that it has a more romantic appeal. Consider the following description given by the character Isabel in a Somerset Maugham novel, *The Razor's Edge*: "it smells of freshly mown hay and spring flowers, of thyme and lavender, and it's soft on the palate and so comfortable, it's like listening to music by moonlight". Sounds heavenly, doesn't it? Another character, Sophie, describes its colour as "the green one sometimes sees in the heart of a white rose".

Zubrowka's romantic appeal is also emphasised by the fact that some believe bison grass to possess aphrodisiacal qualities ("Bison Brand Vodka — The Legend"). Perhaps this association came about when the European bison, which feeds on the bison grass, came back from the brink of extinction to repopulate and live in various protected areas in Poland. Regardless of the reason for its appeal, Zubrowka is one of the top-selling vodkas in Poland and the world, thus causing some conflicts with regard to ownership of its distribution rights.

The Polish Alcohol Industry and Privatisation[1]

With the liberation of Poland from communism and the need to modernise the economic landscape of the nation, Poland's leaders embarked on a massive project to privatise the economy in order to make it more competitive. A variety of industries made this transition, and in the early 1990s, the Polish Spirits Monopoly was broken up into 25 autonomous firms (PVWS, 1999). This, however,

[1] This section can also be found in an academic study entitled "Poland's Industrial Policy in Preparation for European Union Accession" (2002/2003), which was prepared in partial fulfilment of a B.A. (Hons.) degree at the National University of Singapore.

raised the problem of allocating rights to produce the bigger Polish brands because each had assumed themselves co-owners of the near 200 brands that the Polmos state monopoly had possessed.

The solution was an auction at which the individual Polmos companies could bid for the brands of their choice with points they had been allocated upon appraisal. At the end of the auction, the top two vodkas, Wyborowa and Zubrowka, went to Polmos Poznan and Polmos Bialystok, respectively. These Polmoses now hold the right to produce these spirits exclusively. Unfortunately, they still did not have the right to export these spirits, as that right belonged to Agros Holdings S.A., a former state-owned foreign trade agency (Business News from Poland, 2001) and one of the largest companies in the food and beverage sector in Poland. With a €350 million turnover, its main functions include production and distribution through leading brands in the market ("On 17 April", 2001). In fact, Agros held the monopoly to export and the rights from foreign registration of about 20 trademarks for almost 40 years (Ratajczyk & Styczek, 2000).

In 1991, the Polmoses began to demand the return of those rights, and although understandably reluctant, the firm came up with a compromise in which they would relinquish their rights to all but two of the brands, Wyborowa and Zubrowka, as well as supplement it with a cash settlement. This did not go down well with the Polmoses, and a claim was filed against Agros, which was later dismissed by the Warsaw Provincial Court (PVWS, 1999).

Progress, however, has been made with regard to the ownership of these export/distribution rights. Agros and Pernod Ricard, a world leader in the spirits and wine markets ("On 17 April", 2001), concluded a joint venture agreement in 1999, where 37% of the capital share in Agros Holding S.A. and 74% voting rights were transferred to Pernod Ricard ("Pernod Ricard in France and Agros", 1999). Following this, a compromise was reached regarding the ownership of trademark rights. Agros agreed to give the trademark rights of almost all brands of Polish vodka to their respective producers. (*Business News from Poland*, 2001) At the same time, Pernod Ricard was in the process of negotiating the purchase of Polmos Poznan, the producer of the top-quality vodka, Wyborowa. The purchase was completed in 2001 with the acquisition of 80% of the capital of Polmos Poznan for 300 million zlotys (approximately €82 million). This purchase tied in with Poland's privatisation plan and helped inject much-needed capital investment (*Business Wire*, 2001).

In addition to this, Pernod Ricard also signed a five-year renewable agreement with Polmos Bialystok regarding the distribution of Zubrowka in Europe, but which excludes Russia and Poland (*Business Wire*, 2001). Having made a breakthrough in the Polish spirits market and being one of the top operators in spirits and wine — ranked number one in the euro zone, number two in Asia Pacific as well as in Central and South America and number six in North America — Pernod Ricard has indeed much to be proud of. How then does this company achieve what it sets out to do?

Pernod Ricard

With the merger of two French companies, Pernod Ricard was founded in 1975 and has since then developed one of the richest portfolios in the industry through internal growth and clever acquisitions, including that of Polmos Poznan, producer of Poland's top vodka, Wyborowa. The key to its success lies in its corporate strategy, which ensures that it only goes after the big fish, and that means looking only at big brands. It also pays attention to developing strong local or regional brands as well as wholly owned distribution networks in major markets. This means that there is great emphasis given to being the best in the market. Furthermore, it allows employees to be independent in a highly decentralised organisation ("Pernod Ricard: Company Strategy"). Pernod Ricard prides itself on dealing with products with strong cultural roots (think Zubrowka), which is why its decentralised organisation is so advantageous. It allows decisions to be made according to what is most suited to the market. Such specific decision-making also allows problems to be dealt with more efficiently. At Pernod Ricard, the holding company develops the overall strategy, while the subsidiaries deal with specific everyday affairs ("Pernod Ricard: Company Organisation").

The company has certain values that it feels are important for its success. It believes that these common values form the backbone for the progress of the company, which is quite diverse in its culture, products and traditions. Pernod Ricard believes in sociability, as it encourages the sharing of ideas and thoughts. It also encourages friendships, which can make the workplace a more enjoyable place to be in. It also helps that sociability is related to the nature of their products.

At Pernod Ricard, a passion for entrepreneurship is appreciated, as it supports their decentralised organisation. Entrepreneurship implies initiative, which important in learning about and acting upon consumer preferences and the marketplace.

The existence of a decentralised organisation also calls for one to value integrity. This means that conducting business in an open and ethical way is appreciated. With fewer tendencies towards corruption, a company should run into fewer problems and inspire trust in its customers, employees and the general public, thus allowing for greater success.

Pernod Ricard certainly sets great store by the passion for excellence. Representing only leading brands, Pernod Ricard is set on delivering only the best-quality products, placing emphasis on innovation and progress ("Pernod Ricard: Company Ethics — Values"). Only the best is good enough at Pernod Ricard.

It is therefore no surprise that Pernod Ricard does its best to attract and retain its culturally diverse employees. How does it do so? Well, it encourages empowerment through its decentralised organisation, which allows one to use initiative, so as to achieve professional fulfilment and exercise personal responsibility within a common code of conduct. This calls for some measure of autonomy so as to allow subsidiaries to cater to local desires.

Another employee-friendly measure is profit sharing. Many of the group's subsidiaries possess an employee compensation plan that coincides with personal or company performance so as to encourage employees to give their best. Executive compensation consists of stock options related to the companies they manage, thus encouraging hard work and dedication. The measures must work because dedication is certainly evident in the fact that average seniority is more than 10 years in general and more than 15 in France, resulting in a higher level of experience and expertise that certainly improves the overall well-being of the company ("Pernod Ricard: Company Ethics — People"). This well-being is further preserved with training programmes for employees that are set up by each subsidiary.

Corporate Challenges

Zubrowka might not be directly controlled by Pernod Ricard, but the fact that its distribution rests in the hands of the illustrious spirits company implies that certain standards must be maintained, which in turn entails in all likelihood changes that must be implemented and challenges that must be surmounted so as to ensure that Zubrowka does not lose its current position as a unique and much sought after vodka.

Zubrowka's association with Pernod Ricard must therefore compel its producer Polmos Bialystok to improve its professionalism and ensure that Zubrowka's quality retains the excellence and quality of flavour that first brought it to the attention of Pernod Ricard, which deemed it worthy to be included among its other lofty and notable brands of spirits (e.g., Chivas and Martell). This allows Zubrowka to benefit greatly from the marketing endeavours of Pernod Ricard, which works conscientiously to thrust its products up into the ranks of world renowned must-haves.

In a bid to guarantee that product quality is of impeccable standards, stringent quality controls are necessary, and presumably both Wyborowa and Zubrowka are subjected to such measures to improve their international marketability, which in turn helps increase their profitability. This is indeed a marked difference from the past, where a number of distilleries would produce Wyborowa and Zubrowka vodkas without a thought as to any uniformity or quality in production.

With Zubrowka now being marketed on an international scale by Pernod Ricard, where once it was predominantly a domestic product, one can expect to see increased sales and profits. Certainly, with Pernod Ricard now in the picture, the Polish vodka industry and, more specifically, Zubrowka Bison Brand Vodka can look forward to a brighter future, where one can also reasonably assume improved quality and management.

Conclusion

We have thus seen how the Polish vodka industry has developed over the past few years. The process has been trying, what with the long drawn-out battle between Agros and the Polmoses regarding export rights. The privatisation process has not been easy, but the efforts to do so have reaped some rewards. Certainly, such efforts will go a long way in establishing a good reputation for Poland's vodka, which has much promise, especially if we consider brands like Zubrowka as the standard of the exemplary quality we hope to experience in the future.

Pernod Ricard has certainly set the privatisation of the spirits industry in Poland on its way and with measures such as those discussed above; it is no wonder that Pernod Ricard is such a lucrative company. Their strategy of finding the right people to contribute their talents to the company while adhering to a common set of values, combined with a strategy aimed at excellence, inspires confidence in the future of the two brands they have taken under their wing, Wyborowa and Zubrowka. Indeed, with their steadfast efforts in introducing the two brands into the international market, it seems like the privatisation of the Polish spirits industry is off to a great start.

However, caution is advisable with regard to the continuation of the vodka industry's privatisation process. While Polmos Poznan represents an encouraging success story, problems should not be discounted, especially considering the Polish government's efforts in 2001 to sell off an 80% stake in Polmos Bialystok, the producer of Zubrowka. A number of firms including Pernod Ricard have expressed interest, but doubts regarding the viability of Pernod's offer have risen amidst concerns about Poland's competition regulations. One must also take into consideration that the domestic vodka industry faces the additional trials of cheaper, illegal competition from home brewers and neighbouring countries, not to mention a weak local market that makes sales difficult.

As if this were not enough, the government seems to be fixed on selling off all of its remaining distilleries at the same time. This could make redundant existing efforts in the quest towards privatisation, especially since it is believed that only about six of the more than 200 brands of spirits are viable in the long run (*BBC News Online*, 2001). The future of Zubrowka and the Polish vodka industry thus hangs in the balance, as efforts continue to be made in a bid to privatise Poland's vodka industry. With great care and determined commitment, anything is possible, and Zubrowka just might take the world by storm.

The Next Two Decades: Troubles in Vodka-Land

The story does not end here, as one might expect in the Wild East of Europe around the primaeval forests of Bialystok near the borders of Belarus.

As we learnt, Pernod Ricard in October 1999 had purchased 80% of Agros Holding S.A., Poland's then largest agro-food conglomerate, which also held the marketing and brand rights to Zubrowka and Wyborowa. So far, everything seemed mostly settled. Yet in the Sejm, Poland's parliament, in Warsaw, national passions were enflamed that two of their most precious and drinkable assets should be in the hands of foreigners, Poland's bit for EU membership (which happened in 2004) notwithstanding. So, in July 2000, they promptly renationalised the brands, sensing Zubrowka and Wyborowa back to their previous owners, the state-owned distillers Palmos Bialystok and Palmos Poznan, respectively. Pernod Ricard, which still wanted to enhance its deficient vodka portfolio with a premium brand, concluded the mentioned marketing agreement with Palmos Bialystok in July 2001 for a period of five years, for which it paid $72 million.

In the meantime, two former American international cattle traders and adventurers, William O. Carey and Jeffrey Peterson, had started a cattle export business in 1990, called Carey Agri, in liberated Poland, but they soon found trading in beer and liquor with few taxes and rules to be more lucrative and enjoyable. So, the two cowboys set up the Central European Distribution Corporation (CEDC) with a legal seat in Bala Cymwyd, Pennsylvania, but operating mostly in Poland. Intoxicated by first successes but always short of serious capital, they began their buying spree of distilleries, breweries and distribution centres by first acquiring Palmos Bialystok in 2005. In July 2006, they renewed the marketing agreement with Pernod Ricard for 10 years for 70 countries, except for Poland, Germany, the U.K. and the U.S., which they would handle themselves. As they were soon $400 million in debt, with U.S. venture capital not forthcoming, CEDC took a Russian business partner, Roustam Tariko of Tatar origin, as its largest shareholder. He, in 1998, had founded "Russian Standard Vodka", which soon became the largest vodka producer in Russia and by 2007, as Russia's vodka king was estimated worth $5.5 billion and cultivated the extravagant lifestyle of a medium-sized oligarch. By April 2013, CEDC was close to insolvency and was delisted from NASDAG. Tariko then forced his American partners to render full control to him to avoid bankruptcy.

Late in 2013, he also terminated the marketing agreement with Pernod Ricard, handing it over to his own Lixir Group, which also did the marketing in France. As Russian fairytales never have a happy ending, by 2017 Tariko's fully owned private bank had difficulties servicing $450 million in Eurobonds, and his personal wealth was estimated to have shrunk to a modest $1.1 billion. Equally, with a national-conservative and anti-Russian PiS government in power in Warsaw after the Russian annexation of Crimea in 2014, it was highly advisable to sell out. This he did in November 2021. Poland's largest food conglomerate Maspex acquired CEDC, with all its breweries, 52 distribution centres, distilleries — including of course Palmos Zubrowka — and a staff of 4,000, for $1 billion. CEDC added a welcome alcoholic component to the Maspex portfolio of 70 brands in the food industry, ranging from pasta and instant food to jams and juices. It now has a 46% market share in the $4 billion Polish vodka market and has become the country's largest importer of liquor and wine.

Despite all the turbulences in ownership and marketing, Zubrowka has maintained its rank as the third leading vodka brand on the global market. It does not seem to have suffered during the 16 years of interregnum from neither American nor Russian management. Five hundred years of tradition are set to continue, even with product relaunches and changing global distributors. Cheers, or rather, *na zdrovyie*!

Bibliography

Note: Any links to online sources were valid as of the publication of the first edition, in October 2004. Many of the pages have since been taken down.

"Bison Brand Vodka — The Legend". http://www.bisongrassvodka.com/the_legend.htm

Business News from Poland. "Agros Agrees to Give Trademark Rights of Polish Vodka to Their Producers", 7 April 2001.

Channels, B. "The New Face of Vodka". http://www.polishvodkas.com/new_face_of_vodka.html

Deibel, J. "Polish Vodka — Which Way to Go?" http://www.polishvodka.com.pl/juergen.html

Eisenberg, G. "Vodka Dreaming in Poland". http://www.polishvodkas.com/miscelany/voddream/

"History of Vodka: Its Origin, Name and Distilling in Poland, Varieties". http://www.polishvodkas.com/history-vodka/fs_consumption.htm

"On 17 April, the Securities and Exchange Commission Complied with Pernod Ricard". http://www.agros.com.pl/english/html/aktual/pres.php

"Pernod Ricard: Company Ethics — People". http://www.pernod-ricard.com/

"Pernod Ricard: Company Ethics — Values". http://www.pernod-ricard.com/

"Pernod Ricard: Company Organisation". http://www.pernod-ricard.com/

"Pernod Ricard: Company Strategy". http://www.pernod-ricard.com/

"Pernod Ricard in France and Agros in Poland Announce Joint Venture". http://www.pernod-ricard.com/

"Poland's Top Vodka Brand for Sale", *BBC News Online*, 27 July 2001.

"Privatisation in Poland: Pernod Ricard Acquires 80% of the Capital of Polmos Poznan–Wyborowa — and secures the distribution of Zubrowka in Europe", *Business Wire*, 17 July 2001.

"PVWS Team". "Polmos Trademarks Sold", 30 July 1999. http://www.polishvodkas.com/news/Polmos_T_Sold.html

Ratajczyk, A. and Styczek, D. "Agros Holdings vs. the Polmoses", *The Warsaw Voice*, June 2000.

"The History of Vodka". http://www.ivodka.com/history.html

Tyler, S. "Vodka". http://www.viewpub.co.uk/drink_feat_vodka.asp

"Zubrowka". http://www.polishvodkas.com/fr_zubrowka.htm

New Literature, 2nd Edition

Ballin, A. "Zahlungsprobleme bei russischer Großbank", *Handelsblatt*, 27 November 2017.

Flallo, L. "La Pologne renationalize les marques de vodka de Pernod Ricard", *Les Echos*, 3 July 2000.

Gilson, S. C. "Central European Distribution Corporation: Hostile Take-over, Bankruptcy Makeover", *Harvard Business School Case* 216/059, March 2016.

Koziol, M. "Geographic Indications and International Trade". http://mandalaprojects.com

Quising, M. "Da ist er, der neue russische Unternehmer", *Die Welt*, 26 September 2000.

"Spiritueux: Zubrowka quitte Pernod pour rejoinder Lixir a partir de fevrier 2014", *Rayon Boissons*, 12 November 2013.

IKEA: The Småland Way Goes Global

IKEA as the route to nirvana, people believing they'll find spiritual freedom through home furnishings.

— Actor Edward Norton[1]

What is the secret to IKEA's success that allows it to capture the imagination of people across 31 countries on five continents? Why was IKEA's annual catalogue, with 110 million copies published in 34 languages, one of the world's biggest press runs until its last printed edition in 2019? What makes IKEA tick? To answer these questions, we must trace its origins.

Origins of IKEA

IKEA is an acronym for Ingvar, Kamprad, Elmtaryd and Agunnaryd. Ingvar Kamprad is the founder of IKEA, Elmtaryd was his farmhouse and Agunnaryd is his home county in Småland, Sweden.

[1] Quote taken from *Life!*, 16 April 2002.

Perhaps influenced by his maternal grandfather, who had owned a very successful local store, Kamprad started doing business from a tender age. One of his first business deals started when he bought 100 boxes of matches for 88 öre and sold them at a price between two and five öre each. Kamprad was an enterprising boy who sold Christmas cards, fish that he had caught himself and even garden seeds.

He sold whatever he believed was in demand and could make him money. As his father constantly lamented the lack of money to realise his many plans, Kamprad decided to start his own firm to help resolve his father's cash-flow problems. Kamprad was only 17 when IKEA Agunnaryd was founded in 1943.

IKEA Agunnaryd initially sold pens, cigarette lighters and whatever Kamprad found a demand for and could sell at a reduced price. These products were later sold through mail order when Kamprad was no longer able to make individual sales due to his booming business. He later switched to furniture retailing as it was more profitable, and the close proximity to furniture makers from where he lived made the switch even easier. He advertised his furniture in a brochure — *IKEA News* — which he published and sent to customers. This was the precursor to his future IKEA catalogue. Kamprad also gave names to furniture because it was difficult to remember order numbers. Note that giving names to furniture had the effect of imbuing each piece with a personality and a life of its own. This innovative act appealed to customers because they could select furniture which corresponded to their actual or idealised lifestyles. Moreover, furniture with names were so much easier to remember than long order numbers, making it easier for customers to place orders. This farsighted business decision certainly endeared IKEA further to customers, who saw it as increasingly customer-oriented. The first piece of furniture to be christened was Ruth, an armless chair.

Kamprad changed his strategy as a result of the cut-throat mail-order business. Rather than competing with his main competitor on price, which would invariably affect the quality of his wares, he decided to compete on the basis of quality. He was therefore convinced that there should be a permanent display of the furniture he was retailing to allow people to see and judge for themselves their quality. Customers would then be convinced of the superiority of his wares, thereby justifying the higher prices. It would be a win–win situation because he would be able to continue running his business while earning and maintaining his customers' trust.

His first furniture showroom was displayed in a second-hand building at Älmhult, Sweden, which was bought from an old associate. Based on Kamprad's decision to buy a second-hand building, one can discern his frugality and belief in avoiding waste — everything has a second life. Despite being born with a silver spoon, virtues such as thriftiness and frugality can be observed in the man himself. Perhaps these virtues were prevalent among many Swedes, yet it was Kamprad who instituted them as fundamental pillars of his company's culture. These values later affected the development of his furniture empire. Possibly believing that his store should possess aesthetic value and aiming to differentiate it from the nondescript buildings in the area, Kamprad's showroom drew inspiration from New York's Guggenheim Museum. It was to be built with a circular design to save space and provide optimal exposure for the displayed items. Furthermore, coffee and buns were to be provided on the opening day because Kamprad believed that "no good business should be done on an empty stomach". Kamprad was only 21 when he became a furniture dealer. He changed the name of his firm to IKEA to emphasise his switch to furniture-retailing.

The Early Years

The showroom, which opened in 1953, was a resounding success. Even before the doors were opened, there were already 1,000 people waiting to enter the store. What was significant was that many people actually made the trek to Älmhult even though it was located in a remote part of Sweden. The use of his catalogue as a means of temptation was a success. Besides, the IKEA logo, which was printed on his brochure covers, was in the colours of the Swedish national flag. This sought to convey that IKEA's products were reliable and clean, while also emphasising its Swedish identity as it achieved global recognition. The idea of allowing customers to walk around and touch the furniture they showed interest in was revolutionary at that time. People loved the idea because it meant giving them a wide selection of furniture to choose from and allowed them to test the items they wanted to buy. In a way, this empowered the ordinary customer — he was no longer hostage to tyrannical furniture retailers. Traditionally, customers had to pay astronomical prices for furniture that they were not allowed to try out before purchasing. Kamprad's radical yet ingenious ideas laid the foundation for the modern IKEA concept.

It was also during this time that Sweden modernised rapidly, leading to an exodus of people from the countryside to the towns. These people needed to furnish their homes as cheaply as possible. In 1954, the Swedish government published the *Good Housing* publication that set regulations for minimum space and stipulated that every room was to serve a specific purpose. In addition, certain furniture were deemed essential in every household.

IKEA's appearance on the scene around that time coincided with the rapid changes that Swedish society was undergoing. IKEA's furniture was affordable, of good quality and aesthetically beautiful, and it was no surprise that IKEA was quickly embraced by the general public with little resistance.

Despite IKEA's success, there were lingering doubts, especially among competitors, that low prices often corresponded to products of dubious quality. They sought to discredit IKEA; however, tests conducted by the esteemed furniture magazine *Allt i Hemmet* in 1964 put to rest those doubts. In the price test, a living room was furnished in two parts: one part exclusively containing IKEA furniture; the other consisting of similar furniture but from other suppliers. The price difference between IKEA's room and that of its most expensive competitor was a whopping SEK 6,000 ($750). The price difference meant a lot to Swedes who were setting up homes for the first time in the towns and suburbs. Choosing IKEA's furniture meant substantial savings on their tight budgets. This is why IKEA appeals to many students, young couples and small families even now for the same reason: quality furniture at affordable prices.

To critics, the assurance that quality and durability could not be guaranteed because of IKEA's low prices. The quality tests conducted by the same furniture magazine, however, vindicated IKEA's claims. Test results gleaned from a Swedish design lab showed that IKEA's furniture was more durable than its more expensive counterparts. Despite being tipped 55,000 times in a machine during a test, IKEA's Ögla chair (which was retailing for SEK 33 then) was still intact, but the more expensive Thonet model (which retailed for SEK 168) was not. It was a vindication for IKEA as it exposed the hollowness of claims made by jealous competitors that cheap products were synonymous with inferior quality. The test results and the implicit endorsement of the eminent furniture magazine further propelled the acceptance of IKEA in Swedish society, even in middle-class homes. It also led to acceptance in countries worldwide when IKEA branched out overseas.

The principal reason IKEA could offer such low prices was by cutting out the middlemen. Further, IKEA does not manufacture the products it designs. To Kamprad, low prices were essential to make a wide range of quality home furnishings available to as many people as possible. Gillis Lundgren, a designer at IKEA, then hit upon the idea of self-assembled furniture when he realised he could pack the legs of a table under the tabletop. In this way, shipping costs would be greatly reduced, allowing these savings to be passed on to customers. Furthermore, customers were also encouraged to pick up their purchases themselves from the warehouse. Savings gained from self-service would be passed on to customers.

The Man Himself

Every employee, or "Ikean", must be well versed in *A Furniture Dealer's Testament*, which was written by Kamprad himself. This framework of ideas was written with the hope that Ikeans would continue to adhere to this concept that has served IKEA well for the past 50 years. It was also hoped that it would keep IKEA uniquely Swedish in outlook, even after Kamprad had faded away from the scene. Then, who was Ingvar Kamprad? What was he like and how did his views shape his company?

Ingvar Kamprad was "the furniture king who does not look like a capitalist". Despite his wealth (he then was reported to be worth $27 billion and, according to *Forbes*, was the world's 17th richest person), he flew economy, travelled second class by train, frequented discount outlets and bought groceries just before closing time when prices were lowest. It also did not matter to him whether he stayed in a hotel room infested with cockroaches or one where the water supply might be cut off in the middle of a shower. To him, having a place to stay was sufficient, despite its shabbiness. Because of the example he set, subordinates did not enjoy better benefits. He professed that if he were to change to a more luxurious lifestyle, his empire would collapse as IKEA's foundations rest on his low-cost concept. Practising what he preached, for Kamprad, was an act of good leadership. It was also a way of telling his employees and the public that he was an ordinary guy just like them.

A shrewd business acumen was surely one of Kamprad's attributes. He believed it was essential to have a restaurant in his store ("no one does good business on an empty stomach") and a childcare facility consisting of a playroom equipped with a pool of coloured balls for children to dive into ("who can do vital shopping with the kids yelling around their feet?"). Toilets were necessary because "a full bladder must not be what decides the customer on buying or not buying something", and a bistro had to be situated beyond the checkout so as to provide the customers with a "calming effect" after their purchases. He also hit upon the idea of selling hot dogs at the bistro based on the "five kronor" principle. This meant that one IKEA hot dog could be bought with just a single coin. In Switzerland, a hot dog cost one Swiss franc, in Germany one euro, in Singapore S$1.50 and so on. This reflected Kamprad's keen business acumen and his desire to make shopping at IKEA both pleasurable and stress-free. To him, making a profit, regardless of the amount, would still be a profit. The customer's satisfaction matters most.

In many companies, the power imbalance between superiors and subordinates can be quite stark. This is not so in IKEA. Kamprad treated his business associates and subordinates like intimate friends. He knew all his employees' names when IKEA started out. As a way of bonding with people when speaking to them, Kamprad would move closer to them, look into their eyes and hug them when the conversation ended. He would also share hotel rooms and engage in conversations about anything with his subordinates late into the night. Or if only a bed were available, he would even sleep head to toe with his partner. This might seem to others as a sign of parsimony; however, for Kamprad, it was a way of strengthening personal bonds and, like the South Europeans, establishing trust. His manner of treating people as if they were family certainly endeared him to his business associates. For instance, two Polish directors reminisced about the time they spent with him in his room, sitting around, holding hands, singing folksongs and making speeches; they loved his Eastern European way of showing emotions. His subordinates tried to behave in a similar way. This has fostered the Ikean spirit of fellowship and of belonging to a family. Clearly, Kamprad's frugal and hearty way of doing things had a significant influence on the company.

The Culture Within

Like Japanese firms, IKEA prefers to recruit employees straight out of school or those who have not already immersed themselves in another corporate culture and would rather train them for the company, by the company and in the company's methods. Young employees would not only keep wage levels down in this cost-sensitive organisation but could also be trained in the company's ways of *ödmjukhet* — being humble, modest and respectful towards their co-workers. In addition, young employees are usually more ambitious and enthusiastic when they first step into the corporate world. They would also be more eager to learn and accept greater responsibilities. This complemented IKEA's culture of vitality and enthusiasm. More importantly, internal training coupled with internal rotation through different jobs would deeply ingrain a common understanding of the organisation. As a result of IKEA's hiring policy, the average age of a store manager is only 34. This implies that new blood is constantly injected into the organisation, making it quite youthful in its outlook and capable of quickly reacting to changes. Finally, it also suggests that bold decisions can be made more willingly and swiftly.

From the outside, IKEA is perceived to have a power culture, where power resides in the hands of one person, the founder. Before proceeding on any task, his subordinates would often ask, "What will Ingvar say?", "Do you think Ingvar would...?" or "Ingvar said that...". They always take into consideration what

Kamprad would think or feel, and often, his words would become law by default. IKEA stores used to close at 6 pm in Sweden, but now they close at 8 pm, following his comments on the futility of operating a store if it were to close just minutes after people got off from work. Like many family businesses, Kamprad resisted listing IKEA on the stock exchange, justifying his stand by arguing that IKEA would have had to make short-term shareholder decisions that might be in conflict with its long-term planning. He feared that too many foreign shareholders would influence the way IKEA operates if it were to go public. Moreover, going public is expensive, as public companies were required to distribute at least a third of their profits to their shareholders. As such, it would not allow IKEA to build up reserves necessary for taking bold decisions, such as its choice to lose money for 10 years just to enter the Russian market. Clearly, Kamprad had an overwhelming influence on his company.

The culture within IKEA is akin to that of a family. Whenever Kamprad spoke to his employees, it was as if a father was speaking to his children and grandchildren. He would always begin with "Dear IKEA family, a great hug to you all" in his annual Christmas message. Kamprad never failed to throw a Christmas party for his employees. What had started off as a party for his initial 30 employees has now ballooned. In the Christmas party of 1998, 1,000 out of 1,600 employees in Älmhult turned up for a dinner featuring Christmas rice, milk, coffee and ginger biscuits. Then, Kamprad addressed his audience, urging Ikeans to continue adhering to IKEA's philosophy. Upon the conclusion of his address, he then shook everyone's hands and presented them with a Christmas gift. Through his meticulous efforts, he successfully built up his firm based on a family-oriented concept, in which fellow employees treated each other as members of a large, extended family. This came about because his family were his first customers and had helped him when his firm grew. For instance, his father would help keep the accounts, while his mother helped with packing. It surprised no one when he regarded his growing firm as his family. Employee loyalty to the firm was severely tested in 1994 when Kamprad faced a series of insinuations, alleging that he had been a Nazi sympathiser some 50 years ago. Naturally, Kamprad denied the allegations. But as a sign of loyalty to Kamprad, then IKEA of Sweden (IOS) sent him a note together with hundreds of signatures of his employees, reading:

> *Ingvar,*
>
> *We are here whenever you need us.*
>
> *The IKEA Family IOS*

This showed, particularly in times of need, Kamprad's successful attempts and efforts to mould his company into a large family where loyalty is valued.

The culture within IKEA is Swedish and more so Smålandish in outlook, even though the company is now a multinational corporation. Kamprad was of the view that the Smålandish values of thriftiness and cost-consciousness that have assisted the company in its nascent stage should be maintained and remain integral to IKEA's management policy. To Kamprad, expensive solutions were signs of mediocrity, and he believed that wasting resources was a mortal sin. As such, management personnel travelled in economy class like he did, shared hotel rooms and so forth. There is even an IKEA guidebook, informing employees where they can get budget hotels and cheap airfares when they go on business trips. Even though urgent appointments must be kept, that should not serve as an excuse for first-class travel, as one executive found out. Kamprad refused to accede to the executive's request, instead "recommending" that he travel by car as an alternative. This reflected that even matters of urgency were not a reason for expensive solutions in this cost-sensitive organisation.

There is also an emphasis on all things Småland that Smålandish specialities, such as sausages with potatoes in white sauce and meatballs with lingon berries, which are sold in IKEA restaurants worldwide. This not only serves to acquaint customers with IKEA's Swedish roots, but it also indirectly and constantly reminds employees of the Swedish work ethic.

IKEA subscribes to a "dress-down" policy. Kamprad's standard business attire consisted of open-necked denim shirts and slacks, along with a blazer for important occasions. Employees dress in a similar way because, in Kamprad's considered view, too much time would be wasted if they always had to think about what to wear. The environment within is quite informal and egalitarian because both management and the rank and file are dressed similarly. This prevents any form of elitism should employees be discriminated against based on their dressing.

Since the culture within promotes egalitarianism, "antibureaucrat weeks" are organised, requiring all managers to work in store showrooms and warehouses for at least one week every year. This is intended to ensure that managers remain firmly well grounded and do not become too disconnected from their subordinates. Moreover, by working together with employees on the shop floor, managers continue to get a pulse of their subordinates' feelings and do not introduce policies that could generate worker dissent.

More pertinently, managers working with their subordinates in the stores together sent a message — the managers are "one" with the rank and file.

Perhaps the people working at IKEA feel as if they are contributing to the well-being of society, and they also enjoy their work because the company suits their way of life. They believe that being altruistic involves providing affordable and quality furniture to as many people as possible. Hence, the staff is not particularly motivated by high salaries.

In fact, salaries, particularly at management levels, are considered "peanuts" compared to their counterparts elsewhere. Staffers joined IKEA because it aligned with their way of life, without worrying about status or fame but with a feeling that "they have now become more in harmony with themselves". As in Swedish society, an informal *du* culture is also prevalent within the company, flattening the hierarchy. As a model worthy of emulation, Kamprad had the habit of walking around in his stores, hugging and clasping his employees. He even requested that they address him by his first name. This further cemented employee loyalty to IKEA because they felt that they were treated as equals and were valued within the organisation.

European Business Culture

The business culture is similar throughout Europe despite regional variations. It is no surprise that IKEA expanded successfully into continental Europe first. Part of it was the result of ingenious marketing strategies. In Germany, the elk symbol was used whenever an IKEA store was launched. It was so successful that it almost rivalled with the brand name. In another move, if there were more than one store opening, one Swedish clog would be given out to customers as a sign of IKEA's gratitude. If customers were interested in getting the other half, they would have to go to the other new store. This resulted in an explosion of sales in Europe. However, it took IKEA 22 years before being able to generate profits in all its 20 stores in the U.S.

The American Business Culture

Initially, IKEA did not realise that doing business in the U.S. was a different ballgame. It expanded too rapidly without fully understanding American buying culture. This even threatened, at one point, to sink its flagship store in Älmhult.

First, the IKEA brand was not sufficiently introduced to Americans. Even though nine out of ten Americans had heard of IKEA, only three of them knew that IKEA is in the furniture business. There was thus insufficient publicity to announce IKEA's arrival in the U.S. The complacency was blamed on the group of store managers who were managing the U.S. stores. They thought that, since IKEA was already a household name in Europe, its brand strength would automatically enable the company to become one in the U.S. too. Part of the blame also rested on the management back home. The management granted managers considerable autonomy in setting up and running the stores; however, they did not realise that some oversight was needed. Both parties also did not take into account the differences in American and European buying habits and their corresponding lifestyles.

A case usually cited involved an American lady walking into the IKEA store in Houston. She liked the bed she was looking at but did not understand what 160 cm meant. In Sweden, a 160 cm bed meant a double bed, but this did not make sense to the American mindset. All the lady (and, in general, the American public) wanted to know was if the bed was king- or queen-sized. As a result, a sale was lost as she walked away without buying the bed. Other examples demonstrating a clash of cultures include occasions when dinner tables had to be redesigned to be huge enough for an overstuffed Thanksgiving turkey, with space for crockery on both sides; or when couches had to be overstuffed because Americans prefer sofas they can sink into rather than sit on like the Europeans. Because of these new demands, product ranges had to be modified to cater to the American market. This contravened the IKEA concept, where uniformity — be it in terms of store design or the retailing of identical items — was demanded throughout its stores worldwide. A little tweaking of the concept was nevertheless justifiable, especially if IKEA wanted to break into the American market. By 1998, all 20 stores in the U.S. were making money after products were redesigned for the American market.

Despite the clash of cultures, positive benefits were reaped. In the U.S., managers drastically lowered the turnover rate of employees and enhanced loyalty. They did so by mandating that sales on one Saturday a year were to go in full to the employees. Each employee would receive a percentage of sales corresponding to their length of employment. So, even the last one hired received something. This inculcated a sense of belonging to the IKEA family, as they were rewarded for their hard work. They felt invested in the continuing success of IKEA in return. This resembles one of the central tenets of Confucianism: reciprocity, which refers to the fact that employees would be rewarded in return for their loyalty to the organisation. This reward system nonetheless raised motivation levels and, as such, was lauded and adopted in IKEA stores worldwide thereafter.

The success of the IKEA concept has also spawned a number of American copycats. STØR was founded to give the impression of a Scandinavian firm and was copying IKEA in almost everything. Firms such as Home Depot and Crate & Barrel have also jumped onto the bandwagon and followed IKEA's concept of offering a wide variety of products at low prices under one roof. Unfazed by the competition and believing in the strength of its concept, IKEA fought back and now offers apartment setups such as "single-mum with infant" to the American public rather than the traditional single-room setting. Flexibility to change and the ability to adapt quickly were notable.

The Empire

Fearful of incurring debt and worried about the survival of IKEA after his death, Kamprad divided his empire into three holding entities: the IKEA Group, the Inter IKEA Group and the IKANO Group.

The IKEA Group is owned by a Dutch foundation, the Stichting INGKA Foundation/Stichting IKEA Foundation. It owns the stores worldwide, except franchises, and everything related to retailing. Inter IKEA owns the concept of the IKEA brand and the group's intellectual property. It also gives approval to open and run a store — either as one of IKEA's own stores or for an outsider as a franchisee with permission to use the IKEA concept under extremely well-specified conditions. If a store manager wishes to deviate from the laid-down concept, be it to eliminate the playroom or to design narrower aisles, he must seek prior approval from the Group. If a franchisee breaks the rules, Inter IKEA has the power and right to take away the IKEA signboard and discontinue all supplies. The groups possess large, hidden reserves to help fund expansion and create a cushion against economic downturns. Kamprad's sons can "control" Inter IKEA by appointing the board of the group, but they cannot own it. This is to prevent any inheritance disputes. More importantly, it aims to bring about financial stability and prevent his family from being taxed too heavily by the Swedish authorities. It is also to ensure that IKEA will endure in his image after his demise.

The only group that the Kamprad family owns is the IKANO Group. It controls Habitat, a home-furnishing chain, and IKANO has investments in financial services, real estate, insurance and banking. It is also an umbrella name for all Kamprad-owned companies not under the control of the INGKA Foundation. A precursor of these three groups emerged when Kamprad set up a series of companies in the 1950s to circumvent the threat of a supply boycott from furniture suppliers intent on crushing this young upstart who was undercutting their prices.

The complex collection of these holding companies was therefore to ensure the survival of IKEA and prevent it from ever being dismantled. It was also meant to forestall the empire from breaking up or being sold off because of succession disputes.

Prospects in 2003

Kamprad had always been seen as the spiritual leader of IKEA. However, in 2003 there was no one who had the charisma and flair to take on his position. Like Virgin's Richard Branson, IKEA was basically driven by the personality and leadership of its founder, Ingvar Kamprad. Whether IKEA would continue to survive after Kamprad's demise was a big question that remained open. IKEA's senior management remained predominantly Scandinavian. Although IKEA's former president, Anders Moberg, was quoted as saying that a good grasp of the Swedish language was imperative in career advancement, there were justifiable fears and worries that as IKEA expanded globally, non-Swedish managers might be recruited, making it difficult or impossible for IKEA to retain its Swedish roots. Already in the early 2000s, a Canadian had been appointed to a position responsible for all the stores in Sweden, and an American advertising manager had been placed in charge of the catalogue business. Whether they and their successors would be able to assimilate into Swedish culture and the Smålandish psyche, which demands management to be simple, people-oriented and non-hierarchical, or whether they would reject it and instead impose their own cultural imprint onto IKEA, remained to be seen in the future.

The Next Twenty Years

Ingvar Kamprad, who since 1976 had been living near Lausanne at Lake Geneva for tax reasons, moved back to his hometown Älmhult in southern Sweden after the death of his wife Margaretha in 2011. Out of the 8,500 inhabitants in his hometown, 2,500 would work for IKEA. In this corporate small town, both the regional HQ and the original first IKEA store covering the Småland region were located. People also worked in an IKEA hotel, the IKEA village and the IKEA museum. For aspiring managers, it was also deemed useful to spend some training periods there with little distraction, in a sort of summer camp surrounded by dense forests. When Kamprad died here at the ripe old age of 91 in January 2018, he was truly surrounded by his own mourning people.

Already in 1982, he had formally retired from his official duties, yet pulled the strings behind the scenes as "senior advisor" and as member of the family council, which ruled supreme over the complex structure of the operational companies, their holding societies and family-controlled foundations. This structure was carefully designed by him to prevent potential takeovers, incorporating checks and balances, and to avoid paying useless taxes. His three sons were slowly groomed for succession within the company. His oldest son, Peter, was more conservative minded and took the helm of the board of trustees of the Ingka Foundation in the Netherlands, which owned much of IKEA. The second son, Jonas, a trained architect, was more interested in furniture and interior design. So, it was the youngest son, Mathias, who was groomed for succession at the supervisory board of the controlling Inter IKEA Holding. In 2013, at the age of 44, he took up the position after his success in the difficult Danish market. Like his father, he reportedly had occasional problems with alcohol and experienced an equally messy divorce; however, he was ambitious and, when needed, showed humility. In the meantime, Kamprad appointed senior managers, all Swedes, mostly from his region, who had served him loyally for meagre management salaries over several decades. Still, the old man would tirelessly continue to inspect his IKEA shops, ensuring that the merchandise was properly arranged, customers were treated courteously, the Swedish canteen food was tasty, the delivery drivers were offered their free coffee, and no waste, dirt or frivolous expenditure was spotted. What was essential was always not what he said, as he remained invariably informal yet courteous; however, one had to read his mind to understand what he actually meant. For old timers of all ranks in the company, this was usually crystal clear and considered law.

Kamprad's wealth was estimated at $58 billion, which had made him easily the richest man in Switzerland (where, in 2009, he had only paid 45,000 Swiss francs in taxes). However, it was all invested in his foundations, which owned the companies, or was stashed away in complex offshore family foundations, leaving his three sons and adopted daughter from his first marriage with a personal fortune of only €75 million and an old Volvo worth €1,500. After steep Swedish inheritance taxes, this meant €9.5 million for each of them.

In his "testament", which he had made public and already implemented in his lifetime, he designed a structure which he had carefully developed over time, intended to remain unchangeable and make IKEA "eternal" (as if there was such a thing in corporate life).

There was to be a "Blue" group engaged in the furniture trading business, covering the shops, the design, manufacturing and logistics. This was controlled by Ingka Holding, which in turn was owned by foundations in the Netherlands and Liechtenstein.

The "Red" group was in charge of investments. It owned the IKEA shops, who, like franchisees, had to pay a 3% royalty charge based on their turnover for the use of the brand name and concept. This expenditure was and is of course tax-deductible. In 2006–2007, for instance, it amounted to €600 million, which was invested in real estate, equity participation, and the financial market. The Red group was controlled by Inter IKEA Holding as a holding company and owned by various foundations (not charities!), such as the Interogo Foundation located in offshore tax havens, including the Dutch Antilles, the Virgin Islands and Cyprus, all controlled by the Kamprad family.

Finally, there was the "Green" group in charge of side businesses, such as Habitat Furniture and the Ikano Bank, all organised under Ikano SA Luxembourg as a holding company owned by the Kamprad family. The all-decisive family council until 2011 consisted of Ingvar Kamprad, his wife Margaretha, the three sons and two advisors, one of whom was a tax expert.

On the face of it, the IKEA Group weathered the demise of its charismatic founder well. The number of shops went up from

340 (2017) in 28 countries to 445 (2020) and 473 (2024). Note, however, that new city shops have become much smaller! Turnover grew steadily from €11 billion in 2003 to €47.6 billion in 2023, with a little bump during 2020 when most shops were closed due to the COVID-19 crisis; however, the evolving online business fulfilled much of the demand from people who wanted to decorate their homes and equip their home offices where they were locked in. Product categories by global sales remained healthily diversified: Bed and bathroom: 22%, living room: 19%, kitchen and dining: 15%, children: 5%, food sales: 5%, others (meaning bedding, towels, kitchen tools, decoration materials, lamps, flower pots, and so on): 34%. The most important markets continued to be Germany (16%), the U.S. (10%), the U.K. and France (9% each), Sweden (7%) and the rest of the world (49%). Japan remained a difficult market, as most Japanese men dislike assembly labour after returning from work, and customers expect salesmen to deliver and set up fully functional furniture in their homes. After a first attempt in the 1980s failed, an expensive second launch in 2006 has so far resulted in 13 shops, of which three are city shops in Tokyo. China, due to a shortage of suitable locations and business permits, is also considered difficult. Russia, again, is a different story. First, IKEA delayed its entry for years since its ethical code forbade the payment of bribes, which were routinely demanded by the Russian officialdom. Once it launched, the Russian middle class enthusiastically embraced the idea of replacing their old Soviet-era furniture. However, when Putin attacked Kyiv in February 2022, IKEA, like so many other Western consumer producers, pulled out, not that Billy shelves had any military value. Its 17 shops had accounted for 4% of its turnover (or $1.8 million), and Belorussian and domestic copycats were no substitutes in quality and service.

Ingvar Kamprad had always insisted on the time-honoured success story of a catalogue mailed out last to 220 million customers. The catalogue would be studied at homes often for months, followed up by a visit to the IKEA shop, which was a purposeful maze of furniture exhibition, holding on to customers for hours and offering cheap but tasty Swedish self-service food. The customers eventually found the exit counters, fully laden with lots of impulse purchases. The new customers, however, wanted to check products online first and get quick service at more accessible city shops. The difficulty for the modernisers at IKEA was that their system had generated margins of 14%, while online traders such as Amazon had less than 2%.

Finally, in 2017, Peter Agnefjall, who had difficulties with the modernisers as CEO, was replaced by company veteran Jesper Brodin. Then, the organisational structure was in for a major overhaul with the purpose of becoming more reactive. The Blue group functions of design, manufacturing and logistics would be sold from Ingka Holding (with 160,000 employees) to the much smaller Red group, Inter IKEA Holding (with 1,500 employees and Mathias Kamprad at the helm). Inter IKEA would thus become the future franchiser, and Ingka Holding, left with only the shops, would become the lowly franchisee. Obviously, this relationship of master and servant appears somewhat at odds with the cherished IKEA ideology of egalitarian "togetherness", and whether it will work against the global online competition of Westwing, Home 24 and the like remains to be seen. It is hoped that the new franchising system will make it easier to find new partners for shops in new markets.

One of the first victims of the reforms was the famous catalogue, which has been accessible only online since 2020. However, not all smart new ideas work. An example is the "Boklok" homes, prefabricated wooden structures which can be quickly and cheaply assembled (by workers, not customers) and grouped in a uniform design as suburban two-story buildings or row houses. They look like similarly built Japanese prefabricated homes with a Scandinavian look and probably have the same life expectancy of one generation — not unlike IKEA furniture. The scheme started in Sweden in 1997 and was followed up in the U.K. in 2013 (where it seemed initially attractive due to high conventional construction costs) but has since been discontinued.

The standard criticism levelled at IKEA is that its folksy, down-to-earth approach contrasts sharply with its hard-nosed approach to systematic tax avoidance, as if this were not a sign of wise frugality. Had Kamprad remained taxable in Älmhult, his children would have had to sell their one and only furniture shop. Then, there are the usual charges of using wood sourced from illegal logging or the demands for saving the rainforests. Now, there is surely not a shred of heavy tropical timber in any of the cardboard furniture sold. The chipboard and compressed wood used are rather made from the leftovers of sawmills. More fundamentally, however, is the observation that IKEA has helped shift the notion of furniture lasting for generations into one of a disposable commodity, which can be trashed at a whim. In response, IKEA opened a second-hand furniture shop in Eskilstuna in 2020, a rather symbolic first sign of its commitment to a "circular economy". In 2024, IKEA also opened an online platform, "IKEA Preowned", which allows direct trade among customers of IKEA furniture (whose shelves bought in student days normally later end up in cellars). Thus far, it only exists in Madrid and Oslo.

The beauty of blue-yellow IKEA blocks on former greenfield sites accessible only by car and hence surrounded by huge parking areas also lies very much in the eye of the beholder. Again, this seems like an outgoing model.

Bibliography

Note: Any links to online sources were valid as of the publication of the first edition, in October 2004. Many of the pages have since been taken down.

Bartlett, C. A. and Ghoshal, S. *Transnational Management.* Singapore: McGraw-Hill, 2000.

Brown-Humes, C. "The bolt that holds the IKEA empire together", *Financial Times*, p. 7, 12 August 2002.

Ebeling, A. "Size matters", 7 August 2000. http://www.forbes.com/global/2000/0807/0315036s2.html

Heller, R. "Hidden wealth", 8 July 2000. http://www.forbes.com/global/2000/0807/0315036s1.html

Heller, R. "The billionaire next door", 7 August 2000. http://www.forbes.com/global/2000/0807/0315036a.html

Heller, R. "IKEA's founder concerned about rapid expansion", 6 January 2003. www.nordicbusinessreport.com

Lewis, R. D. *When Cultures Collide: Managing Successfully across Cultures*. London: Nicholas Brealey, 1999.

Torekull, B. *Leading by Design: The IKEA Story*. New York: HarperBusiness, 1999.

New Literature, 2nd Edition

Anwar, A. "Schwarzes Schaf wird Ikea Chef", *Der Standard*, 5 June 2013.

Collins, L. "House Perfect", *The New Yorker*, 26 September 2011.

"Das komplizierte Netzwerk der Kamprads", *News.ORF.at*, 27 January 2011.

Gamilscheg, H. "Milliarden im Steuerparadies", *Frankfurter Rundschau*, 27 January 2011.

"Ikea has a new CEO", *Reuters,* 24 May 2017.

"Ingvar Kamprads Testament", *Der Spiegel*, 15 March 2018.

Jungbluth, R. *Die 11 Geheimnisse des IKEA Erfolgs*. Bergisch-Gladbach: Bastei-Lübbe, 2008.

Jungbluth, R. "Alter Schwede, neue Milde", *Die Zeit*, 8 November 2012.

Machatschke, M. and Sucher, J. "Ikea. Das unmögliche Erbe", *Manager Magazin*, 8 September 2008.

The Rise and Fall of the Seibu-Saison Empire

It normally takes the third generation to ruin a business empire. The Tsutsumi brothers managed to do that in the second. In fact, Seiji Tsutsumi's Seibu-Saison enterprise, as part and parcel of Japan's bubble economy of asset inflation in the 1980s, was built up and collapsed during a few decades of his own business activities alone, with him as probably the most spectacular protagonist and, ultimately, also victim of the profligate years. After a decade of failed rehabilitation attempts, Seiyo, the company's real estate arm, went down in July 2000 with $5 billion of debts, and Seiji Tsutsumi was forced to divest most of his remaining Saison Group Holdings. His struggling erstwhile avant-garde Seibu Department Store chain had to be merged in 2003 with the equally bankrupt Sogo chain in a desperate attempt by the bankers to somehow rehabilitate both and avoid the stigma of bankruptcy, which would destroy the remaining brand value of the previously upmarket department stores. The Seiyu supermarkets have been swallowed by Wal-Mart since.

Seiji's half-brother, Yoshiaki Tsutsumi, who inherited most of their father's railroad and hotel empire and who most famously more or less bought for himself the Nagano Winter Olympics of

1998, lost similar amounts, but as one of the world's richest men back in 1990, with a then net worth of $16 billion, he could take a $13 billion crash to stay in the black with a more modest net worth of $2.8 billion (2001), according to *Forbes*.

Central to the Seibu saga is the founding father and patriarch Yasujiro Tsutsumi (1889–1965), his three wives and countless mistresses. As a farmer's son, he lost his parents early and grew up in rural Shiga Prefecture. After elementary school and military academy, he mortgaged his grandfather's heritage to study at Tokyo's Waseda University, already as a young family man.

A couple of speculative deals usefully multiplied his meagre funds. His interests at the egalitarian Waseda, which then was a breeding ground of nationalist-minded reformers, were however less scholarly. Yasujiro became secretary to Shigenobu Okuma, who would later become Prime Minister of Japan. In the politico-economic interface so typical of many Japanese developers, he then used his personal and political contacts for his budding business ends. Even during his student days, he bought up cheap wasteland and pastures near the popular elite mountain resort of Karuizawa, which he subsequently developed with vacation houses, leisure facilities and the necessary infrastructure. By the end of the First World War, he had laid the foundations of his future post-industrial leisure empire.

Having set up his own construction companies, Yasujiro was able to profit from the building and reconstruction boom following the Kanto earthquake of 1923. One year later, he was elected to Parliament to fill a seat in his home prefecture of Shiga, which, except for the purge years during the U.S. occupation (1945–1951), Yasujiro held until his death in 1965. As a member of the war-advocating Democratic Party, he rose to the position of parliamentary vice minister as early as 1932–1934. Yet, he remained disinterested in ideology and continued to use his political work almost exclusively for business purposes: to purchase early land earmarked for future development, to takeer competing railway lines in the west of Tokyo (the Musashino and Seibu lines) and to furnish the logistics for supplying I ammunition to the military.

His fear of being expropriated by the victorious Americans as a war profiteer remained unfounded. Instead, Yasujiro bought up cheaply bombed-out land around his Tokyo railway terminals. He also bought out impoverished aristocrats, who could no longer afford to pay inheritance taxes. He demolished their residences and put up hotels of his cheekily named Prince. He also pioneered three new towns along his West Tokyo railways, which subsequently turned into fashionable pricey suburbs.

As a highlight of his political career from 1953 to 1955, Yasujiro Tsutsumi was elected president of Japan's Lower House, a position that was the most tangible recognition of his elevated status amongst Japan's post-war *nouveau riches*.

His open display of polygamy and despotic leadership style — nicknamed "Pistol" for his gunslinging business methods and his speed to firing non-complying subordinates — were public knowledge but did not hurt. He also survived a fairly well-documented vote-buying scandal, and after his sudden death in 1965, he was buried with all honours at a cemetery, which he himself had typically developed profitably earlier.

His business empire was divided unequally between his two unequal sons. Seiji, the older son, was born to a poetess whom Yasujiro had briefly married. S cultured intellectual, he flirted with a communist student group for a while in the post-war years. Disinherited by his father, he was excluded from the CP for leftist deviance and promptly returned to the fold to serve his father, then President of Parliament, as a political secretary. Of his father's business, Seiji was to inherit only a run-down department store at a Tokyo railroad terminal in Ikebukuro.

The vastly more valuable railway lines, hotels, real estate holdings and resorts went to his half-brother, Yoshiaki, who, as the son of Yasujiro's favourite mistress, had inherited his father's ruthless business acumen and autocratic ways. Similar to Yasujiro, he used his student days to develop privately financed swimming pools and ice stadiums. Within two decades, he built his father's inheritance into Japan's leading hotel, ski resort and golf course operator and developer. This helped smoothen political connections, notably with the then ruling LDP's powerful construction-business-oriented Takeshita faction. Yasujiro's electoral district was inherited by a close affiliate, Ganri Yamashita, who later became Minister of Defence.

Resort development in Japan's typically mountainous and fragile environment is usually done in the most ruthless ways. Unspoiled rural areas would be brought up cheaply, the forests chopped up and the landscape bulldozed to make way for golf courses, ski slopes, parking lots and hotel complexes. Yoshiaki, in addition, made sure that the necessary infrastructure was provided for free from public funds.

He also applied this pattern blatantly when purchasing the 1998 Nagano Winter Olympics as president of Japan's Olympic Committee and vice president of the Nagano Organising Committee from IOC President Juan Samaranch.

Yoshiaki's Seibu Group (later renamed Kokudo Group) then already owned most of Nagano's hotels, shopping arcades and ski slopes. The Olympics brought publicly funded highways and a Shinkansen line, which shortened the distance from Tokyo to Nagano to 90 minutes, thus assuring a steady supply of day skiers into this volatile Alpine region from then on. Widely criticised, the construction destroyed rare habitats of endangered species in protected national parks, turned natural rivers into cemented canals and changed unspoiled forests and farm plots into wastelands of clear cuts and concrete. The Olympics helped channel an ever larger share of Japan's $8 billion annual skiing business into the balance sheets of the Kokudo Group, but it also generated unwelcome international attention to Yoshiaki's business methods. Not only issues of unethical environmental practices and political collusion came to the fore, but his idiosyncratic management style was also scrutinised. As *The Japan Times* at the time put it:

> *He is obsessed with frugality and apart from supporting political friends, loathes donating money to anyone or anything. He roams the country in his helicopter, inspecting his empire of hotels, barking orders, keeping his staff on their toes ("I don't need employees with fancy college education", he once said. "I want people who can do what I tell them") and making sure that nothing is wasted. Towels in his hotels are used for an extra year, after which they are used as rags in Yoshiaki's offices.*

Obviously, recycling old towels did not help stem the evaporation of Yoshiaki's real estate values and corporate wealth. Still, he remained a major player in the Japanese hotel (Prince), railways (Seibu), resort and golf course scene. As owner of the leading Seibu Lions professional baseball team and an ice hockey team, Yoshiaki played a major public role.

His rival half-brother, Seiji, retreated from public view after the collapse of his Seiyo development corporation. Before his death in 2013, he had spent his time writing poetry and had run a small non-profit foundation to support the performing arts. In charge of his father's neglected department store in Ikebukuro, then a run-down neighbourhood in the 1950s, he had introduced the products of then unknown young designers such as Yves Saint Laurent and Issey Miyake to his Seibu department store. His modernised stores became early symbols of a status- and glitter-oriented consumer culture, which affluent youngsters embraced once the hardships of the post-war years were overcome. Almost singlehandedly, Seiji anticipated future trends in consumer tastes. In 1963, he started the later immensely profitable Seiyu supermarket chain. In 1968, with his new flagship Seibu Shibuya, he founded a trend-setting consumer palace for the baby boom generation, followed by the trendy Parco shop-in-shop boutique concept for fashionable, affluent teenagers. During the "golden age" of Japan's consumer boom in the 1980s, Seiji unfolded a firework of new business ideas, most of which were novel to Japan: the Seibu Card (1982) – as solid Japanese banks would never credit finance flippant teenagers' consumer fads; department-store-based sales of financial services, such as the Seibu All State Life Insurance' exclusive sales licences with up-market Western brand producers; and a chain of convenience stores ("Family Mart") which stay open for 24 hours.

Seibu *depaatos* were celebrated for art exhibitions, operating trendy in-store restaurants, coffee shops, theatres, concert halls and cinemas. In the 1970s and 1980s, Seibu and Parco were the most profitable and avant-garde amongst Japan's otherwise conservative and overpriced department stores. As a sponsor of avant-garde theatre, including difficult pieces by playwrights such as Kobo Abe, and contemporary art (exhibited in the Seibu Museum of Art), Seiji cultivated an image of liberal intellectual modernity, which not only contrasted well with the gruffly greed of his unloved half-brother but, more importantly, harmonised well with the message of a luxury-oriented civilisation, reflecting Japan's newfound wealth, which was driven by his up-market stores catering to the new bubble boom rich and those living on credit.

Like most of his customers' lifestyle, Seiji's own rapidly expanding empire was built on credit. The high turnover of his store resulted in only smallish profits. and debt service ate up most of the cash flow. During the period of asset inflation of the 1980s, when debt could easily be turned into equity, this posed no problem.

So, Seiji expanded and diversified further, declaring in the fuzzy logic of the bubble's heydays that his group should service "every facet of living". Seiji's Seiyo real estate subsidiary hence began to venture into his brother's business territory by developing up-market shopping complexes, leisure facilities, hotels and condominiums.

In a spontaneous decision, Seiji in 1983 bought the then 98-hotel-strong global InterContinental chain from Grand Metropolitan for $2.2 billion. He expanded it quickly to 187 hotels, adding a super-luxury hotel at the Ginza, which catered to Elizabeth Taylor and the likes. The economics of this entirely credit-financed frenzy was questionable. But surely brother Yoshiaki's pedestrian 56-hotel-strong Prince chain was duly dwarfed.

Seiji's Seibu Group did not collapse overnight. But his message of eternal lifestyle consumerism and overpriced spending excitements looked quickly out of place in a recession-ridden Japan, where people soon rediscovered the virtues of their traditional frugality.

While his retail operations might have survived on their own, the credit-financed capital — wasted on real estate developments, such as resorts and 15 golf courses, for which there was no longer any demand — heavily weighted down the group.

In 1991, Seiji formally resigned. As it was he who had called the shots, the group drifted. Half-hearted restructuring showed little results. Occasional divestments equally had little overall impact.

In July 2000, Seiyo Corporation, Seibu-Saison's real estate arm, went bottom up, forcing Seiji to sell most of his remaining shareholdings. Intercontinental Hotels were sold in 2003 to Bass, a British brewer, for $2.9 billion, all of which went for debt servicing. Forced by the main creditor, Mizuho Bank, the remaining Seibu Department Stores had to dismiss 40% of their 9,000 strong staff. In return for these restructuring measures, Mizuho Bank (under pressure from the Ministry of Finance) was ready to forgive 230 billion yen ($1.9 billion) of Seibu's debts and accept a ten-billion-yen worth of debt for equity swap.

As Seibu's Tokyo locations remained somewhat profitable, despite being no longer the avant-garde of anything, they were merged with the equally bankrupt but undistinguished Sogo department stores. The rest of Seiji's empire (Seiyu supermarkets, Family Mart, Parco stores, etc.) was gradually disposed of.

By 2025, six decades after its auspicious beginning, the Seibu-Saison party was definitely over.

The Next Two Decades

The two brothers continued to go in very different ways. Seiji Tsutsumi, after his 1991 resignation as head of Seibu Saison, continued his writing career under pseudonyms and stayed on as president of the Saison Cultural Foundation, which he had founded in 1987 and which continues to sponsor avant-gardist Japanese theatre and dance, whose enjoyment is of course a matter of taste. There are two English translations of his novels: *A Spring Like Any Other* (New York: Kodansha, 1992) and *Disappearance of the Butterfly* (Honolulu: University of Hawaii Press, 1994). His last and perhaps most interesting work was *Chichi No Shozu* (Portrait of my father; Tokyo: Shinchosa, 2004). During the boom years of the 1980s, he had showered Japanese and U.S. cultural institutions, the modern arts scene and individual artists with millions of grants and opportunities to exhibit, and they did not forget him, since he appears to have continued as a philanthropist of more modest means. So, he stayed on as the President of the International Pen Club of Japan and became a life trustee of the Asian Cultural Council, vice president of the Japan Writers Association and Chairman of the Japan–China Cultural Exchange Foundation. With these functions, honours were not very far away. After having received the prestigious Junichiro Tanizaki Award and the Noma Literature Prize in 1994, he was awarded the Japan Art Academy Prize in 2006 and the Japan Poets' Association Award in 2009. In 2011, he was selected to compose the Emperor's poem to be read out by His Majesty at the New Year 2012 ceremony. Unsurprisingly, he was nominated as a "Person of Cultural Merit" by the Japanese government the same year. In 1996, as a mature student at the tender age of 69, he also received his

PhD in economics from Chuo University in Tokyo for a thesis on "Blueprint for Change – Beyond the Distribution Theory".

Seiji Tsutsumi died in Tokyo in November 2013, aged 86, from liver failure.

While Seiji lost his fortune but continued a highly honoured life at the apex of Japan's cultural scene, his younger brother, Yoshiaki, became a social non-person after falling from the status as the world's richest billionaire (according to *Forbes* during 1987–1990), worth $21 billion, to an impoverished $500 million fortune today and his arrest in March 2005 and house and corporate searches. He was charged with violating the Tokyo Stock Exchange rules by faking his Kokobu holding company's balance sheet for years with the help of seven directors, one of whom committed suicide. The rules did not allow the individual ownership of more than 80% of shares. With the help of thousands of faked employee shareholdings, he had whittled down his ownership of Seibu Railways on paper from 88% to 43%. There were also charges of subsequent insider trading to cover it up in the tune of $216 million. Kokobu was quickly delisted from the Tokyo Stock Exchange, and the forever ultra-virtuous IOC suspended its erstwhile honoured member and generous sponsor.

After this public humiliation, Yoshiaki Tsutsumi pleaded guilty, apologised duly in public and, with a fine of $42,000 and a suspended jail sentence of 30 months, received a fairly mild yet appropriate judgement for what was after all not a capital crime but a gross violation of reporting rules. His companies, Seibu and Kokudo, were also fined €1.4 million and €1.1 million, respectively, sums which probably represented less than their hourly cash flow. So, it was not the mild judgement per se but the reputational damage following the verdict as a convicted criminal that triggered an avalanche of malicious commentaries in Japan and in the international press about this fallen despotic tycoon who thought himself above the law.

After a management reform of Toshiyaki's holding and its 70 companies and their 35,000 worried employees, which was led by Takashi Goto sent from Mizuho Bank as its new chairman, and after the infusion of new outside capital, the old Kokubo holding was restructured as Seibu Holdings, separating the operations of Seibu Railways, Prince Hotels and Kokobu proper. The new major shareholder was to be the rightly named U.S. Cerberus funds, ever eager to pick up suffering Japanese stocks and introduce a no-nonsense U.S. focus on shareholder returns. Toshiyaki Tsutsumi's shares in the new Seibu holdings were reduced to barely 5%. The lesson of this reflects an old wisdom of the Japanese political and business elite: you may cheat, but you should never get caught.

Bibliography

Note: Any links to online sources were valid as of the publication of the first edition, in October 2004. Many of the pages have since been taken down.

"Bubble-era expansion still tormenting Saison Group", *Asahi Shimbun*, 1 February 2003.

"Computer statt Piste", *Die Zeit*, 50/1999.

"Developer's business likely to win gold from Nagano Games", *AP*, 21 February 1998.

Downer, L. *Die Brüder Tsutsumi: Die Geschichte der reichsten Familie Japans*. München: Heyne Verlag, 1997.

Havens, T. R. *Architects of Affluence: The Tsutsumi Family and the Seibu-Saison Enterprises in Twentieth-Century Japan*. Cambridge, Mass.: Harvard University Press, 1994.

Macintyre, D. "Learning to Let Go", *Time Asia*, 31 July 2000.

"Sales will be real test of Seibu, Sogo Merger", *Asahi Evening News*, 28 February 2003.

"Seibu set to receive ¥230 billion rescue package", *Financial Times*, 15 January 2003.

"Seiyo goes bankrupt with 550 billion yen debt", *The Japan Times*, 19 July 2000.

"The Nagano Olympics and the destruction of nature". http://nolimpiadi.8m.com/enolim01.html

"The Tsutsumi Family: Brotherly Hate", *The Economist*, 8 October 1988.

New Literature, 2nd Edition

"Abstieg eines Tycoons", *Manager Magazin*, 29 March 2005.

"Ex-Saison Group Head Seiji Tsutsumi dies at 86", *The Japan Times*, 28 November 2013.

"Japaner Tsutsumi soll ausgeschlossen werden", *Frankfurter Allgemeine*, 19 April 2005.

"Japanischer Firmenmagnat festgenommen", *Frankfurter Allgemeine*, 3 March 2005.

Nishikawa, M. "The Seibu Group — The Fall of the Seibu Empire", *ICDM Pulse*.

"Vom reichsten Mann der Welt zum Kriminellen", *Der Spiegel*, 27 October 2005.

United, the Benetton Way

There are only very few family-owned enterprises which managed to develop world brands. Benetton, an Italian, family-owned enterprise, is one such case. It belongs to a family of four siblings, Luciano, Giuliana (both of whom were the initial founders of the company), Gilberto and Carlo Benetton. The company's roots are intricately entwined with the family's history.

The Benetton children lost their father, Leone Benetton, in 1945 during the Second World War, when all of them were mere adolescents. Luciano, the eldest, was only 10 years old when his childhood ended. He became the *de facto* breadwinner of the family, selling newspapers and panini (sandwiches) at the train station near their house in the morning and bars of soap after school on a door-to-door basis just to make ends meet. Giuliana, the only Benetton daughter and the second eldest, had learnt to knit from children's comics when she was young. She quit school to work in a garment sweatshop to help support the family income. When Luciano grew older, he worked for several years as a retail salesman in the Dellasiegas' clothing store in Treviso, where he lived. As time passed, he began to realise that he and his sister were capable of producing and selling jumpers on their own instead of selling them on commission for other people.

Luciano's enterprise was based on a simple notion: making and selling colourful knitwear which was of commendable quality and which could be bought at a cheap and affordable price, targeted specifically at a previously untapped youth market. In 1955, some jumpers were designed and produced by Giuliana with a home sewing machine in their house. They were given the brand name "Très Jolie". Luciano consequently managed to persuade his employers, the Dellasiegas' brothers, to sell the jumpers, and this proved an astonishing success. What made them saleable was as much the quality of the jumpers as the fact that they were unique in design. Giuliana had produced jumpers that were unseen at that time. Colours that ranged from red to blue to yellow were produced. Consumers greedily drank up all the colours, and the jumpers became so popular that queues were often formed outside the stores. The reason for their popularity was that customers were tired of the sombre dark colours like black and grey, which were typical of the post-war era. Subsequently, Giuliana would design the woollen models (when the current trend was for acrylic pullovers) and be in charge of fabrication, while her brother would handle the marketing side, acting as a commercial representative. It was then too that Luciano succeeded in his efforts to improve the quality of the wool used to produce the jumpers. For this, he travelled to Scotland to learn how the Scots manufacture the wool to remove the "itch" caused from wearing it. He also managed, together with the help of Adalgerico "Ado" Montana, a dyeing specialist, to invent a method of dyeing a whole jumper after it was finished rather than dyeing it in parts, as it was more cost-efficient to do so. (The original method was to dye the jumper in its constituents rather than as a whole since dyeing it whole would cause the jumper to shrink.)

In 1955, there was only Luciano, Giuliana and a sewing machine. Ten years later, the company had a hundred and fifty employees, with all four Benetton siblings working full time in the company: Luciano was in charge of sales and advertising, Giuliana was responsible for clothing designs and the coordination of preparations for productions, Gilberto was in charge of administration and Carlo was the head of the manufacturing process.

The first store that sold exclusively Benetton knits was opened in Belluno in the quietest part of town. It was a 50/50 venture with a friend named Piero Marchiorello. The shop was named "My Marke'" so as not to risk the real brand name of Très Jolie to market failure. The store became a tremendous hit with the youth of Belluno. After opening a few more stores, Luciano Benetton decided that it was possible to build up a network of retail stores manned by potential partners selling exclusively Benetton products. He introduced a franchising system similar to that of McDonald's and Coca-Cola's. Young potential entrepreneurs who were eager to cash in on Benetton's success could do so. This is where Luciano's "gentleman's agreement" (Mantle, 2000, p. 241) came in. Despite using a franchising system so closely associated with American companies, Luciano's franchising system was unique in the sense that, unlike the American style of franchising, which was based on a voluminous amount of documentation, agreements with store owners were signed with a simple handshake, without a written contract, and this agreement was based on mutual trust — similar to the first agreement that the Benettons made with Marchiorello in the beginning. Also, the franchisees had an added advantage. They need not pay any royalties to Benetton if they made profits or used the brand name. However, it was done on condition that the stores sold exclusively Benetton products with a no-return policy, and they had to buy the store equipment designed by the Benettons' architect, Tobia Scarpa. Moreover, it was Luciano who ultimately made the decision to approve the store location, and he had the right to periodically supervise the store.

By the early 1970s, the company had opened stores all over Italy. The whole decade showed a tremendous increase in turnover:

revenues in 1971 amounted to a total of 1.1 billion lire, which subsequently skyrocketed to a value of 100.4 billion lire. Net income passed from 0.3 million lire in 1971 to 3.1 billion in 1979. In order to increase production efficiency and meet the increasing consumer demand for the clothes, Luciano devised a system of subcontracting the manufacture of the clothes to small family-owned workshops, which employed no more than 20 workers who were paid on the basis of the number of garments they produced. Benetton provided the raw material, the design and the manufacturing plan, which left the subcontractor responsible for bringing in the equipment and the workforce. In 1973, nearly 80 subcontractors worked for Benetton, which minimised the company's investments in capacity. As sales volume increased, subcontractors were coordinated by a series of small factories partially owned by the Benetton family.

Retail stores also increased in numbers. To better coordinate and keep an eye on the retail stores, Benetton decided to build a chain of stores hierarchically coordinated by agents. These agents were personally selected by Luciano himself and were responsible for sourcing more young entrepreneurs keen on opening a Benetton shop. They were also in charge of organising the presentations of new collections to retailers, taking down their orders for "flash", that is, unplanned (Mantle, 2000, p. 122) collections (which actually revealed Benetton's ability to respond to abrupt changes in consumer demand) apart from the usual ones and relating all these information to the Benetton headquarters in Ponzano.

In the 1980s, the Benettons' main strategy was that of internationalisation and diversification. This was done to capture larger share of the consumer market, which was coherent with Luciano's strategy of empire-building. The former "McDonald's of the jumper" (Mantle, 2000, p. 126) now not only produced knitwear but also casual wear, jeans and menswear. The stores operated under the names of Benetton, My Market, Sisley, Jean West and Tomato. Sisley, for example, was acquired in 1978 to create an independent collection targeting a market segment higher than that of Jean West (also another jeans-producing brand under Benetton). Further diversification had brought about the creation of other forms of Benetton merchandise, including maternity wear for women, clothes catering to children ranging from three to twelve years of age under the brand 012, which was introduced in 1978, casual men's and women's wear as well as a broad selection of accessories like cosmetics, perfumes and shoes, offering a full range and wide selection of Benetton style and quality that catered specifically to almost all age groups.

In 2000, the company had Benetton outlets in about 120 countries around the world, with an international retail network of 5,000 stores. Further diversification of the products had resulted in the evolution of subsidiary brands such as The Hip Site, Sisley for teenagers and the sportswear brands Playlife and Killer Loop.

Also, as business expanded overseas, the notion of franchising arose. Benetton subsidiaries in respective countries were managed by local entrepreneurs who became the franchisees. Apart from overseas expansion, Benetton also began diversifying its products as it extended its business abroad. Brands such as Sisley and Killer Loop were specifically targeted at the youth market. There is also a clothing line for pregnant women. Further, innovation in logistics resulted due to Benetton's desire to increase efficiency and reduce product wastage which occurred when a sales order required the manufacture of Benetton products. Despite internationalisation and diversification strategies and attempts at innovation, Luciano Benetton, at the time of writing, was still the head of the company, with the Benetton family still fully controlling the business.

Advertising Campaigns

All over the world Benetton stands for colorful sportswear, multiculturalism, world peace, racial harmony, and now, a progressive approach towards serious issues (Giroux, 1994, p. 6).

Luciano Benetton was constantly attuned to the changing needs and attitudes of consumers. Unlike the consumers of before, current consumers were more aware of their social environment and also more environmentally or socially proactive. He realised that consumers were no longer buying a product simply for its uses but buying a product for what it represented and what attributes of a product also appealed to their sense of an individual identity. He wanted to project the image of Benetton as more than just a manufacturer of products. Benetton had to symbolise a lifestyle and a worldview to stay in tune with consumer needs. Moreover, a global image was of utmost importance to Luciano since 70% of the profits were derived from the international markets. There had to be a common global image for product identification that linked all Benetton shops together for business to grow. In 1972, Benetton conferred its advertising campaigns to the Eldorado agency, which decided on a poster campaign. Hence, in 1982, photographer Oliviero Toscani from the Eldorado agency started working with Benetton, and before long, the label had acquired a certain notoriety.

Benetton adopted the "multi-racial" theme since it was in tandem with the theme of colour in Benetton clothes. At first, the posters focused on depicting a celebratory mix of kids and adults of various races dressed in colourful ethnic clothing with a sense of simplicity and happiness with the slogan "Benetton: All the colors in the world!" attached.

The posters changed and became increasingly provocative. These posters under Toscani's artistic direction became extremely controversial and generated a huge amount of publicity for Benetton. Some examples of Benetton's posters were: a picture of a dead AIDS victim surrounded by his family with a Christ-like aura, a poster of a priest and nun kissing and a poster of a blood-stained shirt and army fatigue-pants of a dead, unknown soldier. The list goes on, but although this might have generated a lot of negative publicity for the company, it had achieved its purpose. Sales almost always increased when Toscani's controversial posters were advertised. It was known to decrease when tamer advertisements were used instead.

To put it negatively, Benetton's advertising launch was an attempt to commodify culture and to boost sales by trying to revive the dried up image of the company in the eighties. This was based on the growing notion that consumers now did not buy the product but rather bought what the product aesthetically represented. Put positively, Benetton Group's advertising campaigns were meant not only as a means of communication but also an expression of our time. The advertisements contained a diverse range of universal themes of racial integration, protection of the environment and AIDS. Through their universal impact, they have succeeded in attracting the attention of the public and stood out amidst the current clutter of images. The campaigns have gathered awards and international acclaim. Likewise, they have provoked strong reactions, sometimes vicious, other times plain curiosity, confirming once again that they are always a focal point of discussion and of confrontation of ideas.

However, critics have attacked Benetton's advertisements as blatant exploitation of people in horrifying situations. One American critic, Henry Giroux, in his book *Disturbing Pleasures* called it hyper-ventilating realism, which basically equates to a realism of sensationalism, shock and spectacle, commenting that the advertisements simply register rather than challenge the dominant social relations reproduced in the photographs. Two racially marked ads which sparked sharp criticisms and attacks on Benetton were used by him to substantiate these claims.

The first depicts a black woman and a white baby. The black woman is shown wearing a crimson cable knit cardigan pulled over her shoulders, which exposes her right breast. Her hands reveal traces of scar tissue and her nails are trimmed short with the baby shown suckling on the black woman's breast. Given the legacy of colonialism and racism against black people in America, it was inevitable that the photo would be interpreted as an imperialist coding, as it privileged an offensive reading of an ingrained racial stereotype of the black enslaved wet nurse. Though this advertisement was pulled from billboards in the U.S., it ironically won Benetton many awards across Europe, including Le Grand Prix de L'Affichage in France.

The second ad portrayed two hands, one white and the other black, being handcuffed together. Critics had not dismissed the possibility that the poster depicted a false and calculated sense of equality. In reality, it only served to reinforce, at least at the level of consciousness, that crime, turmoil and lawlessness were fundamentally a black problem.

Benetton's Company Culture

Since Benetton is an Italian-owned company, much of Benetton's style of management is similar to the approach that the Italians take to business. Benetton, being family-owned, reflects the relative importance of family to business and life in general. There is a strong sense of familism within the family, with personal loyalties given to the immediate and extended family. Trust with outsiders is not easily built, and this is the reason why personal networking is of the utmost importance in Italian business circles. Luciano himself "was an indefatigable world-class networker, known from the White House to the Kremlin" (Mantle, 2000, p. 205). People who became franchisees of Benetton in the international arena were mostly of Italian descent and were usually friends of friends who personally knew the Benettons. Indeed, there seemed "an impression of favoritism towards friends and friends of friends" (Mantle, 2000, p. 127). This method of networking within trusted circles and forming business partnerships only with people whom Benetton trusted was exemplified when Luciano tapped into the American market by approaching the

Italian Chamber of Commerce and enlisting the help of an American-Italian individual named Sal Salibello. Also, the first Benetton shop to open in Prague was attributed to the help of "friends who found [them] a path through the bureaucracy" (Mantle, 2000, p. 137). An Anglo-Italian businessman close to the Benetton family once said in response to rumours that Benetton was linked to the mafia.

> *There is a culture which goes very deep in Italy, and which the likes of American investment banks don't always understand. It is a culture of who you know, and of using this knowledge. It may appear crooked, in the sense that it depends on who you know, but it is also a defence against far greater crookedness (Mantle, 2000, pp. 270–1).*

The issue of trust is again highlighted when it is found that the family had maintained a full hundred percent control of the company through Edizione Holdings. Twenty-five percent of shares were placed in flotation on the Milan stock exchange. This strategy was adopted to transform Benetton from a family-owned company into a mature corporate enterprise. However, ultimate control of Benetton Group Spa belonged to Edizione Holdings (the parent company). Unsurprisingly, the nexus of power lies in the hands of the four siblings, who were the directors of Edizione and no outsider could gain access to that power: "Benetton was and is like a mountain whose summit was above the clouds. At the top, which was effectively invisible, this was and always will be purely a family company" (Mantle, 2000, p. 119).

The level of patronage evident in Italian businesses can also be found in Benetton. Indeed, Italians in authority feel a sense of obligation to employees and even non-employees who belong to their personal network. Luciano, for example, employed his childhood friend Nico Luciani as the director of the Benetton Foundation, even though they had been estranged from each other for 25 years. The notion of friendship which accompanied business relations was also evident when the Scarpas, long-time family friends of the

Benettons who were their main architects, broke off all personal and business relations with Luciano and family when Luciano separated from his wife, Teresa, and married another.

Luciano also adopted a personal approach to the management of Benetton, which is a common trait of Italian business culture. He saw Benetton as more than just a company; to him, it exemplified the principle of entrepreneurship, hard work and initiative and as a symbol of how far the family had come. This personal pride in the organisation was shown when Villa Minelli, a mansion that Luciano had dreamt of living during his childhood, was bought and converted into the headquarters of Benetton. His hands-on approach in the business was also well known. He was committed to the active role he took in locating the stores and supervising the shops personally from time to time, often being away from the headquarters in Italy to inspect the shops. He would know where to locate the stores since he spent a lot of time observing people and their shopping habits.

According to *Management Worldwide*, "the [Italian] captains of industry are powerful, privileged individualists, whose reputations colour their organizations", and they also like to focus "on those aspects of the business which interest them and which they judge to be important, and leaving the rest to others" (Hickson & Pugh, 1995, p. 81). This was definitely true of Luciano Benetton. Certainly, Luciano was and is the most famous Benetton in the Benetton company, and he made himself in charge of sales and marketing while leaving the other departments to the other siblings to handle.

Luciano was known for detesting the structures of bureaucracy. In 1981, Aldo Palmeri, a former Bank of Italy officer, became the chief executive officer of Benetton. This was an apparent move to keep investors happy since they wanted greater transparency within the company and were wary of the Benetton "quart-partite" control of the company. The arrival of Palmeri resulted in the growth of a bureaucratic style which overlapped and sometimes conflicted with the dominating entrepreneurial and informal Benetton culture. The strong involvement of not only Luciano but all the Benetton siblings in operations contributed to the maintenance of styles. This informal and personal style, which also physically manifested in Luciano's casual attire for business, is a characteristic of the low power distance typical of a familial Italian business culture.

Luciano encouraged the entrepreneurial spirit in his employees. He personally saw to the employment of subcontractors and distribution agents. The original selection criterion for selecting subcontractors which Luciano adhered to was to see if there was any presence of an independent entrepreneurial spirit in the subcontractors. He also looked to see if there was any potential in the person for growth and whether the person possessed in-depth knowledge in manufacturing. In this, Luciano seemed to be almost always accurate, as he seemed to possess this innate ability to see if a person had untapped potential. The sub-contractors were given relative freedom in their operations of employing the workforce and buying equipment. In choosing distribution agents, acceptance criteria demanded a thorough understanding of the company style of management, a sense of mutual understanding between the management and the subordinate agent, in-depth knowledge of the market, a dedication to the business idea, entrepreneurial spirit and a sense of loyalty.

Indeed, since Luciano also gave a relatively large amount of freedom to his employees to take their own initiatives and realise their creativity, they often felt empowered enough to be motivated. Motivation was also enhanced by the implementation of reward schemes for the employees. As such, Benetton employees often possessed a strong level of loyalty and commitment to the company. However, herein lies a paradox: although entrepreneurship and initiative were seemingly valued qualities in an employee, Luciano often conducted "cleaning the network" sessions on retail shops around the world. It was a process in which "agents and shops were regularly observed and, where necessary, their performance [was] adjusted". This was accomplished with "a ruthless clarity of vision that was at odds with the image of the 'gentleman's agreement' that Luciano still liked to imply was unchanged since the early days of the business" (Mantle, 2000, p. 241). Certainly, the informal "gentleman's agreement" could have allowed Luciano Benetton to attain greater control of the distribution-end of production.

Despite this, Alessandro Sinatra in *Corporate Transformation* wrote that there are several reasons for the formidable success of Benetton. The first was the idea of using creativity to try to be innovative in the face of the scarcity of cash. In the beginning, the constant lack of financial capital led to the implementation of the most important design principles and resulted in original solutions. This idea of using creativity when cash was scarce became one of the tenets of Benetton's philosophy and is evident in the employment of subcontractors in manufacturing, the franchise agreements in retail, the advance made in the dyeing process and, subsequently, the highly advanced information and logistic systems. The continuous emphasis on cost-efficient methods is also due to the influence of the locals in agricultural Treviso on the importance of frugality and cost-effective methods. The last reason is due to the foresight of Luciano, who saw the potential in the retail market and took the initiative to seize the opportunity. He came up with the business idea and saw it through till the end.

The Next Two Decades: The End of Benetton as We Know It?

In the 1990s, the Benettons could do no wrong. They had 7,000 shops (mostly franchisees) in 120 countries, some 10,000 employees of their own and a turnover of €2 billion. Their textiles benefitted from the "made in Italy" image, being hip and cool and positioned in an affordable range just below Gorgio Armani. The two main brands were Benetton for the global medium-fashion segment for men and women, and Sisley, a fashionable line for men, women and children, popular especially in East Asia and Australia. There were also Undercolours of Benetton: underwear, pajamas and accessories. A multitude of other brands such as Killer Loop, Play Life and Jean's West were tried but later either ended or sold off. Around 1990, Benetton also bought participations in Nordica, an Italian ski boot maker, in Rollerblade (U.S. inline skates) and Prince Sports (U.S. tennis wear), all of which, with no synergies in sight, were sold off in 2004.

One of the three brothers, Gilberto Benedetti, wanted to be more than a textile merchant and insisted that the family holding Edizione should diversify and plough Benetton's profits into infrastructure investments to benefit from the Berlusconi government's privatisation policies. It started in 1995 with a stake in Autogrill, the caterer running restaurants along Italy's motorways. In the year 2000, it was the motorways, Autostrade per l'Italia, themselves, a stake which Edizione in 2003 increased to 84%. The toll system worked like a licence to print money, provided little cash was spent on maintenance. Thus, in 2017, the newly named Atlantia made a profit of €2.4 billion out of a turnover of €3.9 billion for the Benetton family — surely more exciting than selling colourful sweatshirts. The profits were used for further acquisitions in the airport business, including the purchase of Nice airport, for sizable stakes in Spanish motorways, the Spanish toll road operator Abertis, the telecom group Cellnex and in the Channel tunnel operator Getlink. Then, in August 2018, the poorly maintained Morandi Bridge in Genua collapsed, killing 43 people. It took the Benettons two days to apologise and accept their moral responsibility. Though they were politically well connected, the government felt compelled to threaten revoking Atlantia's concession. Soon afterwards, in October 2018, Gilberto, the mastermind of the diversification drive, who was also a director at Mediobanca and with Pirelli, the tire maker, died aged 77. Forbes estimated his personal wealth then at $2.7 billion.

By July 2020, the Benettons announced their gradual exit from Autostrade.

In 2008, the oldest brother, Luciano, announced his retirement as chairman of the Benetton group, which then still produced profits of €155 million, and groomed his son Alessandro for succession. Alessandro, who was CEO from 2012 to 2016, had the company delisted from the stock exchange, with Benetton SrL becoming the sole shareholder. However, losses mounted even after reducing staff by 25% to 7,300, and after reaching minus €81 million in 2016 and following violent disagreements over uncle Gilberto's diversification drive, Alessandro resigned and was shifted to the honorary position of president of Edizione Holding.

All other 13 offspring of the four founding brothers and sister were equally not considered top management potential. Today, only two Benettons are in director positions.

After another series of losses and management exits, 82-year-old Luciano returned to the helm, promising the return to profits, a refurbished brand and brighter shops. With him came his sister Giuliana, again in charge of styling and design, as well as Oliviero Toscani as their controversial art photographer and abrasive communication strategist. It was he who had produced posters with kissing nuns and priests, men in U.S. death cells and blood-drenched clothing during the Bosnian war. This he continued in 2011 with faked kissing scenes between Pope Benedict XVI and Iman Ahmed al-Tajied, Presidents Obama and Hu Jintao, Prime Minister Netanyahu and President Abbas, and so on. He was however fired again, when, in February 2020, in his typical tactless fashion, he told RAI radio, Who cares about the victims of the Morandi Bridge?

This time, these provocations failed to generate the wanted free publicity, new sales and profits. Rather, competitors such as Zara and H&M won the market shares which Benetton lost. By 2023, sales stood at $1 billion — about 50% of what they had been two decades ago. Losses stood at €230 million. With 3,500, the number of shops had also halved. Staff had shrunk from 10,000 to 6,400. With only 12% of sales through e-commerce, Benetton had clearly missed the boat.

Once Luciano learnt these figures, the now-89-year-old, with the usual drama, announced his second, final resignation in May 2024, claiming that he had been cheated by his managers. In June 2024, the last Benetton left his post as chairman, befittingly at its lavish headquarters, the noble Villa Minelli near Treviso. Apparently, he had always covered the annual losses accruing since 2012 from his own deep pockets, estimated at $3.5 billion. In August 2024, his younger brother, Carlo, died of cancer. He had taken care of the family's extensive agricultural interests. Once Luciano is no longer around to finance his passion, it is difficult to see why the family holding Edizione should continue to finance a loss-making fashion business, which currently accounts for only 2% of its portfolio. Potential buyers be aware.

Bibliography

Giroux, H. A. *Disturbing Pleasures: Learning Popular Culture.* New York and London: Routledge, 1994.

Hickson, J. D. and Pugh, S. D. *Management Worldwide.* London: Penguin Books, 1995.

Mantle, J. *Benetton: The Family, the Business and the Brand.* London: Little Brown and Company, 2000.

Sinatra, A. *Corporate Transformation.* Norwell, Massachusetts: Kluwer Academic Publishers, 1997.

New Literature, 2nd Edition

Benetton Group. *Integrated Report 2022.*

"'Ich bin betrogen worden' Luciano Benetton zieht sich aus der Leitung der Modegruppe zurück", *Neue Zürcher Zeitung*, 3 June 2024.

Kness-Bastaroli, T. "Die alte Benetton-Garde übernimmt wieder das Ruder", *Der Standard*, 2 February 2018.

Reski, P. "Der Bankautomat der Benettons", *Cicero*, 20 August 2018.

"The Benettons: Italian magnates who went from sweaters to roads", *Reuters*, 15 July 2020.

"'Unerträglicher Schmerz': 82-jähriger Luciano Benetton will seine Firma retten", *Die Presse*, 31 January 2018.

Nike Just Did It

If you have a body, you are an athlete...
And as long as there are athletes, there will be Nike.

Company History

In 1962, a young business student by the name of Phil Knight was inspired to write a school paper after overhearing staff from the *Oregon Journal* debate whether Japanese Nikon cameras would one day replace the expensive, German-made Leicas. A middle-distance runner for the University of Oregon, Knight argued that if low-cost Japanese producers could manufacture good-quality running shoes, the price differential would open up a new market, undercutting European manufacturers such as Adidas and Puma. Though Knight graduated and went on to work as an accountant, he set out on a summer trip in 1963 and travelled to Japan, where he met the managers of the Onitsuka Company, which produced Tiger running shoes. Stirred by the sight of the cheap, lightweight shoes, which were decent imitations of their European counterparts, Knight was motivated to purchase samples, which he brought home to show his old track-and-field coach, Bill Bowerman. The legendary Oregon coach was impressed enough to agree to invest $500 in a partnership, and the two contracted with Onitsuka and bought 1,000 pairs of Tiger shoes under the name of Blue Ribbon Sports (BRS) (Katz, 1944). Retailing the shoes out of the trunk of his car at sports meets, Knight sold $8,000 worth of shoes in just a year. He immediately quit his job and ordered more stock. Knight hired a small team of salespeople, who were like-minded competitive runners, and BRS gave them the opportunity to hold a job, make a decent living and enjoy running.

In 1966, Bowerman, who was always experimenting with new ways of making lighter shoes, shipped Onitsuka one of his own designs that consisted of a soft, nylon upper instead of a leather one. The resulting shoe, the Cortez, was a huge hit in track-and-field circles despite the taunts and laughs from Adidas representatives. By 1969, BRS had sold a million dollars' worth of shoes; however, its overly dependent relationship with Onitsuka had become shaky. and Knight's fears were validated when the Japanese began to look for bigger distributors and threatened to pull out of the business affiliation. Knight was forced to either sell his stake in the company and face legal action or find another way to produce the shoes. Thus, along with his small team of employees, who had begun to design and innovate a separate line of shoes, Knight decided it was time to take a big risk and strike out alone. After severing ties with Onitsuka for breach of contract and locating a local factory in Exeter, Knight joined forces with the Japanese trading company Nissho Iwai (which provided them with credit) and began to sell the shoes under a new name and trademark. During a particularly restless dream, the image of the Greek goddess of victory came to Johnson, and the name Nike was quickly adopted. With the help of local student Caroline Davidson, who was paid $35 for her design, a fat checkmark was also incorporated as the new logo. The logo was initially disliked because, unlike Adidas' stripes, which supported the arch, and Puma's, which supported the ball of the foot, the checkmark was only purely decorative. However, the "Swoosh", as it was nicknamed, would later become one of the world's most recognised symbols and prove vital to Nike's phenomenal success.

Early Competition in the Athletic Footwear Industry: Adidas — Letting Market Advantage Slip Away

Based in Herzogenaurach, Germany, Rudolf and Adolf Dassler designed and marketed their Adidas brand of shoes under the Adidas Company. An established footwear manufacturer, its breakthrough came during the 1936 Olympics when the famous medallist, Jesse Owens, agreed to wear Adidas shoes. This initiated a marketing strategy that associated running shoes with famous athletes, thereby setting a precedent for other athletic shoe manufacturers. However, in 1949, the brothers fell out and went their separate ways. Adolf stayed with the Adidas line, while Rudolf set up the Puma Company, which became the world's second-largest manufacturer. Adolf continued to innovate and develop a variety of shoes, including the spiked soccer boots that were instrumental in Germany's World Cup win over Hungary in 1954. Adidas dominated international sports meets with its great variety of superior products. For example, 82.8% of medallists at the Montreal games in 1976 were equipped with Adidas, giving the company tremendous publicity. Adidas' lead seemed insurmountable, diversifying into athletic apparel, sports bags, tennis racquets, swimwear and even ski equipment.

During the 1970s, the American athletic footwear industry experienced exceptional change and growth, fuelled in part by the 1972 Munich Olympics and increasing concerns with physical fitness. The publication of scientific studies such as Dr. Kenneth Cooper's *Aerobics* and James Fixx's *The Complete Book of Running* endorsed the physical benefits of jogging and became monumental bestsellers. The footwear industry was then largely dominated by Adidas and Puma. However, by the end of the decade, the little upstart company that was Nike had outstripped all its competitors, including Reebok, LA Gear, Converse and New Balance. How did Nike surpass Adidas, which stood on the threshold of dominating the entire market, and more importantly, what were the ingredients of Nike's success in these initial years?

In a classic case of miscalculation, Adidas had underestimated the entry and aggressiveness of competitors in the U.S. market and lost out on the recreational boom of the century. As an experienced manufacturer, it dismissed its new rivals as weak opportunists and complacently believed that they would not pose any serious threat to the market leader. It also underestimated the growth of the market for running shoes, which it had dominated for four decades. During that period, the market had only seen slow, stable growth, and Adidas was sceptical of the durability of the boom. However, with the preponderance of magazine articles and television programmes promoting a healthy lifestyle, the notion of exercise became an activity one did for fun and self-discovery. Adidas was not the only player to be caught off-guard. Other U.S. firms that were traditionally strong in the industry also misjudged the market opportunity, notably Converse and Uniroyal's Keds. While Adidas strayed into other product lines, Nike remained focused at the forefront of the industry, with major commitments to research and development, so as to introduce the most technologically advanced shoes on the market. Nike took full advantage of the industry's favourable primary demand and offered an even wider product line than Adidas. By offering a wide variety of styles at different prices, Nike appealed to all kinds of runners. It was able to convey the image of a comprehensive shoe manufacturer with a readily recognisable trademark. Most of its manufacturing process was contracted out to Asian firms, allowing flexible, short product runs at low cost.

Consequently, Nike did not have to establish a large infrastructure with high fixed costs, leaving it resistant to changes in demand (Hartley, 1998). These techniques were not unique to

Nike, for it imitated Adidas rather than becoming a revolutionary innovator. However, it simply did it better than its competitors and, true to its early Japanese influence, it became a case of the imitator outdoing the original.

Nike's Growth and Development

During the early 1980s, Nike sales grew from $270 million and exceeded $1 billion by the fiscal year-end of 1988 (Hartley, 1998), boosted by the creation of a patented "waffle sole" and a cushioning system known as Nike Air. These technological developments attest to Nike's early commitment to research and product development. Demand for Nike's soared to a point where distributors could place orders up to six months in advance under the Nike "Futures" system, which cut inventory costs and guaranteed delivery. In the 1982 Forbes Annual Report on American Industry, Nike was ranked the most profitable firm in the past five years. At the same time, the company went public, making Knight an instant millionaire with a net worth of almost $300 million. However, the 1980s also saw Reebok emerging as Nike's greatest competitor. Part of the reason was that Nike was slow to respond to the fast-growing market for women's aerobic shoes, choosing instead to focus on male-dominated basketball. This failure to appreciate new trends in the industry and a lack of perception concerning women's fitness needs caused sales and profits to sink by 18% and over 40%, respectively, between 1986 and 1987. Yet, unlike Adidas, which never managed to regain its lead, Nike fought to remain the dominant player.

While Nike's core business was traditionally made up of running shoes, it also began to diversify into other areas. Under its footwear segment, basketball shoes accounted for nearly a third of all sales by virtue of its universal appeal and popularity amongst male teenagers. However, Nike expanded its range to pursue the market for soccer boots, children's footwear, cross-trainers, tennis, aerobics and even golf shoes. Nike also successfully forayed into the outdoor footwear category with its own line of hiking boots, sandals and "All Conditions Gear" (ACG). Nike also began to promote its line of athletic apparel, which included men's and women's clothing, warm-up suits, team-licensed attire and, more recently, outfits for women's yoga classes. Nike also entered the market for casual wear with its purchase of Cole Haan Holdings Inc. in 1988. Cole Haan now produces high-quality, casual luxury footwear and accessories. In addition, Nike also produces its own line of eyewear, time pieces and heart monitors. The company's acquisitions include Tetra Plastics Inc., which manufactures the plastic compound used in Nike's Air cushioning system. In addition, Bauer Nike Hockey, based in Montreal, Quebec, is the world's leading manufacturer of hockey equipment and a wholly owned subsidiary of Nike. The company's research, design, and development centre, as well as manufacturers, are based in St. Jerome, Quebec. Nike has also partnered with Hurley International, a premium teen lifestyle brand based in California, in its efforts to truly consolidate its position in the sports industry. Hurley sells $70 million worth of T-shirts, cargo pants and surf shorts annually, capitalising on a craze for surf and skateboard gear. According to Matt Powell, a consultant to athletic shoe retailers at Princeton Retail Analysis, Nike wasn't considered authentic in the skate and surf crowd; thus, this move has been applauded.

Corporate Culture

Nike's belief is that every individual is an athlete, and that includes its own employees. In order to be a "Nike guy", one has to "get it", which can mean anything from having an aggressive attitude to an unquenchable thirst to win. Nike's corporate culture tends to project masculinity, with its emphasis on assertiveness and individuality. Its male-dominated management could also be the reason why it has not traditionally done well in the women's market, unlike Reebok. At its headquarters in Beaverton, Oregon, the buildings surrounding a seven-acre artificial lake are named in honour of influential athletes such as Michael Jordan, Bo Jackson and Steve Prefontaine. Posters and sports paraphernalia adorn the interior, making it seem more like a college campus than a corporate headquarters. Nike's workforce is made up of fit, healthy and surprisingly youthful employees attired in informal wear rather than business suits. Many are former professional athletes, collegiate competitors and even former Olympians who still continue to pursue recreational sports. Corporate videos describe the working environment as "a factory for fun" and "being in a playground". The corporate "we" is regularly and sincerely used and new recruits receive a catalogue of Nike's values: use structure to promote innovation, stay flexible and adaptive and challenge the status quo. Smoking is prohibited on the grounds, and employees are rewarded and encouraged to ride bicycles to work instead of driving. The sheer athleticism and competitive mindset that characterises its corporate culture have even permeated the administrative vocabulary of employees, who use terms such as "quarterbacking" a committee. Sports metaphors are also prevalent elsewhere, with employees regarding work weeks and fiscal quarters as countdowns on a game clock or a seasonal game. A career with Nike has effectively become an extended sports moment for some. In return, Nike provides its employees with state-of-the-art facilities, including hairdressers, massage parlours, fully equipped gyms and a comprehensive daycare centre (Katz, 1994). The isolation of the headquarters has led to it being nicknamed the "berm", outside of which lies the real world.

The Nike attitude and the anti-establishment image it conveys comes from its roots as the entrepreneurial underdog that snapped at heels of a bureaucratic and sober Adidas. Its corporate heritage includes a shared determination to work for the company cause without taking oneself too seriously. This has sometimes been interpreted as corporate arrogance, with critics claiming that sports and business should remain separate entities. Along with its meteoric rise to the top of the industry, Nike also had to deal with the anti-Nike establishment. It has been denigrated as a cult organisation that holds too much power over the athletes that it endorses, thereby spoiling the game. During the 1992 Olympics held in Barcelona for example, the Dream Team, which included basketball heavyweights such as Jordan and Barkley, refused to take to the medal stand as the American anthem played. The reason behind the players' defiance was that the official awards ceremony jacket had the Reebok emblem on it. The stand-off, which was wrongly perceived to be a carefully orchestrated corporate strategy, caused immense public controversy, as the athletes had placed corporate loyalty before patriotism. Although the incident arose entirely out of the players' own initiative, Nike executives later commented that "Michael Jordan holds us to our values", attesting to the company's ability to inspire loyalty. Attitude surveys held by the James H. Joerger firm confirm this by ranking Nike as having the highest level of corporate loyalty and acceptance of company policy ever recorded. A similar Business Week survey rated Nike 13th for most improved productivity out of all the Standard and Poor 500 companies.

Organisational Structure

Nike's top management in 2003 included Knight, one of the original founders of the company. Bowerman passed away in 1999 after his retirement, leaving Knight as the company's CEO and from 2004 as its chairman of the board. A sports enthusiast and the epitome of a sports fan, he had an unconventional management style, hating negotiations and preferring informal discussions and meetings. Yet, it was obvious that he was well qualified to run the company, given his passion and determination for sports and his educational background, which boasted an MBA from Stanford. Reputed to be a recluse who rarely entertained interviewers, Knight lent his enigmatic aura to the rest of the company. Other notable executives included Mark Parker, president of Nike Brand, Tinker Hatfield, vice president of Special Projects and Dennis Colard, vice president of Global Operations.

Nike, in 2001, employed 22,000 people worldwide, from its Nike World Headquarters in Oregon and Nike European Headquarters in Hilversum, The Netherlands, to almost every region around the globe, including Asia Pacific, the Americas, Europe, the Middle East and Africa. Including manufacturers, shippers, retailers and service providers, nearly one million people helped bring Nike products to consumers everywhere. Of the 11,000 Nike employees located in the U.S., about 5,000 worked in Oregon at the World Headquarters, Wilsonville Distribution Center and numerous retail venues. The original Nike European Headquarters opened in Amsterdam in 1980. The current European headquarters, a state-of-the-art complex designed by William McDonough & Partners, opened in 1999 in Hilversum, The Netherlands. Nike Partners is the subsidiary in charge of dealing with local distributors located in Eastern Europe and Middle East, including Israel. Nike's latest addition, Africa, came under the administration of the European region in the middle of 2000. Eleven offices were located in the Asia Pacific region, including Australia, China, Hong Kong, Japan, Korea and Singapore.

Nike's organisational structure has been described as a matrix, mixing its entrepreneurial past with its current status as a global corporation. It does not fall into any recognised, standard organisational structure and seems to be more of an Oriental hybrid, given its association with Japanese firms. Although it is generally streamlined in order to foster autonomy, it retains a formalised management structure so as to facilitate accountability and responsibility. Nike's mission is to design, develop and merchandise its products and is a market-driven company. Its focus is on research and development to produce high-tech shoes and other equipment to meet future trends. Research and testing takes place in the Nike Sports Research Lab (NSRL), where accomplished scientists study athletes in motion and the ways in which they are affected by various shoe, apparel and equipment design during specific activities. Key areas of research included the biomechanics and physiology of performance enhancement and injury prevention. The NSRL also accommodates the Environmental Chamber, which can imitate various conditions that athletes face in order to improve the design of fabrics. A notable feature in Nike's operations is that it does not see itself as a manufacturer. Instead, Nike outsources all its production to contract manufacturers in Asia. This has resulted in it being labelled a "hollow corporation", as it is essentially nothing more substantial than a design company that depends on other firms for production.

Manufacturing and Labour Pains

Manufacturing overseas has been a familiar practise for Nike. Almost all of its footwear is produced in Asian factories based in Taiwan, China, Indonesia and Thailand because of lower labour costs, less union involvement and fewer government regulations. These management contracts are critical to Nike's operations as they ensure a reliable supply to all retail outlets under its Futures program. The independent contractors provide several advantages, namely greater flexibility to control inventories, lower capital requirements and more accurate sales forecasts. However, this dependency on foreign contractors also means that Nike is vulnerable to political instability, exchange rate fluctuations and criticism of its treatment of employees. In recent years, Nike has faced accusations of unfair labour practices. Human rights groups and labour unions claimed that Nike has profited from child labour and paid its employees below the minimum wage. In 1998, negative publicity was generated by the "discovery" of Pakistani children stitching Nike soccer balls for six cents an hour, which further tainted Nike's corporate image. Workers in Asian factories were allegedly exposed to harmful chemicals, physically abused by supervisors for not meeting production targets and were not paid for overtime. In addition, their living quarters were cramped and dirty, and they were apparently paid less than $1 daily. These accusations were true to a certain extent in some factories; however, such criticisms had a tendency to focus on perceived malpractices of a wealthy multinational corporation instead of the broader social and global context.

Although wages were meagre by Western standards, workers earned a steady income that was much higher than subsistence agriculture, which remains the main form of employment in developing countries. It would be fallacious to insist that the minimum wage in a Third World country be comparable to that of a developed nation. In fact, these very shoe factories were responsible for dramatically lowering poverty and unemployment levels and paving the way for industrialisation. Jobs at shoe factories were actually considered desirable because they provided additional benefits such as meal and transport allowances, and there were never shortages of applicants. Furthermore, the heavy reliance on female workers brought about a social transformation in some Asian societies by empowering women with the ability to earn their own income. The factories that Nike contracted were often run by ethnic Chinese, who dominated the business communities in Asia (Litvin, 2003). Their Confucian management styles often conflicted with workers of non-Chinese origin, for example, Indonesian workers would often complain of verbal abuse from aggressive Chinese bosses. However, this was a cultural issue which stemmed from historic tensions and miscommunication, rather than Nike's management style.

It can be argued that Nike was not even responsible for these issues because it had no ownership of the factories, nor did it dictate the terms of employment or set wage limits. Government policies in developing nations encouraged and even provided incentives for such factories because of the billions of dollars' worth of investments and revenue that were generated. However, because of Nike's high profile and its huge profit margins, the company, rather than the respective governments and officials, was singled out for condemnation (Litvin, 2003). These same factories also produced shoes for Reebok and Adidas, yet the media sought to highlight only Nike's involvement in what has been termed a contortion of corporate responsibility. Nike bashing was thought to be a means of justifying opposition to successful multinationals, and the company took the blame for the entire industry. Some human rights groups even obscured the fact that their motives stemmed from a protectionist desire to save their own jobs, which were threatened by cheap, foreign labour. Yet, Nike accepted these responsibilities in its stride and introduced its Code of Conduct. The Code stipulates the maximum working hours per week, provides compensation for overtime, prohibits the employment of children under the age of 16 and ensures the general health and safety of workers. All Nike contractors are also required to sign a memorandum of understanding, requiring compliance with local government regulations. Factories are also open to inspection by independent organisations and schemes for free education and business loans to workers are also available. While significant improvements have been made, there is no global consensus on labour standards, leaving Nike open to continued criticism and an ethical dilemma. Yet, this situation also serves to illustrate Nike's powerful ability to effect positive change along a broad spectrum of society.

Interestingly, just as Nike's geographical distance from its manufacturing plants could not protect it from the labour controversy; it has also meant that Nike is not immune to other conditions that affect Asia. In 2003, the outbreak of the SARS virus in China and other parts of Asia had a significant impact on the company's production. Orders were rescheduled, on-site visits replaced by communication via e-mail and the entire manufacturing process effectively slowed down. This incident only served to highlight again Nike's heavy reliance and dependency on these Asian factories and how significant they are to its business.

Ingredients for Success

In a world where image is everything, the Nike "Swoosh" is one of the most recognisable symbols in the world. It is integral to understanding Nike's success and corporate culture because it is a commercial symbol that has given the Nike brand global omnipresence. The "Swoosh" has become so familiar to the public that Nike signs its advertisements only with its icon because they are so confident that it will be recognised without any text. It has become a cultural icon that Nike relies on to increase its brand value, recognition and status. No other athletics company has achieved this level of brand identification. In order to illustrate this point, ask anybody what the name of Reebok's logo is and they will probably draw a blank. In fact, Reebok's logo is named the vector; only it is not as readily recognised or desired by consumers. Nike, along with its advertising agency Wieden & Kennedy, now focuses on keeping the logo highly visible in its advertisements. The company's advertising and promotions budget has been estimated to be 10% of its annual revenue in order to firmly lodge the symbol in public consciousness.

So, why is the Swoosh so important to our understanding of Nike's business culture? The reason is that it goes hand in hand with the good old American philosophy: "Just Do It". Nike does not simply sell running shoes; it sells consumers a way of life and this is the core of its success. The inspiration that the swoosh stands for, along with the motivation and determination behind its philosophy, is something that everyone can relate to, whether you are an athlete or not. Nike uses the language of empowerment in order to motivate its consumers. No matter who you are, what colour your hair or skin is, what physical or social limitations you are confronted with, Nike convinces consumers that it is possible to achieve. It tells people to get up, take control of their lives and act. The simple yet highly effective logo and mantra have come to represent athletic excellence, achievement and hip authenticity. Behind the "Just Do It" slogan lies a very American ideology; yet with globalisation, what was once an American ideology has become a universal aspiration. The idea of a level playing field that allows you to compete not only in sports but in every aspect of life goes back to the early American pioneer spirit and desire for success. The expression sells to the world the great American dream and promotes its work ethic by telling consumers that if you are motivated and competitive enough, you will excel and conquer. In this way, Nike has created a personality and an attitude for itself by encapsulating a very human desire to achieve. By cleverly using a very simple tagline and logo, it has managed to turn a lifestyle into a commodity.

In today's athletic industry, companies no longer gain a significant advantage from the actual manufacturing process. Therefore, in order to stay competitive, one must focus on selling an image in order to gain value. As we have seen, Nike is not a manufacturing firm but a company that concentrates on developing and marketing its products. One of its most successful marketing strategies is the use of celebrity endorsements to promote its products. The most famous of all was Michael Jordan, who was enlisted as a spokesperson in Nike's basketball advertisements. These television commercials conveyed a theme of human transcendence by capturing Jordan in mid-flight. They also provided Nike with an identity and enticed viewers with the tagline "it's gotta be the shoes". The creation of a superhero image and its association with Nike were crucial to propelling both Jordan and Nike to the top of the industry. The Air

Jordan line of basketball shoes became one of Nike's most popular and lucrative innovations, selling over $100 million in its first year alone. Jordan himself became an instant role model for youths and inspired them to follow the American Dream. This reinforced Nike's image of performance and achievement while, at the same time, imbuing it with a personality that consumers could relate to. Nike's shoes stood for fame, success and reaching the impossible: if you wore Nike's, just maybe you would be empowered with the ability to fly like Jordan. This psychological and emotional connection was a powerful marketing tool that translated into billions of dollars' worth of sales. Nike has also been consistently advertised by a stable of talented, top athletes, including Andre Agassi for tennis, Bo Jackson for baseball and Tiger Woods for golf, thus appealing to a broad spectrum of consumers who want to emulate their heroes. Nike has also harnessed popular culture, in particular music, to promote its products. Catchy tunes such as Monty Python's "Always look on the bright side of life", accompanied images of athletes such as Ronaldo in various stages of distress and injury, reinforcing the notion that there is no gain without pain. Keen to avoid its earlier mistakes, Nike has also tailored commercials to capture the women's fitness market. Instead of using sexually exploitative advertising or stereotyping, Nike has sought to represent the empowerment of women. Commercials have a more narrative style and use motivational discourse to convey inspiration. The use of female celebrities, such as soccer player Mia Hamm, represents Nike as an advocate of gender equality in sports.

The Competition

According to the Sporting Goods Intelligence newsletter, it is estimated that at the end of 2002, Nike had 39.1% of the U.S. athletic shoe business, Reebok had 12%, New Balance had 11.6%, and Adidas-Salomon AG had 9.6%. While Nike continues to rule the footwear industry, analysts say Reebok has a good chance of at least doubling its share in the next few years and thus poses the biggest threat to Nike's business. Since Paul Fireman regained control in November 1999, Reebok has increased sales, its capital and its exposure in the marketplace. In the fourth quarter of 2002, Reebok's total sales gained an unprecedented 14.8%, reaching $763 million. Apparel sales in the U.S. grew 48.1% to $145 million. According to a Lehman Brothers report in February 2003, Reebok has had 11 consecutive quarters of sales increases. In December 2000, Reebok and the National Football League announced the formation of an exclusive partnership with the NFL's restructured consumer products business. The NFL granted a ten-year exclusive licence to Reebok, beginning with the 2002 NFL season to manufacture, market and sell NFL licensed merchandise for all 32 NFL teams. The agreement also gave Reebok exclusive rights to develop a new line of NFL fitness equipment. In August 2001, Reebok formed a ten-year strategic partnership with the National Basketball Association under which Reebok would design, manufacture, sell and market licensed merchandise for the NBA, the Women's National Basketball Association and the National Basketball Development League. Beginning in the 2004 season, Reebok had the exclusive rights to supply and market all on-court apparel, including uniforms, shooting shirts, warm-ups, authentic and replica jerseys and practice gear for all NBA, WNBA and NBDL teams, thereby encroaching on Nike's traditional basketball and football territory.

Since 2003, Reebok has been hurrying to fill the empty shelves in more than 2,500 U.S. branches of Foot Locker Inc., a gap opened up by a rift between Nike and Foot Locker, the largest athletic footwear chain in the world. In February 2002, Foot Locker told Nike the store wanted to reduce the number of Nike's Air Jordans, Shox and Air Force Ones that sell for more than $100. The move, which reflected reluctance amongst teenagers to buy expensive basketball shoes, came at Nike's expense. Foot Locker told Nike it wanted to reduce its marquee shoes from 12% of the chain's business to 6%, and cancelled $150 million in Nike orders. Nike later denied that it had pulled back on existing orders or punished Foot Locker with late shipments, as had been reported. However, the relationship with Foot Locker has been testy since the beginning of 2004, and Nike has already been busy finding alternative chains. Foot Locker is no longer a primary distributor for Nike's marquee and launch products. Nike's Hall of Hoops displays in Foot Locker stores were replaced by Reebok's Above the Rim, featuring RBK shoes endorsed by Reebok's Allen Iverson. Reebok has also filled the vacuum with more of its Classic line, part of the "retro" look that has been successful for sneaker brands such as Converse and Puma, responding to the American market's need for nostalgia.

Although Nike has always been historically able to reinvent itself and surprise industry watchers, its competitors are catching up fast. Despite the refusal of competitors such as New Balance to cash in on marketable celebrities, other companies such as Reebok and Adidas have copied Nike's lead and recruited their own athletes for endorsements. Watching the television these days, it is hard to differentiate between an Adidas commercial and a Nike commercial, as they both use generic inspirational imagery, slogans, music and athletes. Adidas sponsors Zinedine to endorse its soccer boots, while Nike sponsors Ronaldo. Adidas' latest A3 running shoe boasts technology that cushions the foot and maximises energy use just like Nike's latest Shox technology. And to top it all, Reebok's corporate website shares the same grey, black and orange colour scheme as Nike's, further blurring the distinction between the two! A global homogenisation of consumption means that there is very little substance or technological advantage that differentiates a Nike product from that of a rival. Thus, marketing, image and the "cool factor" remain very important when targeting consumer groups, especially the youth segment. It appears that in an industry that seems to have reached market saturation, the only real difference is whether a customer prefers to be seen in a Swoosh, vector or three stripes.

The Next Two Decades

In the next two decades, Nike, however, went from strength to strength. Turnover grew about five times from $10.7 billion (2003) to $51.2 billion (2023). Profits naturally developed somewhat uneven, yet multiplied by 10: from $500 million (2003) to $5.1 billion (2023), much to the joy of shareholders, as market capitalisation multiplied from $11.8 billion (2003) to $160.5 billion (2023) by a factor of 15, as the world's leading supplier of sports goods by far. It now controls 62% of the U.S. market for sports shoes. The secret of this? Nike simply more or less stuck to its core sales portfolio of sportswear, accessories, fitness trackers and smart watches. The only acquisition was the Converse brand for $300 million in 2003.

As the main promotional avenue the big-ticket sponsoring of spectator sports continued unabated: basketball, soccer, golf, tennis, long-distance running and skateboarding. In 2012, Nike became the main sponsor of the American Football League (NFL), and in 2027, it is due to become the official supplier of the German soccer federation DFB, replacing arch-rival Adidas, by paying twice its offered amount, namely €100 million a year. Most successful among its sportsmen-branded lines are the Michael Jordan "signature shoes" sold at $2.6 billion in 2014, plus Jordan apparel for more than $1 billion to his fans, which Nike managed to turn from baseball, where it is worn by other NBA players, into a lifestyle brand. With similar intentions, Nike offered Le Bron James in 2014 a lifetime contract, whereupon it sold $340 million worth of James-shoes the very year.

In 2008, Phil Knight published his ghost-written memoir *Shoe Dog*, which Warren Buffet called "the best book I read last year" (2017). Also, Bill Gates reviewed it favourably, as it described well the "messy, perilous, chaotic journey, riddled with mistakes, endless struggle and sacrifice" from a $50 startup to global success, as there were no single "5-step programs" with checklists offered on "how to" bookshelves. Knight, who comes across as friendly, shy and introverted, often wears sunglasses at public events and is a man of few words ("say it in 25 words or less" was a command to his children). He basically advocates a hands-off approach and the avoidance of micromanagement to let collaborators' ideas flow unhindered.

In December 2004, Knight, then 66, stepped down as CEO after 35 years at the helm of Nike but remained chairman of the board. His immediate successor was William Perez, who had been CEO of S.C. Johnson & Son, a detergent maker, but left after barely a year to lead Wrigley's. Mark Parker, the next CEO, would survive. He had made his in-house career in design and development and had been president of the Nike brand before. In 2016, he also joined Disney as a director and, in 2017, took a 71% salary cut as poor sales the year earlier forced the layoff of 1,000 workers.

By 2016, Phil Knight, then aged 78, retired as chairman of the board, a function in which he was succeeded by Mark Parker. He set up a new company called Swoosh LLC, which would hold most of his shares, with decisions taken by its four directors of which he was one, with his family owning still 20% of Nike. His son Travis, born in 1973, joined the Nike Board to be groomed for succession. Travis Knight, during his student days, had dabbled as a rapper and later made animated children movies, such as Bumblebee, Boxtrolls, Kubo — the brave Samurai and Masters of the Universe, which were also given awards. Once daddy bought his studio, it was renamed Laika, the previous owner was fired, and the son was promoted to CEO. Thus far, however, he has shown little visible interest in Nike and has been rarely seen wearing its outfits.

Phil Knight, whose net worth according to Forbes varies between $47 billion (2023) and $37 billion (2024) — a big difference to ordinary mortals, but it does not really matter in this league — with his wife Penny through the Knight Foundation has donated $3.6 billion to charity, plus $500 million to his *alma mater*, the University of Oregon (B.A.) and Stanford University (MBA) each, as well as $400 million to rebuild the historical Black Albina neighbourhood in Portland (Oregon). With so much generosity, some honours came in return. Thus, in 2012, he was duly admitted to the "Naismith Memorial Basketball Hall of fame" for his merits to promote basketball around the world and, in 2015, was elected to the American Academy of Sciences.

As a registered Republican, Knight should be expected to be on the socially conservative side, yet Nike, as a corporate policy, has endorsed all the tenets of contemporary political correctness. With its evident commercial interests in college sports, which on U.S. campuses play a much bigger role than in most of the rest of the world, the company is sensitive even to the silliest of college protests and boycott calls. Like for all sellers of apparel and shoes, the evergreen issue since decades is working conditions amongst the hundreds of subtractors in China, Bangladesh, Pakistan, Vietnam and Indonesia if it is not the cotton in Xingjian or in Central Asia, which are regularly fed by horror stories, real or made up, produced by the usual NGOs or well-meaning freelancers. Nike, apart from inspecting the 785 plants of its hundreds of sub- and sub-sub-contractors and their 650,000 workers, ranging from Korea to Thailand and Turkey to Mexico (and the U.S.), themselves has responded by publishing names and addresses and inviting anyone to inspect them unannounced. Publicly egged on by Michael Moore, Knight even conceded that he would henceforth insist on a minimum working age of 18 at his Indonesian subcontractors' plants. Please note that the minimum working age in the U.S. stands at 14.

With the Russian attack on Ukraine in February 2022, Nike also felt compelled to close its 116 shops in Russia and to end all franchising business. Again, it was not selling military boots, nor do Russian troops wear its sports attire. Yet, as demand for elusive Western products remains strong, parallel imports beyond control of Beaverton (Oregon) continue, albeit at steeper prices. As dictatorships and wars inevitably end someday, hopefully rather sooner than later, but not always with the desired results, business awaits redevelopment.

Bibliography

Note: Any links to online sources were valid as of the publication of the first edition, in October 2004. Many of the pages have since been taken down.

"2003 to see major tech strides in US athletic shoes", *Market News Express.* http://www.tdctrade.com/mne/footwear/footwear019.htm

Aaker, D. A. and Joachimsthaler, E. *Adidas and Nike — Lessons in Building Brands: Brand Leadership.* New York: Free Press, 2000.

Back, B. J. "Nike campaign pointing toward a future with football", *The Business Journal*, 17 May 2002. http://portland.bizjournals.com/portland/stories/2002/05/20/story2.html

Dukcevich, D. "Nike's Got Global Game". http://www.forbes.com/2002/09/18/0918nike.html

El Kahal, S. *Nike: Ethical Dilemmas of FDI in Asia Pacific Business in Asia Pacific: Texts and Cases.* New York: Oxford University Press, 2001.

Goldman, R. and Papson, S. *Nike Culture: The Sign of the Swoosh.* Thousand Oaks, California: SAGE Publications, 1998.

Grigsby, D. W., Gaertner, S. and Roach, K. "Nike, Inc.", in Grigsby, D. W. and Stahl, M. J. (eds) *Cases in Strategic Management.* Oxford: Blackwell Business, 1997.

Hartley, R. F. *Nike: Riding High with a Great Image, Marketing Mistakes and Successes.* New York: John Wiley & Sons, 1998.

Horrow, R. "If the shoe fits: sneaker wars heating up", *CBS Sports Online.* http://cbs.sportsline.com/general/story/6211588

"How Nike got its game back", *Business Week Online*, 4 November 2002. http://www.businessweek.com/magazine/content/02_44/b3806118.htm

Katz, D. *Just Do It: The Nike Spirit in the Corporate World.* Holbrook, Mass.: Adams Pub., 1994.

Kitchens, S. "Footwear in Flight", *Forbes Online*, 15 April 2002. http://www.forbes.com/global/2002/0415/061.html

Litvin, D. B. "The contortions of corporate responsibility: Nike and its Third-World factories", in *Empires of Profit: Commerce, Conquest and Corporate Responsibility*. New York and London: Texere, 2003.

Rozhon, T. "Former sneaker king making a comeback", *International Herald Tribune Online*, 7 March 2003. http://www.iht.com/articles/88965.html

Strasser, J. B. and Becklund, L. *Swoosh: The Story of Nike and the Men Who Played There*. New York: Harcourt Brace Jovanovich, 1991.

"When to run with Nike", *Business Week Online*, 18 April 2003. http://www.businessweek.com/technology/content/apr2003/tc20030418_2274_PG2_tc109.htm

White, R. K. "Nike, Inc.", in Peter, J. P. and Donnelly, J. H. (eds) *Marketing Management: Knowledge and Skills*. Boston, Mass.: Irwin/McGraw-Hill, 2001.

New Literature, 2nd Edition

Badenhauser, K. "How Michael Jorden still makes $ 100 million a year", *Forbes*, 8 December 2015.

Brettman, A. "Phil Knight takes steps away from Nike; will leave as board chairman", *The Oregonian*, 30 June 2015.

Gates, B. "An honest tale of what it takes to succeed in business", *Gates Notes*, 5 December 2016.

Knight, P. *Shoe Dog. A Memoir by the Creator of Nike*. New York: Simon & Schuster, 2008.

"Nike reagiert auf US-Studentenproteste wegen Arbeitsbedingungen", *Der Standard*, 31 August 2017.

"Sportartikelriese Nike stellt sich an den Pranger", *Die Welt*, 15 April 2005.

Nokia: Connecting People Through a Disconnected Past

Until the 1980s, Nokia was a Finnish company, in the 1980s Nokia was a Nordic company and in the beginning of 1990s a European company. Now, we are a global company.

— Jorma Ollila
President and CEO, Nokia (1997)

Nokia's rise to global prominence is nothing short of astonishing. From its humble origins in Finland, Nokia has grown into a global company and a brand greatly admired by companies and employees all over the world. Yet, Nokia's runaway success was not an overnight miracle but one that has been borne out of numerous failures and successes, trials and errors before becoming what it is today.

In 2001, Nokia was the world leader in mobile phones and the leading supplier of mobile and fixed broadband and Internet Protocol (IP) networks. Equally impressive were Nokia's net sales, at €30 billion in 2001, and its some 17 production totalled facilities in nine countries and R&D centres in 14 countries, where it employed nearly 52,000 people worldwide.

In order to understand in depth how far Nokia has come, we need to trace Nokia's origins and history. We will also focus on the two prominent leader figures, Kari Kairamo and Jorma Ollila, who have both shaped Nokia with their own unique brand of management. As Nokia is synonymous with design and technology, we will also look into the aspects of design, marketing and telecommunications technology of Nokia. As Nokia's success is driven by Nokia's employees, this chapter will not be complete without examining the work ethics and attitudes of "Nokians" and the company's policies towards its employees.

Origins of Nokia

For many years, the world outside Scandinavia was misled by the Nokia name into thinking that it was a Japanese company. Many people today find it hard to believe that Nokia used to produce toilet paper and rubber galoshes. And some will be astonished to learn that Nokia is not a "new economy" company but one that can boast of a 160-year history. Nokia was originally started in 1865 with the founding of *Nokia Aktiebolag* (Nokia Forest and Power) by Fredrik Idestam, a 25-year-old mining engineer. He imported the pioneering groundwood techniques from Saxony into Finland and revolutionised the making of paper. Since Finland is blessed with lush forests and water-power resources, Idestam seized the opportunity to set up his wood pulp plant along the river Nokia, which had actually derived its name from a dark, furry weasel known as a nokia.

However, the current Nokia Group was only officially formed after the merger of Finnish Rubber Works (*Suomen Gummitehdas Oy*), the Finnish Cable Works (Kaapelitehas Oy) and Nokia Forest and Power in 1966. Although Nokia has become a substantially large company, there was little value added from the merger in 1966. Instead, much effort and management time was consumed having to coordinate the newly enlarged operations. The 1960s was an equally interesting period for Nokia because it was Nokia's first venture into electronics. Although Nokia treaded slowly into the electronics industry, it laid the foundation for Nokia's modern-day success in digitalisation. Despite the entry into electronics, cable products to the former Soviet Union remained a major contributor to Nokia's earnings. Unknown to many outside Finland, Nokia began to import computers into Finland, and it also manufactured electronic equipment for the modest Finnish defence industry. In the 1970s, Nokia produced the popular office computer, Mikro Mikko, and it grew to become one of Nokia's major divisions in the 1980s. Another important, far-reaching decision was to produce digital telephone exchanges. It was a bold move because it pitted Nokia in direct competition with the more established Ericsson's core business.

While the growth of Nokia's electronics business was attributed to clear and sound objectives, it owed its success partially to the domestic industrial policies in Finland. A new wave of deregulation and internationalisation was sweeping across the world. The ripple was first started in Europe by former British Prime Minister Margaret Thatcher in her crusade for free competition. This notion gradually spread to other countries, including Finland. Although the deregulation of the financial markets in Finland resulted in an economic boom in the 1980s, this was followed by deep recession in the late 1980s.

The Cold War period proved particularly challenging for Finland, as it had to straddle between trading with the Western democracies and the Soviet Union. Finland committed itself to economic cooperation and integration within Europe through the European Free Trade Agreement (EFTA) and later (since 1995) the European Union while supplying products to the former Soviet Union. It has managed to maintain that image of "neutrality" so remarkably well that Finland has never been regarded by the West as pro-communist.

The Kairamo Era

Two individuals were instrumental to the success of Nokia: Kari Kairamo and Jorma Ollila. Kairamo was Ollila's predecessor, and it was he who single-handedly steered Nokia's transformation from a purely traditional company to an electronics company from the 1970s to the 1980s. Kairamo first joined Nokia in 1970 as vice president of Nokia's international affairs division. He was a charismatic and inspirational leader who subscribed to the virtues of hard work and constant learning. As the 1970s–1980s were a transitional period for Nokia, it offered the golden opportunity for Kairamo's trailblazing streak to emerge. Unlike his predecessors, Kairamo foresaw Nokia's future beyond the shores of Finland and the need to conquer new markets to ensure Nokia's survival. When he became managing director and CEO of Nokia in 1977, Kairamo introduced reforms to allow Nokia to compete on the world market. Traditional formalities and processes gave way to speed and immediacy. Change and flexibility soon became important attributes of Nokia.

Kairamo pushed Nokia onto the path of competitive advantage. He wanted Nokia to be more productive, efficient, innovative and manage its resources carefully in order to gain a competitive advantage. Kairamo's vision of transforming Nokia into a competitive company was unprecedented at a time when the notion of comparative advantage held sway. Until the mid-1980s, internationalisation was dominated by the idea of comparative advantage, in which labour, natural resources and financial capital were regarded as the most important factors in determining a company's continuous success.

At the beginning of the 1980s, Nokia set out to expand its consumer electronics and telecommunications business with renewed vigour. Part of Kairamo's grand plans for Nokia was the acquisition of companies as a way of rapidly expanding Nokia. Kairamo wanted to turn Nokia into a Japanese-like conglomerate with a presence in diverse industries. Kairamo believed that time and money would be saved if they acquired established companies instead of spending time investing and cultivating new companies. More significantly, Kairamo identified the electronics business as a core business and invested heavily in buying key electronics companies. With that objective in mind, Kairamo acquired Mobira, Salora, Televa and Luxor of Sweden, and Nokia soon became a major producer of TV sets, monitors, and computers. Between 1983 and 1984, Nokia was transformed from a diversified industrial conglomerate into an electronics company.

Unfortunately, the acquisitions in the 1980s proved costly for Nokia. When Nokia bought two television set manufacturers in Central Europe in 1987, it sank Nokia further in the red. By 1988, things seemed to be going terribly wrong. Profits were trickling away. The rapid buying spree seemed to have exhausted management resources. The strain became evident when the management, including Kairamo, began to make misjudgements, and Nokia had to grapple with unprofitable electronics divisions. The management also became split internally, and decision-making sometimes reached an impasse. On 11 December 1988, Kairamo committed suicide. Although the motive for his suicide was not fully explained, it was quite clear that the losses Nokia was making, an overworked schedule and dashed hopes contributed to his death.

Kairamo left Nokia with a dual image. While he led Nokia into its major losses and mistakes, it was undeniably his inspiration and focus on internationalisation that paved the way for Nokia's bold ventures into telecommunications and mobile phones, as well as its subsequent conquest of the global market.

Restructuring Nokia

After Kairamo's death, Simo Vuorilehto was appointed chairman and CEO of Nokia. He embarked on the streamlining of Nokia's businesses and dismantled the internal board, replacing it with an executive board. Overall management was further streamlined by placing each member of the new internal executive board as head of a business division. Between 1988 and 1989, Nokia shifted its activities from aggressive buying to selling. Vuorilehto sold off Nokia's basic industrial units but did not sell or divest those businesses he considered strategic, in particular consumer electronics, data communications, mobile phones and telecommunications. However, Nokia failed to turn around amidst the sea of tumultuous changes in the world between 1988 and 1991. The Soviet economy collapsed, and the overheated Finnish economy plunged Finland into a deep recession.

The New Visionary: Ollila Takes the Helm

While Kairamo had been ambitious in diversifying Nokia, Jorma Ollila was bold in divestiture. Jorma Ollila took over the helm from Vuorilehto in spring 1992. He was then president of Nokia Mobile Phones (NMP) before being appointed CEO.

At 41 years, Ollila was a youthful, energetic leader, and he was responsible for shedding Nokia's non-core information technology and basic industry operations to focus on telecommunications.

Before Ollila joined Nokia in 1984 as vice president of international operations, he served as a member of the board in Citibank Oy, the bank's Finnish subsidiary. In 1986, he became chief financial officer at Nokia, and in 1990, he led Nokia Mobile Phones (NMP) unit.

Restructuring at Nokia did not start with Ollila. It began soon after Vuorilehto became CEO in 1988, but Ollila continued and completed this phase. Ollila understood the strategic importance of NMP, and he also knew that mere restructuring would not suffice; Nokia had to refocus.

On 1 July 1991, Finland became the first country in the world to introduce the wireless digital GSM network, which could carry data in addition to high-quality voice. But it was not unexpected. Nokia had prior experiences with analogue telephones. The Mobira Talkman was the first car phone made by Nokia. The first handheld phone was also produced by Nokia. Since then, the telecommunications and mobile phones divisions have been growing.

The Scandinavian countries provided the preliminary testing ground for Nokia's telecommunications technology before they were released to the rest of the world. In 1981, the world's first cellular mobile telephone network, the Nordic Mobile Telephone network (NMT), was introduced in Scandinavia. The introduction of NMT was important for Nokia because its immediate consequence was to create a market for Nokia to test its telecommunications products. By the late 1980s, Nokia had become the largest Scandinavian information technology company through the acquisition of Ericsson's data systems division.

The rapid growth in the mid-1990s presented a cash-flow problem for Nokia. It was in 1994 that Nokia was listed on the New York Stock Exchange. This helped finance the tremendous growth of Nokia. It also meant that Nokia's share ownership moved overseas, mainly to U.S. investors during the 1990s. This was a dramatic departure from the past when Nokia has been owned by Finnish commercial banks, such as the Union Bank of Finland and *Kansallis-Osake-Pankki* (National Bank, KOP). This also meant that Nokia was answerable to a wider distribution of shareholders instead of having to consult the major banks on management-level decisions. This freed Nokia from potential conflicts between management and the commercial banks.

By 1994, Nokia had grown so rapidly that it needed to address the question of profitability and growth. Alarm bells started ringing when profits fell below budget in 1995–1996. Yet, Ollila and his team looked for solutions quickly — improving the production chain. The improvements were achieved through more efficient inventory control, and the old centralised inventory system was replaced by a new regional demand/supply process. Nokia called the new, leaner worldwide logistics system the "Integrated Supply Chain". Another important improvement was the move to outsource mobile phone parts to suppliers.

Nokia's Strategic Intent

No politics, a lot of trust, realism with equality between people, titles are not important — teamwork with openness is. There is a Finnish word, nöyryys, which means humility, humbleness that you take pride in the past but don't project it into the future.

— Dr Matti Alahuhta
President, Nokia Mobile Phones

Ollila's vision was extraordinary. By the end of the 1990s, Nokia's brand was synonymous with product innovation, flexibility and rapid responsiveness. For Nokia, the key to all strategic considerations was simple: to listen to the customer. Yet, Ollila knew right from the beginning that the customer is a moving target. Between 1986 and 1991, Nokia created a foothold in key European markets by relentlessly pursuing emerging and deregulated markets. Unlike the mobile subsidiaries of Ericsson, Siemens and Motorola, Nokia's mobile unit was considered mid-size. But for what it lacked in scale and scope, it gained in speed and timing.

Nokia emulated Japanese companies; it was constantly on the lookout for new markets in telecommunications and internet technology advantage. So far, Nokia had built strategic alliances with new wireless technology companies to deliver cutting-edge mobile phone platforms, such as Symbian and WAP. Ollila's new focus was on integrated wireless and internet products — "combining mobility and the Internet and stimulating the creation of new services" became Nokia's new direction.

Ollila also shuffled his senior management and moved them out of their comfort zones. He believed that cross-fertilisation would help learning across the companies. In turn, Nokia's senior management believed that an elitist management hierarchy could disenfranchise the organisation.

Nokia's persistent determination to focus on the cellular business has distinguished the company from its rivals since the 1990s. But Ollila was not alone in crafting the strategic direction; he discussed and debated strategic issues with a small circle of veteran Nokians and the group executive board, whose teamwork served as a model for other teams within Nokia. One of Ollila's strengths was not to monopolise power and decision-making but to delegate his authority.

The New Nokians

The objective (at Nokia) is to always have decisions made by the people who have the best knowledge.

— Dr Matti Alahuhta
President, Nokia Mobile Phones

In 2001, Nokia had a youthful workforce with an average age of 32. It has nearly 52,000 employees worldwide. Almost 41% are located in Finland; 24% in other European countries and 16% in the Asia-Pacific. Attaching and retaining the best and brightest talent is vital in Nokia — employees are paid above-average wages and receive a 5% bonus if annual profits achieve 35%. And about 5000 executives are given stock options.

As a result of the Finnish penchant for an egalitarian, flat organisation structure, Nokia is similarly not only less hierarchical than most large corporations but decidedly anti-hierarchical. The practice of meritocracy management nurtured an environment of creativity, entrepreneurship and personal responsibility.

Kairamo and Ollila believed in continuous training and learning. To this end, Kairamo devoted himself to education issues and promoted them vigorously. Ollila channelled large amounts of funds into Nokia Research Centres (NRC) and training for employees. He valued his employees and viewed them as assets to Nokia. In 1981, Kairamo said:

> *Finland has quite a few resources. Briefly put, there are 2 of them: the people and the trees. Exports are obligatory in the future as well. Things must be sold abroad, so that living conditions will remain good domestically. This, in turn, requires that we have extensive experiences in international business.*

Human resource issues are treated as strategic issues. Strong corporate culture and values are entrenched in the *Nokia Way* — a brochure distributed to all old and new employees. The *Nokia Way* played a critical role in communicating the company's vision, strategy and values. It also gave rise to the slogan "Connecting People". Contemporary Nokia was built on Kairamo's dictum that people should replace trees.

Nokia has encouraged an environment that nurtures creativity and the collective realisation of individual ideas. Despite its rapid growth. Nokia has continued to stress a corporate culture more typical of an independent, innovative and creative startup. The objective has been to maintain this culture no matter how large the company has become. The values were also important to impart a sense of cohesiveness to Nokia offices around the world. These values include:

- ◊ a drive to achieve customer satisfaction;
- ◊ respect for the individual;
- ◊ willingness to achieve and belief in continuous learning;
- ◊ encouraging sharing (information and responsibility) and openness (to each other and to new ideas).

These values are extended consistently worldwide with some local differences. Additionally, Nokia recognises three fundamental principles: serving the society in which the company works; protecting the environment and working according to strict, ethical principles.

When Ollila promoted Nokia in the late 1980s to 1990s, his maxim was to focus on telecommunications and mobile phones. Has the corporate culture of Nokia changed? Yes, but the change is not drastic. Today, Nokia is still advocating designing phones with the consumers in mind (human technology) and making it fun and accessible. Nokia phones are selling well today because of their functionality and user-friendly interface.

The corporate culture is still dominated by the visionary Ollila. He still seeks out new markets to conquer by customising phones according to consumer needs in different markets. Nokia has also spearheaded or initiated pioneering research into 3G technology and aggressively persuading countries to adopt the 3G technology.

Nokia still remains rooted in the anti-hierarchical, relatively flat structure in which ideas are valued. However, with enlarging markets and growing number of employees, it is expected that this flat hierarchy may not be as attractive to talented individuals seeking promotion and status. The Finnish egalitarian culture pervades Nokia — although it creates a sense of equality and loyalty, it may not be as attractive for ambitious employees. But Nokia has recognised this problem and reacted by allocating stock options.

Not only is the power distance in Nokia low, it is a fairly feminine culture which is concerned with the working environment, conditions and welfare of the employees. Although slightly less aggressive in marketing nowadays after having established a large global market share, it still continues to spend a substantial amount on marketing annually. Nokia continues to make us of wide-ranging media from TB to print.

On the research and development side, Nokia has joint ventures and partnerships in developing new telecommunications standards, and it spends quite a lot on training its employees.

However, one major problem for Nokia is competing technologies such as the CDMA in South Korea and a different standard in Japan. Moreover, several strong competitors such as Sony Ericsson, Matsushita and Mitsubishi Electric are also spending a lot on joint research and marketing to stake out a larger market share.

Having paid much for the 3G licences, there are concerns as to whether the 3G technology will take off. There may be a risk of being parochial and over-focusing on the 3G technology instead of exploring viable alternative technologies.

Furthermore, Nokia appears to be battling for more countries to adopt the 3G technology so that they will be compatible with Nokia mobile phones. Nokia is still concentrating on its mobile phones and networks without any intention to diversify. As to whether Nokia can continue to maintain or exceed its current foothold in the mobile phone industry will depend how dynamic and efficient it is in adjusting itself to market conditions and consumer expectations.

Nokia Research Centre

Nokia's R&D unit has played a central role in the company's new product development efforts. By the end of 1999, almost one-third of Nokians worked in R&D. Nokia did its utmost to integrate R&D into the whole corporate process. It actively participated in works of standardisation bodies and various internationalisation projects in cooperation with universities, research institutes and other telecommunications and mobile companies. Nokia established R&D centres worldwide in order to tap the knowledge there and commercialise the products for those markets quickly.

The roots of Nokia Research Centre (NRC) date back to 1979. Since then, it has developed several programmes such as an electronic mail system called NoteX. However, in the 1990s, the NRC's role increased substantially under Ollila.

By 1999, R&D investments grew to FIM 10.6 billion. Nokia's R&D strategy was to develop generic platforms that could be quickly adapted to different standards. Even in R&D, Nokia focused on software development because software is the principal component that adds value to the handset. This approach fitted well with Nokia's overall strategy of speed to market with innovative products that covered multiple standards.

Nokia also recruits its new employees from student trainees working at Nokia. In the late 1990s, some 1,000 students annually prepared their theses while working at Nokia.

While rivals like Motorola and Ericsson pursued and developed new technologies (upstream innovation), Nokia focused on listening to its customers (downstream innovation). Listening to customers became the sole distinctive characteristic of Nokia's R&D. For example, Nokia purchased semiconductors from suppliers instead of pouring R&D investments into them so that it can concentrate on other areas such as network standardisation and technology alliances.

Upstream Innovation

Around 1992, Nokia's team of 25 researchers, scientists and managers embarked on a secret project codenamed Responder. The purpose: to combine internet, computer and telephone technologies to produce a portable machine that converge all three capabilities. The final result was the Nokia 9110 Communicator launched in 1996 — the world's first pocket-sized mobile office, which allows users to send e-mails, receive and send faxes, conduct conference calls and surf the internet. Although the Communicator was not a runaway commercial success, it anchored Nokia's image as an innovative company.

By 2000, the competitive environment of mobile phones was increasingly global and highly volatile. New product and process development had become the focal point of competition. To ensure its continual leadership in cellular technology, Ollila urged Nokia into key technological coalitions. Nokia's process chains remained highly focused. It consisted of three basic categories: R&D, upstream innovation (platforms/standards, logistics), and downstream innovation (branding, segmentation, design).

Branding and Marketing to Niche Markets

By the end of the 1990s, the mobile market was rapidly expanding and many people were buying their first phones or upgrading their old ones. Nokia introduced colourful snap-on covers in the mid-1990s. Today, they come in an assortment of colours with snazzy names like zircon green and electric purple to reflect different moods and lifestyles. Following the colours was graphic design. Nokia hired emerging young artists from Europe and America to design the snap-ons. Yet the market is segmented. While some consumers base their purchase decisions on the snap-on covers, business users prefer functionality.

Nokia excelled in market segmentation. Throughout the Kairamo era, Nokia relied on decentralised marketing for its exports but the direction was ambiguous. But Ollila focused Nokia on global consumer segmentation. Nokia cleverly segmented the markets according to different consumer lifestyles. The advantage for Nokia is that it can now tailor its phones to suit and complement the needs of a particular niche. As the reliability of Nokia phones became established, consumers began to base their choice of phones on the designs and user interface over technical capabilities.

Marketing plays a crucial role in Nokia. Design has always been important at Nokia. Back in the 1960s, Nokia produced brightly coloured rubber boots for the hip, fashion-conscious consumers.

Today, Nokia's interchangeable clip-on phone facias come in a variety of designs and colours. The design of Nokia mobile phones was given a clear direction when Ollila decided to set up the Nokia Design Centre in Los Angeles in 1995. Nokia hired Frank Nuovo as its chief designer and vice president. Nuovo designed the Classic 2100 cellphone, which was to become the breakthrough phone for Nokia. Nuovo has worked with major brands including BMW before and has myriad experience designing for a wide array of products — furniture, consumer electronics, car interior, medical equipment and even instrument panels for power stations and computers.

Nuovo hired young designers form art schools in order to keep in touch with the latest trends. The designers were encouraged to form work teams to produce well-thought-out designs. Nuovo also recognised the aesthetic appeal in simple Scandinavian designs and incorporated them into many Nokia designs. Finnish designer Marimekko and Sony were among Nuovo's inspirations for design. The result is the creation of highly appealing and attractive phones. With the lower costs of owning a mobile phone and making a call from mobile phones, Nokia phones no longer became solely used for business. It has become a mass-market product, like a Swatch wristwatch.

Nokia led in the market because its product cycles had decreased over the years. Nokia introduced about 20 new products each year. In April 2000, Nokia's 8860 arrived in Hollywood with a glamorous marketing blitz — the elegant phone was spotted on celebrities from Nicole Kidman to Christie Turlington. Overnight, owning a Nokia phone became hip and fashionable not only in the U.S. but all over the world.

In 1905, Nokia evoked a river in Finland. By the 1990s, Nokia became a global brand name coupled with its slogan "Connecting People". It has not always been the case in the past. Today, it stands alongside Coca-Cola and Nike as an instant globally recognised and highly valued brand. Nokia's most intensive brand-building efforts were between 1993 and 1995. Nokia employed all possible channels and tools for its global branding strategy. In addition to print advertising, Nokia invested heavily in television advertisements and sponsored MTV and the Science and Technology programme on CNN.

Conclusion

By combining high-end technology and trendy, forward-looking design in mobile phones, Nokia managed to corner a huge global market share in the telecommunications industry. However, the other phone manufacturers caught up in this regard. In order to stay ahead of the competition, any mobile phone manufacturer has to reinvent itself and take bold risks in revolutionising future forms of telecommunications. Such thinking has always been Nokia's maxim. Nokia's vision of "putting the internet into everybody's pocket" was one such maxim. But it's not just placing the internet within the everyday reaches of the common man but to make it relevant and consumer-friendly to the end user. By combining mobility and communication, Nokia managed to stimulate the creation of new services and products, thus revolutionising how people communicate and do business. Digital convergence was the new buzzword in Nokia.

From rudimentary prehistoric cave-wall paintings, which were the first signs of human communication in a non-technological age, to the MMS technology pioneered by Nokia, we seem to have come full circle in our exploration of how we choose to relate to our fellow humans. A simple picture paints a thousand words. Perhaps by keeping communication in its simplest form, Nokia had managed to stay at the forefront of the telecommunication industry.

A key aspect of Nokia's success was its uncanny ability and willingness to "listen to the customer". This capability has been perfected into an art form — through excellent strategy, structure and maximising human resource allocation. Nokia's future in 2003 was dependent on the 3G standardisation across the world. It faced steep competition from other mobile phone manufacturers such as Japan's NTT DoCoMo, Panasonic, Sony and South Korea's Samsung. But this future was only possible if 3G standardisation was adopted in most, if not all, countries. In 2003, 3G standardisation was still in its infancy, although interest in it had been expressed in most parts of the developed world. As long as Nokia stayed focused with its winning formula of combining user-friendly technology and sleek design, there was no doubt that Nokia's star would continue to shine. Such were the prospects in 2003.

The Next Two Decades: What Went Wrong?

For Nokia, the next two decades turned out to be a rollercoaster from boom to almost bust, with a complete change of the product portfolio in the quicksand of high-tech innovation and competition. Between 1998 and 2011, Nokia had been the world's largest producer of mobile phones and smartphones. At its peak, in 2000, it represented 4% of Finland's GDP and 21% of her exports. Nokia's shares in June 2000 stood at €65, pushing the company's worth to €243 billion. In 2016, the share price was at €4.2, and Nokia was valued at €65 billion.

Under Jorna Ollila's chairmanship (1992–2006) since 1992, there has been an exclusive focus on digital mobile phones and telecoms systems. All other business lines were sold off. In 1998, 41 million mobile phones were sold, surpassing its then strongest competitor Motorola (which has disappeared in 2011 — today, known as Lenovo). In the mid-2000s, the mobile phone market stagnated at high levels. In 2007, Nokia sold 33 million phones, holding a world market share of 40%, yet was also hit by the recall of 46 million faulty cellphone batteries. At the time, the major producers focused on improved displays, cameras and sizes. In 2005, it had developed a Linux-based software system called Maemo, which it marketed in the Nokia 779 internet tablet, and after purchasing Navteq in 2007, added navigation systems to its phones. In 2004, Nokia had become the largest shareholder of Symbian, whose software it used until, in 2008, it took over "Symbian Foundation" fully.

By 2011, however, the iPhones and Android phones developed by Apple and Samsung, respectively, hit the market. Apple had used its experiences from desktop PCs to develop touch screens, which proved extremely popular. Symbian smartphone sales started to fall, first losses occurred, and by 2012 Samsung took over as the world's largest smartphone producer. Nokia replaced its Symbian operating system with "Lumia", developed by Microsoft's Windows system, but the hoped-for turnaround failed while losses doubled, as its world market share for smartphones fell from near 50% to 5.8% (2012).

Nokia, which already in 2008 had moved production from high-cost Germany — the closure of its plant in Bochum (for the opening of which Nokia in 1995–1999 had received €60 million in state subsidies) proved very unpopular and even cost it 18% of sales in Germany — to low-cost Romania and Hungary, by cutting 10,000 jobs in research and production and moving manufacturing from Canada and Finland to East Asia. When this proved insufficient to stem losses and improve sales, in 2014, the entire mobile phone business, including patents, services, mapping devices and the CEO in charge, Stephen Elop, was sold to Microsoft for a mere €5.4 billion, which changed its brand name to Microsoft. Nokia factories in Beijing and Dongnan were closed, and the remaining production equipment was moved to Hanoi. About half of the remaining 25,000 employees were dismissed. Billions had to be written off. The crisis of 2011–2014 was surely a unique case where a single product company and world leader was knocked out in the space of a few years by the single product innovation of a competitor, which it had ignored beforehand.

It was tragic that Nokia engineers, in fact as early as in the 1990s, had developed smartphones prototype. This however was refused market development by a conservative management for fear of cannibalising its own successful products — by no means an experience unique to Nokia! If internal stories are to be believed, an ever-changing top management obsessed with quarterly returns practised a very aggressive style, rather barking orders at subordinates and setting one research team against the other to compete for the same objective, with people fearing for their jobs. At the same time, there were long internal tedious and acrimonious debates on new product introductions, which led to inevitable delays. Clearly, not the way how to run a company, not even a dog kennel, let alone one at the forefront of innovation.

Nokia now moved into telecom infrastructure. Already in 2007, it had been the third-largest telecom equipment provider after Alcatel-Lucent and Ericsson-Marconi by creating a joint venture with Siemens as Nokia-Siemens networks. It then purchased the 49% share of Siemens and in 2014 took over the Franco-American Alcatel-Lucent for €15.6 billion to pursue its new, again temporary, almost single-minded focus on networks. Part of the deal were the famous Bell Laboratories in Murray Hill (New Jersey), the world's largest private research institute for communication technologies, which having won nine Nobel Prizes fitted ill with Nokia's insistence on quarterly profit figures and instant deliverables. As a result of these efforts, Nokia in 2018 became — temporarily — the world's largest network supplier ahead of Ericsson, Huawei and ZTE.

After having expanded its geographical card services and concluded user agreements with Amazon, Groupon and Oracle, in 2015, Nokia sold its map service "Here" to Daimler, Audi and BMW as its online route planner MAP 24 (originally developed by

Navteq, taken over in 2007), covering 196 countries. One billion mobile devices currently use those of "Here" and Navteq.

Also, a security device (like a firewall) which had been developed in-house was sold to Check Point. Nokia had also developed digital health products and, in 2016, even purchased the French producer Whitings for €170 million, selling activity trackers, fitness watches, devices for measuring body fat, temperature, blood pressure, etc., which however did not always work. Hence, after write offs of €141 million, this line was sold off for €30 million in 2018. Nokia also sold off its IP video streaming to the Canadian Volaris Group in return for a minority shareholding in Volaris in 2019.

As if these twists and turns of ever-changing top managers had not been enough, after Microsoft exited from its Lumia business in 2018, Nokia in 2019 returned to the mobile and smartphone business, albeit only as a licensing brand name giver (which had been returned by Microsoft). In fact, Nokia has also licensed its brand name for TVs, laptops and earphones. The new smartphones are managed by HMD Global, run by former Nokia managers who had previously dealt with Nokia mobile phones, paid for the brand name and by chance are also headquartered in Nokia's huge Espoo HQ complex near Helsinki. The phones, however, are produced and marketed by Foxconn, Taiwan's huge contract producer of electronics. For the purpose, it had bought Microsoft's production site in Hanoi for $350 million to make new "Nokia" phones and popular retro versions, thus going full circle.

Since 2020 Pekka Lundmark as new CEO has reorganised Nokia into four major business operations:

◊ Mobile networks to develop new technologies for service providers, industry and the public sector to create critical wireless networks.
◊ Network infrastructure as services for established telecom providers to enable a new wave of digitalisation.

◊ Cloud and Network Services (CNS), providing solutions for change of communications service providers (CSPs) and enterprises to cloud native software and core networks.
◊ Nokia Technologies invents and markets technologies to improve intelligent devices and offers new uses, and licenses them to producers, as we have seen in the iPhone case (2014–2016 by Microsoft, and since 2017 by HDM Global).

And how did the mobile infrastructure focus fare thus far? In 2019, Nokia delivered 5G network infrastructure for the Swiss Salt mobile. Taiwan awarded Nokia a $450 million order to build its 5G network as the sole supplier. NASA gave it a $14 million order for a 4G network to communicate with astronauts on the moon. So far, they are not there yet. But in 2021, Nokia did not manage to get any contracts for 5G radio access network in China. Rigged contracts predictably went to Huawei and ZTE, with a symbolic 12% share to Ericsson. At the same time, Samsung also beat Nokia on the North American market with a contract with Verizon.

A serious ray of hope is the general distrust which European, North American and Australian governments rightly entertain as regards the reliability of Huawei and ZTE as government-affiliated network providers, which are increasingly banned from public procurement. In Europe, this leaves only Ericsson and Nokia as reliable partners in the future.

Thus, there is a continuation of unpredictable losses (-€59 million in 2019) and profits (€885 million in 2020) due to the prevalence of mega contracts, replacing the theoretically steadier retail business of iPhones, and the continuous pressure to cut costs, which is bad news for a R&D depended company. It is easy to set sales targets for car salesmen and fire the 10% least performers or close the 10% least-selling burger joints. But how do you set targets for an R&D centre which undertakes basic research, which management hardly understands? At Nokia, they also faced their regular cuts, and frustrated scientists would rather opt for quotes in academic journals to prepare for a more rewarding and less stressful university career. The loss of competitiveness is the mid-term consequence, apart from the overall outfall of continuous staff dismissals, management and product changes. Total employee numbers stood at 132,000 in 2010, at 55,000 during 2013–2015 and at 87,000 in 2023. How could any corporate culture worth its name survive in this human resources rollercoaster?

In 2023, again, a weak turnover left top management envisaging €1 billion in savings with up to 14,000 global job losses. One small way was to outsource service management with 500 employees. But how did Nokia conceptually react? Well, it opted for a "comprehensive rebranding" — like all managers who are at wit's end. A new logo was needed to showcase "B to B innovation leadership" and to finally move away from Nokia's mobile phone image (which they were still licensing) for the digital transformation towards 6G. Also, internal procedures and structures were to be "simplified". Who would ever have thought of this? Nokia also ended its business in Russia (2% of turnover) duly in 2022. But the war in Ukraine upped the chances for lucrative military contracts, in which Nokia, in terms of military uses for safe mobile wireless communications, remains well placed, or at least it once was.

Needless to say, that politically correct Nokia advanced its goal of CO_2 neutrality to 2040. If you go out of business, this virtuous goal can be reached handily.

Bibliography

Häikiö, M. *Nokia: The Inside Story*. United Kingdom: Pearson Education, 2001.

http://www.nokia.com

Kulkki, S. and Kosonen, M. "How tacit knowledge explains organizational renewal and growth: The case of Nokia", in Nonaka, I. and Teece, D. J. (eds) *Managing Industrial Knowledge: Creation, Transfer and Utilization*. London: Sage, 2001, pp. 244–269.

Steinbock, D. *The Nokia Revolution: The Story of an Extraordinary Company that Transformed an Industry*. New York: AMACOM, 2001.

Vikkula, K. "Nokia: Two directed issues, one private placement and one euro equity issue", in Oxelheim, L. *et al.* (eds) *Corporate Strategies to Internationalize the Cost of Capital*. Middleton, WI: Copenhagen Business School Press, 1998, pp. 199–213.

New Literature, 2nd Edition

Erle, C. "Erfolgreiches Sterben: Das Beispiel Nokia", *Umweltdialog*, 28 July 2017.

Morris, I. "Nokia CEO lays out 5G turnaround plan as shares tank", *Light Reading*, 29 October 2020.

Morris, I. "Nokia faces long road to mobile recovery", *Light Reading*, 4 February 2021.

Morris, I. "Nokia has cut 11,000 jobs in effort to boost profit", *Light Reading*, 5 March 2021.

"Rüttgers jagt die Subventionsheuschrecke", *Die Zeit*, 17 January 2008.

"The rise, dominance and epic fall — a brief look at Nokia's history", *GSM Arena*, 12 August 2015.

"Vom Handy Marktführer zum Smartphone Nachzügler", *Kleine Zeitung*, 21 June 2016.

Sony: Made by Morita

The story of Sony's post-war success does not quite follow the popular "rags to riches" pattern. In 1944, the future founding fathers, Masaru Ibuka, a civil engineering contractor, and Akio Morita, a Navy lieutenant with an engineering degree from Osaka University, met in a task force charged to develop a heat-seeking missile for the Japanese Navy. Their work was too late to change the course of war, but the duo turned out to be the perfect complement to each other: Ibuka, an impulsive tinkerer and technical explorer, and Morita, a marketing genius with a keen business acumen and a drive for recognition and success.

Both came from well-off and well-connected families. Ibuka's father-in-law was governor of Niigata Prefecture, and Morita, as Akio Kyuzaemon Morita the 15th, was to be head of the household of a prosperous sake-brewing family from Nagoya, which also produced miso (fermented soy bean paste) soup base and soy sauce. Morita grew up in affluence in pre-war Japan and, throughout his life, as an absentee chief (while his brother managed the family business), his word was law as a traditional household head.

When Ikeda and Morita set up their Tokyo Tsushin Kogyo (Tokyo Telecommunications Company) in the ruins of Tokyo in 1946, Morita's father contributed most of the capital, and the company's board of advisors was packed with influential people with good financial connections. Hence, placing stock and obtaining credit were never a problem (Nathan, 2000, p. 24). The fledgling company started out with radio repair and producing Ibuka's invention of a voltmeter driven by vacuum tubes. Amidst the visionary exuberance in a survivor's atmosphere, Ibuka then decreed as the corporate philosophy the principles of an engineer's company (valid in Sony until today): "to create an ideal work place, free, dynamic and joyous where dedicated engineers will be able to realize their craft and skills at the highest possible level". As a rare gift, Ibuka in fact managed to kindle and harness the innovative spirit in his engineers. They soon produced magnetic tapes and tape recorders, which were invented by Grundig and Telefunken during the war in Germany. When in 1952, the company wanted to move to transistors, the Ministry of International Trade and Industry (MITI) temporarily blocked the move by vetoing the payment of $25,000 as licensing fee. In 1957, the first pocket-sized transistor radio appeared, which, with 1.5 million units sold, made Sony soon a market leader in this modest segment.

Morita made his first visit to the U.S. in 1953, which for him was an overwhelming experience. Catching up, acceptance and success in the U.S. became a lifelong obsession. In the mid-1950s, he changed the corporate name to a mixture of "sonus" (sound) and "sunny", thus arriving at "Sony".

In 1963, Sony produced its first colour TV Chromatron under a licence purchased from Paramount. As it had difficulties mastering the new technology, high losses resulted. In 1966, they discovered RCA's improved system, which in 1968 Sony adapted to its "Trinitron Colour TV" and, after several agonising years, moved on to Betamax technology. Ultimately, in 1978–1980, Sony lost the

Betamax battle in the home video market to Matsushita's VHS, which was more affordable and offered longer playtime. Morita's advocacy of the Walkman and the eight-millimetre video camera, both huge commercial successes, rescued the company.

In 1963, Morita and his family had moved to New York for a year. While he resided at the exclusive Upper East Side, he wanted to observe the all-important U.S. market firsthand and build up Sony's U.S. subsidiary. Unlike other Japanese companies which managed their overseas subsidiaries with expatriate Japanese managers by remote control from headquarters, Sony hired mostly local managers (based on a "man's word", not on detailed contracts) and insisted mainly on building up business, not on showing earnings. For advisory and management functions, Morita curiously hired exclusively American Jews. One of them is quoted as saying, "He (Morita) seems to have felt that Jews were smart, imaginable and very compatible with the Japanese in temperament" (Nathan, 2000, p. 61). Nathan correctly sees this as "naive stereotyping" (p. 62), suspecting that Morita felt the need for tough allies and hired hands for Sony to survive in the U.S. business jungle. Often, after a while, these hands would turn against him, however, having raided his accounts, switched sides or made extravagant renumeration requests.

In 1976, Ibuka *de facto* retired and, as an honorary chairman, wrote bestsellers on technical education for children. Many of the new technologies such as laser (for compact discs) and parallel signal crossing (for computers and integrated circuits) were no longer accessible to him. Sony in the 1980s was in fact run by Morita as a chairman since 1976 in an autocratic one-man show with little checks.

As the story of Sony's U.S. subsidiary with its periodic management purges shows, Morita as an autocrat was able to delegate, but he never abdicated. In 1982, Morita appointed his handpicked successor Norio Ohga, a Tokyo- and Berlin-trained accomplished musician as his successor. Ohga, who had entered Sony in 1959 at bucho (director) level, created the shallow "cutie pie boom" for teenagers rather than promoting European classics or Japanese enka ballads.

Reputed as tyrannical and aloof, his focus was on modern marketing and stylish design — the "Sony look", with premium placement and a polished look of the logo. When Morita had achieved the Walkman, it was Ohga who pushed for the digital age with the compact disc and forced his engineers to use the general-action laser. Since 1982, Ohga had made most of the operational decisions (including moving Sony Europe's HQ famously to Potsdamer Platz in reunited Berlin), subject to final approval by Morita.

Since the Betamax disaster, Morita had insisted on acquiring the music and cinematographic software to complement Sony's traditional hardware (if they had both at the time, in his view, the calamity would not have happened). Hence, Sony USA in 1987 purchased CBS records (with performers such as Michael Jackson, Bruce Springsteen and Barbara Streisand) and in 1989 bought Columbia Pictures, Columbia Pictures TV, Tristar Films and the Loews Theatre chain for $3.2 billion plus $1.6 billion in assumed debts.

To Sony's surprise, this purchase, then the largest of a U.S. company by the Japanese, created a lot of public resentment, which was already fuelled by the takeover of vast tracks of prime real estate in Florida, California, Hawaii, the acquisitions of Firestone Tyre, the Rockefeller Centre, etc., by Japanese investors aided by the strong Yen of 1985–1990.

It quickly transpired that Columbia had been purchased at a level almost twice the original share price. Sony was seen by U.S. sellers as "hungry, cash rich and naïve about the movie business" (Nathan, 2000, p. 187). It is unclear (and doubtful) whether due diligence was undertaken prior to the purchase. As chairman, Morita was known to believe in the synergy of music, films and Sony hardware. His dream of owning a Hollywood studio and sharing its glamour made Sony pay the asking price (much like Seibu-Saison would buy Intercontinental Hotels and many other big-ticket ill-fated Japanese foreign acquisitions of the bubble years). Sony's board, which was packed with 30 Sony directors, duly rubber-stamped the deal with no awkward questions being asked.

Colombia was subsequently renamed Sony Pictures Entertainment, and a five-year history of costly troubles ensued, which was greatly enjoyed by the U.S. public. Sony USA paid the best salaries for its top executives and, given the high turnover of its quarrelsome senior staff, also faced the highest severance payments. It had twice the overhead costs of other studios and, through overspending and a lack of commercial successes by 1993, lost at the rate of $250 million p.a. Yet, as Sony was keen that the studio was seen to be run by Americans, the Japanese continued with their hands-off approach, while U.S. senior staff continued to milk this generous entity with apparently little scruples (Nathan, 2000, p. 278) or incentives to succeed.

Sony USA ventured into a range of new businesses: the Viva music channel; Sony & Warner, which syndicated music programmes to radio stations; and Sony Signatures, which did merchandising with Sony stars, and created a series of Sony multiplex theatres from San Francisco to Berlin. Only when losses mounted with the need to write off debts of $3.4 billion in 1994 was Sony USA's chief, Michael Schulhof, finally fired.

Already in the 1970s and 1980s, Morita had coveted top positions in international fora such as the U.S.-Japan Economic Relations group and the Trilateral Commission, and was proud to be on the international advisory boards of Pan American, IBM, Morgan Guarantee Trust, etc. He enjoyed hobnobbing with famous has-beens on the international policy and party circuit and to be seen and photographed with Henry Kissinger, Mike Mansfield, Otto Graf Lambsdorff, etc. As one of the few Japanese executives who could argue their case well abroad, Morita was liked and respected.

Despite extensive socialising with celebrities, artists, politicians and businessmen at home in Shibuya and in New York, Nathan observes an "illusion of familiarity" (p. 81), as Morita felt obliged "to act as the most international understanding businessman in Japan", while in reality, he was rather a conservative autocrat of the traditional mould, who insisted on primogeniture (favouring his first-born son Hideo), had his share of polygamous adventures and generally entertained a nationalist world outlook. Morita's vision for Sony Japan was to control electronics manufacturing and development, while Sony International in New York should handle marketing and software. In his last active years, Keidanren's private economic diplomacy with Europe and the U.S., and the advocacy of Japan's national business interests were his main concerns. The objective was to become elected as the chairman of Keidanren, Japan's association of big business, a position which so far had been reserved for chairmen of Japan's established Keiretsu companies like Mitsubishi, Mitsui or Sumitomo, but not for recent post-war upstarts like Sony.

After tireless efforts, tragically, Morita was felled by a stroke in 1993 (one year after this had incapacitated his old partner Ibuka) just the day prior to his foregone election to Keidanren's prestigious chairmanship. Without regaining his physical functions, Morita died on 3 October 1999.

Ohga, his chosen successor, turned over the chairmanship of Sony, by now a $45 billion operator, to Noboyuki Idei in 1995. Idei, a Waseda economics graduate with extensive marketing experience in Western Europe dating back to the late 1960s, insisted that Sony remained driven by the vision of its founders, but that its management should become professional instead of being guided by personal friendship. There was no longer any sign of an inferiority complex towards foreigners, which Morita displayed, nor of the self-indulgence and showiness which both Morita and Ohga liked.

Sony has moved into the age of corporate normalcy. But would its Japanese management mainstream (which had since been able to produce a couple of new PlayStations) deliver strokes of genius like the transistor radio, the Walkman, the handycam or the CD player?

Sony was always an eager provider of corporate visions, not all of which were sound. During 2002–2005, then Chairman Idei pursued the vision to integrate ("network") its electronics, media and software business in order to exploit the convergence of television, mobile phones and the internet. Sony would cease to be a classical audio-visual appliance manufacturer and entertainment provider and move towards internet-linked audio-visual devices, games and computer equipment. PCs, TVs, camcorders and mobile phones are all supposed to be transformed into "gateways to networks". TVs are being reborn as centres of broadband entertainment. Sony's Vaio computers already function as TVs and can play compact discs as well.

The big-price question remains: how to make money on the contents side? The PlayStation was a closed system. Everything had to be bought, but the net by definition is free.

A massive reorganisation followed. Audio-visual and IT divisions, hardware and software providers were to be integrated. In what Idei termed "localised globalisation", Sony organised its 168,000 employees into three regional hubs: Tokyo/Shanghai, London/Berlin and New York. Sony Europe, for instance, aims to ensure closer cooperation of its electronics, music, film, games and mobile communications (Sony Ericsson) departments through a top management committee. Sony Pictures Entertainment and Sony Music (promoting Bruce Springsteen, Jennifer Lopez, Shakira, etc.) were merged to "Sony Music Entertainment", forming the world's third-largest music company. Its chief music mogul, Tommy Mottola, was promptly forced out.

The regional hub concept was supposed to overcome the fragmented country organisation by "regional empowerment" (Idei). This was also meant to attract and retain the best of the younger local staff and to avoid them getting frustrated by Japanese corporate bureaucrats.

From 2002, Sony's profit margins hovering around 2.5% were below expectations. The company faced multiple pressures: the commoditisation of computers, mobile telephones and home entertainment as well as piracy and copyright protection problems for its music business. Canon and Samsung moved into Sony's neglected Camcorder business. Market shares were being lost in its core electronics sector. Also, on the Chinese market, for premium electronics, the Koreans were quicker. In the new synergised fields, there would be competition from established operators from all sides: electronics, media and software. Even back in 2003, nobody was making decent profits in these once glamorous areas.

Earnings from films and cable TV were notoriously volatile. Successes such as *Spiderman* and *Men in Black* needed sequels. A large chunk of Sony's operating profits in 2002 was generated by PlayStations and PS2 consoles. As sales could be expected to level off before long, an ever more elaborate PlayStation Portable was made public. The head of the successful games division and president of Sony Computer Entertainment, Ken Kutanagi, was duly promoted executive vice president, a sure indication of greater things to come. It could also have been indicative of Sony's future as an electronic toy maker.

The Next Two Decades: Entertainment Troubles

Sony was no exception to the troubles high-tech companies encountered at the interface of a rapidly evolving innovative scene with fickle consumer tastes and needs and its own bureaucratic hierarchical apparatus and tribal departmentalisation — so typical of Japanese companies with their life-long employment systems. Most Japanese electronics producers, such as Matsushita (now Panasonic), Hitachi and Mitsubishi Electric, after the boom years of the 1980s lost their drive and competitiveness thereafter. Sony as an innovative maverick was no exemption. In the 1990s, it still turned out 500 new products per year, often with only incremental improvements and innovation, thus cannibalising its own products on the market. Yet, it has survived in a somewhat better shape thus far…

Today, its core businesses are PlayStations, image sensors, entertainment electronics and its music and film business. So, essentially, as predicted, it has become an electronic entertainment conglomerate and, after Hitachi and Panasonic, remains Japan's third-largest electronics company with 110,000 employees and a turnover of €61 billion (2022).

Sony Music Entertainment (previously, CBS Records) in 2004 remained merged with Bertelsmann Music Group (BMG) until Bertelsmann withdrew from the music business. After Columbia Pictures had been bought from Coca-Cola for $3.4 billion in 1989, a consortium of four investment societies, led by Sony and Comcast, a cable network provider in 2005 purchased Goldwyn Meyer and its subsidiary, United Artists, thus rounding the contents side of Sony.

In the 1990s, digital cameras, image sensors and digital camcorders were produced and sold in great numbers. Since 1996, they have also used lenses from Zeiss (Germany). Sony was also a supplier of image sensors to other Japanese camera makers: Canon, Fuji Film and Konica Minolta. In 2006, Sony acquired the camera business of Konica Minolta and subsequently put its own Alpha A100 camera based on Konica Minolta technology on the market. Following the Olympus accounting scandal in 2012, in which $1 billion of losses had been covered up by inflated prices for takeovers, Sony invested $500 million in the decapitated camera maker and, with a 11.5% share, became Olympus largest shareholder (which it divested in 2019). In a joint venture ("Sony Olympus"), Olympus delivered the lenses and Sony the image sensors. Olympus also provided Sony access to its sought-after technologies in medical devices.

By 2019, Sony, with a global market share of 20.2%, had become the world market leader, ahead of Nikon.

On PlayStations, after disagreements with Nintendo, Sony began its own exclusive models. After losses mounted with PlayStation 3 in 2006, as they were sold below production costs, they turned profitable again once the costs for its hardware were reduced. The success story continued with PlayStations 4 (2013) and 5 (2020).

On mobile phones, in the 1990s, it was still in a joint venture with Siemens, producing rather over-engineered heavy devices, for which Sony only had supplied the batteries. After Sony ended the cooperation with Siemens in 1998, it built its own Digital Telecom Europe (DTE) development centre in Dornach near Munich. Manufacturing was done in Rappoltsweiler (Alsace). In 2001, a joint venture was set up as Sony Ericsson, but due to financial difficulties in 2003–2004, the sites in Dornach (with 300 people being fired) and North Carolina were closed. After Ericsson pulled out in 2011–2012, it became Sony Mobile Communications AB, with its seat in Lund (Sweden), which was also in charge of producing Sony's tablet Xperion and the Sony Reader. Its notebook batteries were also supplied to Dell, Toshiba, Lenovo, IBM and Apple, though in 2006, there were occasional recalls. By 2012, Sony's world market share in cellphones stood at a mere 1.8%.

Also, Sony attempted to push its own standards, such as for memory sticks, digital cameras and microcontrollers in batteries, to prevent access by competing products in these unregulated innovative fields. Similarly, Japan in the cellphone market introduced her own national standards, which, although predictably created a very lucrative domestic market, cut her phone makers off from the world markets. But the smartphone and the Android system developed by Google and offered free of charge and used *inter alia* by Sony Ericsson made this type of self-defeating industrial policy obsolete.

As losses started mounting by 2008, Sony had to offload non-core businesses to revive its consumer electronics. The Walkman of historical fame ("balladeur" in French) using cassette tapes, with 186 million sold units, was already discontinued in 1998. One of the first new casualties was the robot dog Aibo (1999–2006), an electrical toy created with great fanfare and which was supposed to comfort old senile people in their loneliness. Yet, this "cute" talking dog was to be no real substitute for its 150,000 customers for whom seven further years of service were promised — a life expectancy quite short compared to a real dog. The development of a humanoid robot, Qvio, was discontinued, with no one missing him or her. Another erstwhile flagship, Vaio personal computers, was sunk in 2014 due to poor sales, being sold to "Japan Industrial Partners" (JIP), a Tokyo investment society cooperating with the U.S. KKR. In JIP's new "Vaio Corporation", Sony holds a share of 5%. In 2020, JIP actually also took over the camera business of Olympus, which it had given up after 84 years of production after falling sales and mounting losses to focus on medical devices, such as endoscopes.

Next to follow for Sony in 2015 were the Betamax video cassettes, which for 40 years had been in production for the home video market even after Sony, though its system was considered technically superior, had lost its fight against the VHS format. Then, in 2017, the battery business (in which the Chinese also had been very interested) was sold in a company reorganised as "New Co" with 2,700 employees to Murata Seisakusho (Murata Manufacturing), a world leader in electronic components, for a mere €153 million. It had been very research intensive with 1,000 patents but apparently yielded relatively little usable output. The competition in the world market for lithium-ion battery cells, estimated at $18 billion — 60% of which are in mobile devices (smartphones, tablets and PCs) — is very tough with razor-thin margins. Market shares for Sony at the time of sale stood at 7%, those for Samsung at 27%, for Panasonic at 21% and for LG Chem at 17%. Korean mass producers with a weak currency had been at an advantage. At the time, Sony had not yet entered the automotive battery market. Murata then poured $450 million into Sony's erstwhile battery operations, including the factories in Singapore and Wuxi (China), as Sony had delayed their modernisation due to curbs on capital spending. In Japan, it had also taken over 9,000 former Sony employees and relocated them to its new production site in Yokohama. For a while, miffed Chinese regulators had held up the deal.

The loss-making TV business had for years been treated as an untouchable sacred cow. Not only have the flat-screen TVs since 2005, with their cinematic qualities, been indisputably glamorous, but they have also been connected to Sony smartphones and Play-Stations, hence were thought indispensable.

Yet, as Sony's debt after continuing losses was downgraded to junk by the Fitch rating agency late in 2012, its market value went down to below $10 billion, which pushed up borrowing costs and made — very un-Japanese — asset sales more attractive. As part of the "garage sales" by all Japanese electronic producers, who were in dire straits for reasons of their own, Sony's TV business with its employees was also going to be abandoned sooner or later. As a telling sign of things to come, the TV business was spun off into a separate society, with 5,000 jobs cut until 2015. Thanks to a weak yen in 2014, Sony unexpectedly made €82 million in profits, though it was much below expectations. Hence, the loss-making TV and PC businesses were allowed to continue for a period of grace.

Understandably, there were also dramatic management changes, which normally in a traditional consensus-oriented Japanese business setting had been unheard of. Norio Ohga (1930–2011), Morita's man at the helm who had led Sony through the boom years during 1982–1995 and, as a pioneer of the leisure industry through music CDs and Play Stations, had transformed it into an entertainment giant, named Nobuyuki Idei (1937–2022) first as his co-CEO (1999–2003), then as sole CEO until 2005, whereupon Idei briefly became chairman of the board. Idei was succeeded by Sir Howard Stringer (2005–2012), a Welsh-born American executive. He became the first American to run a Japanese company.

Stringer was an Oxford scholar, subsequently emigrated to the U.S. and, as a naturalised American, served as a military policeman in Saigon. Over the next 30 years, he rose through the ranks of CBS from reporter to president (1988–1995), where he was successful with the *Spiderman* series in the media industry and since 1997 had been president of the Sony Corporation of America. Hired as a no-nonsense Anglo-American crisis manager, during his helm losses however mounted. A three-year turnaround plan with thousands of job cuts, the closure of unprofitable projects and the merger of divisions did not yield results. After the Tohoku earthquake of March 2011, exchange rate problems, still having to stick with the unprofitable TV business and record losses in 2012, Stringer threw the towel after four years of losses. He reminisces: "My Sony bosses thought that I could wake up a dinosaur. It was really a bridge too far". Further: "Running a big company is like running a cemetery. There are thousands of people below you, but no one is listening. It was a bit like this at Sony". There was also a "not invented here" mentality, which he had been unable to shake up.

As during the war, Japanese units were excellent at advancing but horribly bad in retreat, which they had never been trained for. Thus, during the boom years with lifelong employment guarantees in the cash-rich major companies, they could branch into all directions and cultivate their compartmentalised business cultures. With seniority-based advancement, they were represented in top corporate decision-making and thus could feel safe. In a crisis mode, with a foreign manager in charge, clearly units and their managers went into a passive resistance mode. Firing long-serving staff members and selling off entire units to the hated competition (where they would be treated worklife-long as sub-humans) were clearly the most un-Japanese way you could think of in a country where most men are still dedicated to a strict Confucian work ethic.

Stringer was succeeded by an in-house manager, Kazuo, Hirai, who first declared his unshakeable commitment to the loss-making

TV businesses. Later, after the successful introduction of PlayStation 4, he announced its three future foci of business:

- ◊ imaging (digital cameras, video cameras and professional equipment);
- ◊ games (PlayStations, video games); and
- ◊ mobile products and communications, including its best-selling brand Xperia in smartphones and tablets.

But a Japanese company would not be a Japanese company if it did not pursue other promising options. One is the medical devices purchased from Olympus once upon a time. And then there is, surprise, surprise, electric cars. In 2020 and 2023, two concept cars in a joint venture with Honda ("Sony Honda Mobility") were presented, called Afeela, as a limousine with internal displays looking like an aeroplane cockpit, including monitors of outside cameras, 40 sensors, automatic door openings and driver assistance ready for automated driving, plus films and games (courtesy of Sony) to be enjoyed during the boredom of highways and local traffic jams. Thus far, this wondrous vehicle, which perhaps someday you could enter fully drunk and ask it to "take me home", like good horses would do in the old days, is yet to see the light of day, except for two prototypes in Las Vegas. First deliveries are foreseen in 2026 in the e-car-allergic U.S. So, please watch this space.

Bibliography

Guth, R. A. and Chang, L. "Is Sony Cool Enough for China?", *FEER*, 2 January 2003.

Morita, A. *Made in Japan: Akio Morita and Sony*. New York: EP Dutton, 1986.

Nakamoto, M. and Burt, T. "Consumer Electronics", Parts 1–3, *Financial Times*, 10–12 February 2003.

Nathan, J. *Sony: The Private Life*. London: HarperCollins, 2000.

"Sony — Surprise", *The Economist*, 3 May 2003.

"Sony, the Complete Home Entertainer?", *The Economist*, 1 March 2003.

New Literature, 2nd Edition

Blasi, M. and Fritsch, D. "Akio Moritas Unternehmensphilosophie", in: Rothacher, A. (ed.) *Die Rückkehr der Samurai. Japans Wirtschaft nach der Krise*. Heidelberg: Springer, 2007, pp. 95–108.

"Das Duell Samsung versus Sony", in: Rothacher, A. *Die Rückkehr der Samurai. Japans Wirtschaft nach der Krise*. Heidelberg: Springer, 2007, pp. 175–180.

Emoto, E. and Kelly, T. "Banks Offer Help Sony Offload Battery Unit", *Reuters*, 28 November 2012.

Haas, K-H. "75 Jahre Sony: Tonband statt Soja-Soße", *Heise-online*, 7 May 2021.

Handel, J. "Ex Sony CEO Howard Stringer on Sony's Failures and Time Inc's Big Challenges", *The Hollywood Reporter*, 25 October 2014.

Henzeroth, T. "Sony ohne Fernseher wird es nicht geben", *Die Welt*, 11 March 2012.

Hopf, E. "Sony verkauft Lithium-Ionen Geschäft an Murata", *Elektroniknet.de*, 16 November 2016.

Kuhlmann, U. "Sony geht unter die Elektroauto-Hersteller", *Heise-online*, 5 January 2022.

Kuri, J. "Sony in der Krise: PC Sparte wird verkauft", *heise online*, 6 February 2014.

Leichtenring, S. "Afeela: Neuer Prototyp des Sony-Elektroautos auf der CES", *Inside EVs*, 5 January 2023.

"Mr. Silberscheibe ist tot", *Der Spiegel*, 24 April 2011.

"Murata to Pour $ 450m Into Sony Battery Ops After Purchase", *Nikkei Asia*, 1 September 2017.

"Olympus gibt sein Kamerageschäft auf", *Frankfurter Allgemeine*, 26 June 2020.

"Sony Chairman Sir Howard Stringer to Retire", *BBC News*, 11 March 2013.

"Sony investiert halbe Milliarde in Olympus", *Der Spiegel*, 28 September 2012.

Sir Richard Branson's Virgins

The Road "Not" Travelled

One of the most recognised names in the U.K., Virgin is a brand that defies the odds and captures the imagination. Never before has a brand been so widely used in sectors that stretch across air travel, financial services, music, beverages, automobiles, telecommunications, retail and fashion. Although one may argue that Hanson, a British-American conglomerate, which makes bricks, cigarettes, industrial chemicals and food, and Proctor and Gamble (P&G), which is engaged in the production of toothpaste, shampoo, peanut butter, paper towels and drugs, are multi-national companies who are also involved in diverse industries, none of them are, however, in the same league as Virgin. Even the likes of Japanese keiretsu companies such as Mitsubishi, which are engaged in the automobile industries, steel-making, consumer appliances, electronics and banking, and Yamaha (music and motorbikes) do not come close to the "magic" of the Virgin brand. The reasons are obvious. Most consumers are either unaware or do not care about the name of the parent company. They buy Hugo Boss fashion and fragrances, use

Pantene shampoo, Pampers diapers and eat Pringles potato chips, but most do not know that P&G made them. Nor can they find P&G shampoo or P&G potato chips. The Virgin name and logo, by contrast, appear on a huge range of products. Virgin Atlantic Airways, Virgin Cola, Virgin Mobile, Virgin Bride, Virgin Megastores, Virgin Direct and Virgin Books are just a few of the many diverse products that carry the Virgin brand name. When asked, most consumers have no problem identifying the Virgin brand. In their eyes, the brand stands for value for money, quality, fun as well as a sense of competitive challenge. Most importantly, Virgin does not merely sell a product, like most other brands. Instead, it sells an attitude! Its consumers have an emotional association with the brand.

Stretching across five continents, from Japan to Singapore, Australia, South Africa, the U.K. and the U.S. in 2001, Virgin Group was composed of around 250 companies of different sizes, industries and locations. They are broadly categorised into eight product functions. The group's total revenues around the world were in excess of £4 billion, and it had around 25,000 employees. Led by adventurous entrepreneur, chairman, and owner Sir Richard Branson, the reach of Virgin is extremely extensive. It was involved in three airlines, two rail franchises, holiday tours, wine and beverages, cosmetics, bridal service, balloon flights, health clubs, cinema chains, internet services, mobile communication, radios, cars, motorbikes, a credit card scheme, a pension fund, a record label, publishing and many others. Given the "shroud of secrecy" in which Virgin Group operates, it is almost impossible to pinpoint the exact number of companies that carry the Virgin name. It is, after all, a private company which is run as a network of holding companies and many off-shore trusts, which are designed to cut costs by minimising the group's tax liability.

The value of the brand and the attitude of its employees appear to be the only things that hold the Virgin empire together. Virgin strongly believes in giving its customers a richer experience through quality and fun by creating new opportunities and turning innovative ideas into reality. The Virgin vision is the desire to be different by being better and by giving better quality, better service and better value to its customers, with a tradition of doing it with a bit of style and having fun. Its mission is to provide premium quality to consumers at first-class discount price.

Virgin also empowers its employees to deliver a quality service and facilitates and monitors feedback to continually improve the customer's experience of the brand. By adding the fun element to business, Virgin is able to stand out from the seriousness and mundaneness attached to many companies, especially the established ones.

The Virgin Chronicle

With the aim to avoid retail rental costs, the company started out as a mail-order record business. Toying with various names, which include Slipped Disc, the name Virgin was adopted for its easy application to many different products and the fact that its founders were all business-world virgins.

Business was booming until labour strikes by the postal service in 1971 threatened to bankrupt the upstarts, forcing them to open their first record shop rent-free in exchange for bringing human traffic for the shoe shop landlord at the cheaper end of Oxford Street. In the same year, Richard Branson bought a manor in Oxfordshire and converted it to a recording studio, adding the third company to the Virgin portfolio. It was also this period when Branson fell afoul of the law, resulting in a fine of £53,000 by the HM Customs & Excise for purchase-tax fraud, which nearly crippled the company.

Embracing a customer-first service attitude, Virgin mail-order and record shop business grew from strength to strength. However, Virgin's business did not take off until 1973, when Mike Oldfields' Tubular Bells topped the U.K. charts and earned Virgin enough profit to purchase Necker, a private island in the British Virgin Islands, to set up Virgin's first nightclub, a gay disco and its Event magazine, and most importantly, to finance the expansion of Virgin Records. Throughout the 1970s until the early 1980s, Virgin Records signed up numerous artists, including the Sex Pistols, Human League, Phil Collins, Boy George, Culture Club and later, Janet Jackson and The Rolling Stones, whose chart-topping successes made Virgin Music Group one of the top independent record labels in the country. In the middle of this period, Virgin Records made its foray into the European market through licensing deals in France.

The success of its music group bankrolled Virgin entry into the air travel industry, with the creation of Virgin Atlantic Airways, beginning its first flight between London and New York in 1984 from Gatwick Airport. The airline later started its first Heathrow service in 1991.

By 1989, more companies which carry the Virgin brand were formed. Virgin Vision (forerunner to Virgin Communications) was set up to distribute films and videos, while Virgin Games was founded to publish computer games software. Virgin Holidays, Virgin Cargo and Virgin Airship & Balloon Company were also formed. Mates Condom was launched, with proceeds going to the Healthcare Foundation. While Vanson Development was created to develop residential and commercial property. A luxury hotel in Deya, Mallorca, was also acquired, spinning off to hotel operations in the U.K. and the Caribbean. Recognition of Virgin's achievement came when the company won a Business Enterprise Award for company of the year in 1985.

In 1986, the Virgin Group, comprising the music, retail and property and communications divisions, floated on the London Stock Exchange at 140 pence and later on NASDAQ over-the-counter exchange in the U.S. in 1987. However, the decision to list the company was an ill-fated one, as the stock market crashed on 16 October 1987, plunging Virgin's stock price from 160 to 90 pence, halting its acquisition of EMI, a rival record label. Together with Branson's dislike of getting permission from institutional investors with regards to Virgin's business decisions, the "burden" of being a listed company placed heavy demands on Virgin and made it difficult for the company to cope with all the formality that institutional investors insisted they adopt. In the end, the initially promising stock listing plunged the company into heavy debt when the company bought itself out from other shareholders with a loan of £182.5 million from a group of banks.

Between 1989 and 1990, Virgin entered into a period of partnership with Japanese companies. Virgin's "flings" with the Japanese began when Fujisankei, a media group, bought a 25% stake in Virgin's music business for £115 million. Seibu-Saison, a travel and leisure conglomerate, also entered into a strategic alliance with Virgin through the purchase of a 10% stake in Virgin Atlantic for £36 million after the outbreak of the 1990 Gulf War. However, disagreements led to Seibu-Saison pulling out of the partnership, selling back its share to Virgin in 1993. Virgin also entered into an alliance with Marui, a department store chain, to establish a 50–50 joint venture company to open megastores in Japan.

This was the same period where Virgin sold off huge stakes in its business to starve off its supposedly perpetual financial problems. Fifty percent of its megastore business was sold to W. H. Smith, while the "jewel in the crown", Virgin Music Group, was sold to Thorn-EMI for £560 million in 1992. Such was the irony that, just a few years ago, Thorn-EMI became a target of hostile takeover by Virgin. However, though selling Virgin Music was a painful decision, the money raised from the deal helped expand the Virgin empire. One of the biggest beneficiaries was Virgin Atlantic, which grew to become the biggest breadwinner of the company and was voted airline of the year by Executive Travel magazine for three consecutive years. In 1999, 49% of Virgin Atlantic was sold to Singapore Airlines.

Following the sale of Virgin Music in 1992 until 2000, the company launched Virgin Radio 1215AM (sold for £85 million in 1997), Virgin Cola and Virgin Bride (the biggest bridal retail shop in Europe), entered the internet market with Virgin.net and bid twice for the franchise to run Britain's National Lottery, promising to give all profits to charitable foundations. The company also acquired MGM Cinemas, together with Hotel Properties Ltd. and TPG Partners, a major U.S. investment fund. Virgin Direct Personal Financial Service was launched in partnership with the Norwich Union, who was later bought out by Australian Mutual provincial, and in 1997 launched its first banking product, Virgin One Account. The company also won the franchise to run two train services under the name of Virgin Trains. Other Virgin-related companies include Virgin Vie, a cosmetics and beauty care company, Virgin Mobile and Virgin Cars.

As we can see, the reach of the Virgin empire is extremely diverse. Many of these companies were formed in partnership with other companies, with Virgin taking a majority interest in the new venture so as not to bear the whole risk of a business by itself. However, to be able to fully see the reason why consumers are so fascinated with the brand and what the company's culture is like, one must look at Sir Richard Branson. Without this peculiar and flamboyant figurehead, Virgin would certainly not be where it is now, entrenched in the hearts of many whose paths crossed with one of the most exceptional brands in the world.

Sir Richard Charles Nicholas Branson

A billionaire entrepreneur consistently featured in Forbes magazine's list of the World's Richest People, Richard Branson had an estimated fortune of $3.3 billion in 2000. Also a daredevil adventurer, celebrity icon, national hero and prankster rolled into one, Branson is the power behind the Virgin "revolution". Flamboyant, fun-loving, caring and a good motivator, his critics would also say that he is scheming, greedy, narcissistic, has a "grasshopper" mind and a womaniser underneath all that public relation skills. However, there is no doubt that he is the company's best advertisement. Other companies like Pepsi may have spent $300 million on an advertising campaign, while Walt Disney may have built its image around Mickey Mouse, none of them could beat Branson, who is able to create free publicity for Virgin through his antics and public relations genius.

Born in 1950, Branson could not read even at the age of eight, as he was dyslexic and short-sighted. Admitted to Stowe School after receiving numerous cramming sessions to make sure he passed his entry exams, Branson never improved to be an academically smart student. When he left school in 1967, his headmaster predicted that he would either go to jail or become a millionaire, both of which came true.

Branson's first brush with business was his *Student* magazine, which had very limited success. However, it evolved to become Virgin mail-order record business, which was his first "real" step into the world of business when *Student* magazine shut down. As we have seen, the 1971 postal strike "forced" Branson to open his first record store, where he fulfilled the first prediction of his former headmaster. For the second part of his prediction, there is no doubt that he achieved it many times over.

Known for his penchant for wearing casual clothing and dislike for business suits, Branson carries an air of informality around him and hates to be caught in an overly formal meeting. However, it can be argued that it is not through his business success story that the world came to know about him, but rather through his many adventures which, often endangered him and threatened to deprive Virgin of its inspirational chairman. Branson broke the Atlantic sea speed record in the Virgin Challenger II in 1987, crossed the Pacific Ocean in a hot air balloon and skidded naked down the Swiss Alps.

He is also notorious for his pranks, which are a lot more practical than intelligent. He is known to have emptied the contents of a fire extinguisher onto guests or his employees and upturned attractive women during parties. One infamous case was when Branson flipped Ivana Trump, then wife of New York property tycoon Donald Trump, upside down at an airline awards dinner. Another incurred the wrath of the late Sir James Goldsmith, a corporate raider and takeover baron, who was pushed into his swimming pool by Branson, even after repeatedly reminding him not to do so before and during the party held at Goldsmith's mansion. Branson is often criticised as being narcissistic. Always wanting to be at the centre of attention, he believes that a party is not a party until he is there to start it. Once, he was stuck in a traffic jam and repeatedly called his hosts every 15 minutes to update them on his whereabouts, saying that he would be there soon to start the party.

As a celebrity icon, Branson is often seen with other more illustrious public figures. He was well acquainted with the late Princess Diana and politicians such as Margaret Thatcher and Tony Blair. In 1999, he was knighted in the New Year's Honours List, not too bad a distinction for a person who once broke the law.

Virgin's Organisation Culture

Using traditional management theory, the essence of an organisation can be divided into seven categories: innovation and risk taking, attention to detail, outcome orientation, people orientation, team orientation, aggressiveness and stability.

The Virgin Group is a highly risk-taking company. It was reported that the company bought over MGM Cinema without due diligence, unaware of its financial and physical condition. Many of the cinemas were reported to be run-down and in serious need of maintenance. The group is also seen, in Wall Street lingo, as a "debt-junkie". The company has no qualms about going into debts in the name of expansion. Many times, this trait nearly led to the demise of the company, until a "white knight" came along at the crucial moment to buy a part of Virgin's assets and refinance the company. This scenario was supposed to have played out many times, from the various partnerships with the Japanese to the sale of Virgin Music to Thorn EMI and the 49% stake of Virgin Atlantic to Singapore Airlines. This high risk-taking nature of the company can be traced to its chairman. As the main decision-maker of the company, the way in which Branson does business reflects his tendency of putting himself in high-risk situations, like his ballooning trips and Atlantic crossing. Therefore, it is not surprising that Virgin has a highly optimistic outlook with regards to the way it does business and its speed in picking up business ideas.

Virgin often boasts itself as one who "seeks" justice for consumers. It prides itself for entering into markets long dominated by monopolies that overcharge their consumers. An example is its very first business venture, where buyers of music records are able to purchase records from Virgin mail-order records at a much cheaper price than from its rivals. The outcome of this marketing strategy was that Virgin came to be often seen in a way in which it wants consumers to see it. However, whether Virgin is really what it markets itself is quite ambiguous, as often the prices which the company charges are not any lower than what its rivals charge. Moreover, there is a need to cover the downside, which relates to what Branson would say.

Virgin is supposedly a very people-orientated company. The company strives in an environment of "business is fun". Employees are apparently remembered by the first name, and everyone is encouraged to walk into Branson's office and give him suggestions on how to improve the company's operation or to come up with a new business idea. Company parties are also held regularly, where alcohol, drugs and sex are supposed to be in abundance. It should be noted that Virgin employees are reportedly not paid well but are attracted to the company because it is fun to work for Branson.

The company is very aggressive in the way it functions. Often, the management is not shy about making use of the media to create free publicity or in giving writs against competitors, which they allege are trying to drive them out of business. When the company first entered the Australian market, it threatened to sue anyone who used the Virgin brand, although there were a few native companies who are registered under that name and had a longer history than Branson's Virgin. Being a very growth-oriented company, Virgin is often seeking to conquer new markets, sometimes with little regard to risk and reward considerations. Its tendency of engaging itself in almost every industry in the world puts it in quite a fragile position. As the Virgin brand is used on almost all its products, the possibility of brand dilution from products that are out of line with the Virgin image may also affect the rest of its business. Therefore, stability is not a word that can be used smoothly in the same breath as Virgin.

Branson is Virgin, Virgin is Branson

To describe Virgin's organisational culture using traditional management models or organisation theories would be "un-Virgin-al" to begin with. To adequately explain the Virgin culture, we should look at three dimensions. Firstly, the most prominent aspect of Virgin is its irreverent attitude towards establishments.

This trait can be attributed to the swinging 1960s, in which Branson grew up. Part of this irreverent image is the portrayal of a "rebellious" Virgin, which can best be illustrated with the "Sex Pistols" incident.

During the Queen's Silver Jubilee celebration outside Parliament House, Branson rented a boat from a River Thames cruise company and sailed down the river with the Sex Pistols in their perpetual drunken state. At the height of the celebration, Branson's procession stopped directly opposite Parliament House and the Sex Pistols started singing their rendition of "God save the Queen"! When they touched shore, the police immediately arrested them, and the incident was sensationalised by the tabloids the very next day. It could explain why Virgin is more popular among the more rebellious part of the population or with working or young middle-class consumers, who have more rebellious attitudes but normally suppress them to be in line with the conformist, orderly majority.

Being irreverent towards the establishment was also acted out in the British Airways (BA) "dirty tricks" incident. By assuming the position of a moral authority, Virgin portrayed itself as the upholder of justice, challenging big monopolies who tried to drive small upstarts, like Virgin, out of business, so that they can continue to overcharge the consumers who were not given adequate choices. Virgin Atlantic, the fun-loving and cheeky airline, which had only one leased plane at the time of the "dirty tricks" incident, was supposedly undercut by British Airways, a former state-owned established airline with 250 planes which, together with United Airlines and American Airlines, had a monopoly of landing slots at Heathrow Airport. Putting itself up against BA, which was supposedly managed like a government administrative department and lacked entrepreneurship, Virgin charged that BA was trying to remove its competitors by engaging in dirty tricks like reading into Virgin's reservation list and aggressively "touting" Virgin Atlantic's customers to switch to BA. When Virgin won the suit, it portrayed itself as the people's company, gaining market share as sympathisers started to purchase Virgin's products. Thus, Virgin adds a sense of challenge and purpose to its image, not only to its customers but also to its employees who see that they are fighting for the underdog, enabling Virgin to continue paying below market rate to its employees.

This image was further enhanced when Branson tried bidding for the National Lottery, wanting to rename it as the People's

Lottery and giving all profits to charitable institutions. Branson also injected imagination and responsiveness for the consumers, providing massage and manicure services on board his airline when requested. And by adding a "cool" alternative image to the Virgin culture, it is no surprise that the brand occupies a special place in the hearts of his fans. Surprisingly, given his many antics and pranks, Branson is on good terms with many celebrities, journalists and politicians.

The second element of Virgin's organisational culture is how it does things the fun and non-conformist way. In Virgin, employees are encouraged to be personal. Dressing down is prevalent, people call one another by their first names and company parties with a lot of drugs, alcohol and sex seem to remain a regular fixture. It is said that money-making is not the motivation that drives the company, but rather customer and employee satisfaction.

The way in which Virgin uses publicity is another major aspect that defines the company's fun and non-conformist culture. The launch of Virgin Coke in the U.S. took place at New York's Times Square, with Branson driving a tank down the street, knocking down a wall made up of Coke cans. Virgin Mobile, on the other hand, was launched in London with a casually dressed Branson sitting in a see-through van surrounded by six nude models holding mobile phones. The use of sex to sell its product is not new to Virgin. Other than Virgin Mobile, Virgin Coke's bottles are made to shape like Pamela Anderson's famous curves, with slogans like: "Open your mouth, I'm coming!" and "You can taste our love every time you swallow!" Semi-naked nurses were also used to launch Virgin Energy. Branson is also known to cross-dress for publicity. He was seen in a bikini, wearing a bridal gown during the launch of Virgin Bride and as an air stewardess on board Virgin Airways serving wine to his passengers.

However, the most outrageous publicity campaign was during the launch of the first Virgin Atlantic service from Heathrow

Airport. Branson, covering BA's Concorde, which was parked at the lobby, with Virgin Atlantic's signature red over BA's logo, boarded the plane in a pirate costume, declaring, "This is our territory". All the above publicity campaigns, though shocking, were cheap but very effective when compared to the millions spent by other, more established companies. Together with the many dangerous adventures that Branson undertook up until today, it emphasises the fun and non-conformist culture of Virgin.

Positioning itself as a large extended family, Virgin culture places its customers and employees first. After the company won the lawsuit against BA, the damage handout from the case was famously given to its employees as the "BA Bonus". During the airline industry downturn, Branson offered to relocate his airline staff to other parts of his empire instead of opting for retrenchment. The bid for the National Lottery, the launch of Mates Condom to educate the young about safe sex and chairing the UK2000 environment group were other ways in which Branson claimed to give power to the people.

The Virgin culture also believes in the empowerment of the individual companies and their employees. It is a highly atomised empire, or as some critics will argue, a huge primitive tribal hierarchy. This is done with the belief that "small is beautiful" and that it encourages entrepreneurship and contributions within the group as decision-making is passed on to individual companies and that it minimises tax liability. Except for Virgin Atlantic, which employs 6,200 people, Branson is said to split a company into two once it has more than 50 employees.

Virgin's Future as Foreseen in 2003

The corporate culture of the Virgin Group underwent minimal changes as it achieved global reach. It still functions the same way it did when it was first created by Branson. If there are any changes, it could be that the increasing size of the empire would cause the organisation to turn into more of a "task" culture. However, the company is still very much a "power" culture company, with Branson calling the shots. As the company increased its standing in the global business world, its culture remains as atomised as it was two decades ago. Except for Virgin Atlantic, the rest of the other 200 plus companies are micro-managed by Branson's lieutenants and only once in a while checked upon by him.

When the company was formed, its aim was to provide quality products at lower costs to consumers. "Power to the People" was a slogan used by Richard Branson during his marketing blitz, which often makes use of free publicity created by the media, notably the British tabloids. An irreverent, rebellious and anti-establishment image took shape as the company grew and, together with the above, is still used to market the company. Fun-loving and informality were never far in association with the brand. Sex, drugs and alcohol are still rumoured to be a big part of the company culture.

As Virgin's fate is heavily tied to that of Richard Branson, it makes one wonder if there will be life for Virgin after the demise of its chairman. As Richard Branson is Virgin and Virgin is Richard Branson, the company may find it impossible to find a replacement for such an inspirational, flamboyant and at times cultist leader. Virgin's survival and growth may rest on how Richard Branson instils his beliefs and image into the Virgin Group. His ability to source out new business ventures with more established partners and take up majority stakes like what he has been doing will also be crucial. Whether he will be successful in doing so may decide if Virgin will hold on to its irreverent and fun-loving image or fade into the business world as yet another of those boring profit-making institutions.

The Next Two Decades

The development of Virgin Group as a holding of dozens of highly diverse companies of hugely different fates remained complex, surely puzzling also to its owner-founder and president, Richard Branson, who had always preached and practiced a hands-off management style. As there are no consolidated accounts, *Forbes*' estimation of Branson's private wealth fluctuating between $4 billion (2019) and $2.7 billion (2024) may serve as an indicator of the group's fortunes, although by 2024, he holds mostly minority stakes in his erstwhile founded companies.

Having sold Virgin Records already back in 1984 to EMI for $600 million to raise funds for his two airlines, Virgin Atlantic and Virgin Blue (since 2011, Virgin Australia), these remained the flagship enterprises of his group, while the other four dozen or so stayed fairly peripheral; either they did well, died instantly, were sold, merged and taken over or simply vanished within a few years.

Virgin Atlantic Airways ("Everyone can take on the world") in 2024 is owned at 49% by Delta Airlines and at 20% by the Virgin Group; 73-year-old Branson remains its president. CEO since 2019 has been Shai Weiss, a U.S.-trained Israeli who had been job-hopping from one management position to the next, none of them in the airline business. With hubs in Heathrow and Manchester and since 2023 part of the world's third-largest Sky Team Alliance, it flies to 30 destinations in the U.K., continental Europe and the rest of the world. There are also seasonal services from Edinburgh. It is administered separately from other Virgin-branded airlines and associated with Virgin Holidays, controlled by the Virgin Group (51%) and Delta Airlines (49%).

In 1999, Virgin Group sold a stake of 49% of Virgin Atlantic to Singapore Airlines for £600 million. Yet, in 2008, Singapore Airlines made it known that it was ready to sell their shares, as they had "underperformed". In December 2012, Delta Airlines bought their shares for a mere £224 million. The loss represented a mere 0.1% dip in the net worth of Temasek Holdings, Singapore Airlines' state-controlled majority owner.

During 2014–2015, the flights to Sidney, Tokyo, Bombay, Dubai, Vancouver and Cape Town were scrapped due to mounting losses. Also, the "Little Red" services, which had been set up to compete with British Midland International (BMI) between London and Manchester, and the Scottish routes were ended. A code-sharing agreement was entered with Delta Airlines to stem the losses on transatlantic flights. In March 2020, COVID-19 struck. As all airlines worldwide were more or less grounded in the pandemic hysteria, Branson and Virgin management asked all staff to take eight weeks of unpaid leave. This was before a hesitant British government announced its "Coronavirus Job Retention Scheme". Yet, in May 2020, 3,000 dismissals were announced, and services from Gatwick discontinued permanently. In June 2020, only cargo flights were possible from London to Brussels. While other politically better-connected airlines were helped in survival by their government (who after all had grounded them), such aid was not forthcoming for a fiercely independent maverick like Virgin. Thus, in August 2020, it had to file for a Chapter 15 bankruptcy protection from creditors in New York. As part of a private €1.3 billion refinancing package, debt restructuring was agreed, and a further 1,350 employees were dismissed.

In 2022, the Russian airspace was closed for all U.K. carriers in retaliation for Europe's ban on Aeroflot. While Virgin had had no Russian destinations, flights to India and Pakistan would take up to one hour longer.

The COVID-19 crisis had come on top of ongoing financial problems. Losses had continued at the order of £132 million (2010) to £600 million (2021), with only occasional small gains in 2011 and 2015–2016. In 2022, with a revenue of £2.9 billion, net losses amounted to £340 million. The number of employees had gone down from 9,600 (2013) to 6,500 (2021), total flights from 30,000 (2014) to 8,000 (2021) and the number of passengers from 6 million (2014) to 1.1 million (2021). Yet, Shai Weiss received the biggest bonus of all European airline CEOs in 2023, probably less for performance achieved than for frustrations suffered. Or a sure sign of Branson's unshakeable dark British humour?

In 2024, on "Trip advisor", Virgin Atlantic, among 16,000 reviews, half of them rated services, punctuality, seat sizes, the quality of food, drinks, inflight entertainment and friendliness of staff as "excellent" — some of Branson's old hands-on service culture may have survived — but the rest were more mixed, up to "never again". A judgement apparently very much in the eye of the beholder.

Much as Virgin Atlantic had taken on the giant and staid British Airways in Europe, so did Virgin Blue ("Bring on wonderful") attack the customer-unfriendly local duopolists Qantas and Ansett down under. After the collapse of Ansett in September 2001, it succeeded in establishing itself as a major inner-Australian airline, linking hubs in Brisbane, Melbourne and Sidney to 33 inner Australian destinations and starting short international flights. In 2005, Virgin Blue was subjected to a hostile takeover by Patrick Corporation, an Australian logistics operator, which corned 62% of its shares, with 25% remaining with Virgin Group. Thereupon, Patrick, in turn, was swallowed in May 2006 by Toll Holdings, which subsequently sold its majority share in Virgin Blue to Air New Zealand, which in 2013 held 23% but kept 1.7%. Virgin Blue then started a series of multiflyer, lounge access and code-sharing arrangements with United Airlines, Emirates, Hawaiian Airlines, Malaysian Airlines, Garuda, Vietnam Airlines, Etihad Airways and Air New Zealand. Renamed "V Australia" in 2008, it offered transpacific flights to Los Angeles and San Francisco to compete with Qantas and United Airlines. So far, Virgin Blue, like other budget airlines (Ryan Air and Southwest — "Southworst" — Airlines) had charged passengers to pay for food and drinks on board, to pay fees for luggage and asked them to book by phone or internet by saving on printed tickets. By 2011, a new CEO, John Borghetti, from Qantas management took the helms and ordered an upgrade to compete better for business-class passengers. The renamed Virgin Australia was to be a hybrid between a budget and a full-service airline, with a new design (the end of "Blue"). The Pacific Blue subsidiary, flying between New Zealand and Australia, was integrated; turbo props for regional destinations were bought, as were wide-body planes for international destinations, with code-sharing with Singapore Airlines.

In 2016, the Chinese HNA Group bought 13% of Virgin Australia holdings for A$159 million, thus opening the way to flights to Hong Kong and Beijing (which ended due to COVID-19 in 2020). Then also, New Zealand Airways sold its Virgin Australia shares and ended the partnership — only to resume it in 2024. The new CEO, Paul Scurrah, starting in 2019, had to do damage control over the COVID-19 crisis, as from March 2020, when only inland flights were possible. Like with Virgin Atlantic, this had come on top of earlier financial difficulties. So, he asked for A$1.4 billion in emergency credits from the government. When this was not forthcoming to any significant extent in April 2020 and even inland flights were grounded, Virgin Australia was suspended from the Australian Securities Exchange and entered into "voluntary insolvency". Already in June 2024, Bain Capital, which specialised in taking over suffering quality stock, acquired Virgin Australia, reducing the share of Virgin Group to 5%, announcing to cut down the airline to size and forcing Paul Scurrah out by October 2020 itself.

By April 2022, a new partnership was announced with United Airlines, ending the one with Delta after 20 years. In October 2023, it was announced that the airlines had become profitable again after 11 years of losses. In June 2024, state-owned Qatar Airlines declared its interest in a share of 20%. Since airlines are considered "critical services" in Australia, such a purchase must wisely first be screened and approved by the Australian Foreign Investment Review Board. Throughout its short and turbulent corporate history, first Virgin Blue, then V Australian and Virgin Australia had always been prominent in sponsoring sports teams and using their planes as paid-for flying advertisement boards for other consumer goods, thus creating free PR for themselves as well — just as Richard Branson continued to do.

Among the almost innumerable companies and joint ventures which Branson founded under the Virgin brand — they start from Virgin Active (fitness clubs in South Africa, the U.K. and Southern Europe) up to Virgin Wines (for online wine sales) — as mentioned above, most seem to have disappeared, sold or taken over. From his multiple memoirs and business testimonials, it seems to have been enough to chat him up with a brilliant-sounding business idea, best over a few drinks in his sky-high in-flight bars. Detailed business plans apparently were not necessary, as Branson did not need banking loans, but paid his share as an early venture capitalist for the joint venture from his own pocket. The main thing was that it should be fun to attack whatever business giant in whichever business line with a smart product in an unforeseen flank. Until such an angry giant, like Coca-Cola, woke up after he had outsold Coke in the U.K. and had all his Virgin Colas removed from British supermarket shelves, like Tesco's.

Two of his further creations stand out: Virgin Mobile USA, founded in 2000 in San Francisco, and Virgin Galactic, set up in 2004 in Las Cruces (New Mexico).

Virgin Mobile, with headquarters in Kansas City, was conceived as a low-market pay-as-you-go (no contract) mobile virtual network operator, a joint venture with Spirit Corporation. At its height in 2007, it had 8 million, mostly young, customers and 500 employees. Its 27.5 million shares were sold at $15 each. Whereupon the company went downhill, most staff were subsequently dismissed, and when Walmart stopped its retail presence in 2019, the remaining customer base was integrated with Boost Mobile in February 2020. End of story.

Virgin Galactic was supposed to open the outer space, or rather suborbital space, to exclusive tourism. The initial idea was to allow six passengers for the price of $200,000 each (with a down payment of $20,000) the adventure of three minutes of weightlessness at the height of 80 kilometres. Later, after a few deadly accidents and complications, in 2021 the ticket price was increased to $450,000, as the number of rich, risk-loving passengers had to be reduced to four. Virgin Galactic's Spaceport America opened in 2011 in New Mexico, but for a fee it is also open for scientific excursions. The Virgin Group still holds 26.3% of its capital.

As for the rest of Virgin-branded companies, the main criterion is who is still alive, who is not and who is taken over.

Virgin Orbit after a failed restructuring was sold in parts.

The family-friendly fitness chain Virgin Active was sold (80%) in 2015 to Brait SE.

◇ Brussels Airlines is now part of Lufthansa.
◇ Virgin Money (which offered Virgin credit cards and financial services) was sold to Nationwide Building Society in 2024.
◇ Virgin Records, the founding company, as mentioned, was sold to EMI.
◇ Virgin Megastores were taken over by HMV.

No longer in existence seem to be the following:

◇ Virgin Cinema, Virgin Games, Virgin Trains, Virgin Lightships, Virgin Student, Virgin Hyperloop, Virgin Clothing, Virgin Shop and Virgin Travelstore.

But still in existence, one way or the other, were the following:

◇ Virgin Oceanic (a submarine operator), Virgin Cosmetics, Virgin Books, Virgin Balloon Flights, Virgin Comics, Virgin Drinks (Virgin Cola and Virgin Vodka), Virgin Flowers, Virgin Holidays, Virgin Jewelry, Virgin Radio, … until Virgin Unite (a charity).

Undeterred Branson claims that these multiple, mixed adventures have not been able to do damage to the Virgin brand name.

In six easy-to-read short volumes, Branson has left his two-volume best-selling autobiography (the first until 2006 and his "second life" thereafter) and business wisdoms and insights, mostly consisting of his stories as a delinquent schoolboy who skipped university and business school and funny, encouraging business anecdotes. Much seems written by a ghostwriter or to have been dictated in a very haphazard way in a "how to" style ("Five secrets to starting a business"). One of them is never to work in an office and never to trust a banker. All this is meant to be inspiring to startup entrepreneurs who have already sufficient cash in their pockets (and are ready to lose some). But given the current prospects of his Virgin Group, with minority shareholdings in two mostly loss-making airlines and a very uncertain outlook for suborbital tourism, it is patiently not. His companies, for better or for worse, will probably be net zero carbon by 2050, as promised, provided that Virgin Galactic has also gone out of business by then.

Yet, there is still the 30-hectare tourist paradise of Necker Island in the Virgin Islands, owned by Branson, where a small luxury hotel and Balinese-style bungalows cater for the really affluent. Who wants to share a business idea with the master of the island over a drink or two?

Bibliography

Bower, T. *Branson*. London: Fourth Estate, 2000.

Branson, R. *Sir Richard Branson: The Autobiography*. London: Pearson Education Ltd, 1998.

Dearlove, D. *Business the Richard Branson Way: 10 Secrets of the World's Greatest Brand Builder*. 2nd ed. Oxford: Capstone, 2002.

The Economist, 11 January 1997.

Jackson, T. *Virgin King: Inside Richard Branson's Business Empire*. London: HarperCollins, 1995.

New Literature, 2nd Edition

Branson, R. *Screw It. Let's Do It. Expanded. Lessons in Life and in Business*. London: Penguin, 2006.

Branson, R. *Business Stripped Bare. Adventures of a Global Entrepreneur*. London: Virgin Books, 2010.

Branson, R. *Like a Virgin. Secrets They won't Teach at Business School*. London: Penguin, 2012.

Branson, R. *The Virgin Way: If it's not Fun, It's not Worth Doing*. New York: Penguin, 2014.

Branson, R. *Finding My Virginity*. New York: Penguin Random House, 2018.

Schmidle, N. *Test Gods. Virgin Galactic and the Making of a Modern Astronaut*. New York: Henry Holt, 2021.

Toyota: The Reluctant Multinational

Toyota Motor Corporation was founded by the Toyoda family in 1937. In 1997, it was the world's third-largest carmaker, holding 9.5% of the global auto shares after General Motors and Ford and by far the leader of all Japanese carmakers (*Business Week*, 7 April 1997). It is famous for being the most innovative automotive manufacturer in process technology and the most efficient in product development. Yet, Toyota lagged behind when compared to its other major Japanese competitors in international production and regional headquarters (Kumon, 1998). This was due to its prudent strategy of avoiding risky overseas ventures, the importance of its home market and its ultra-conservative financial and management policies, which might be a consequence of it being a traditional Japanese family business by origin. Fortunately, there was a change in the attitudes towards overseas investments when Toyota selected Hiroshi Okuda as the first non-family president of the company.[1] Other than investing in the automobile industry, Toyota is involved

[1] The first non-Toyoda in 45 years to hold this position in 1999, Okuda moved to the chairman's position (until 2006), *The Wall Street Journal*, 11 January 1999.

in other business segments, which include factory automation, semiconductors, design and manufacture of prefabricated housing, financial services, leisure boats and IT-related businesses and telecommunication.

In order to understand the company, it is helpful to look at their corporate motto. Toyota's motto stipulates creating an affluent society and improving the quality of life through the automobile (Basu, 1999). Therefore, Toyota emphasises the quality of its products which will be offered to consumers at a reasonable price. It also aims to be a good corporate citizen by donating money to five main sponsorship activities: education, international exchange, environment, arts and culture and local communities.

Origins of Toyota Motor Corporation

The founder, Sakichi Toyoda, son of a poor carpenter, set up the Toyoda Automatic Loom Works in 1926. He was also known as the King of Inventors, who had 84 patents for his inventions. He was a humble person who lived by the maxims of labour, gratitude and service, which would serve as the guidelines for the group's policies and activities (Toyota Motor Corporation, 1988). Kiichiro Toyoda, his son, majored in mechanical engineering and saw how popular cars were in the U.S. and Europe. Therefore, he decided to set up his own automobile company, Toyota Motor Company, in 1937 using capital obtained from the sale of the rights of his father's automatic loom to a British company, the Platt Brothers. The first prototype automobile was produced. It was a Model A1 passenger car with a Type A engine.

However, after the Second World War, Toyota was on the brink of bankruptcy due to high inflation. It decided to seek help from the Nagoya Branch of the Bank of Japan. But the rescue came at a very high price, as the marketing organisation had to be split off as an independent company, Toyota Motor Sales. Worst of all, a labour dispute culminating in a two-month strike took place in 1950 in response to the substantial personnel cuts initiated by the bank (Basu, 1999). It was only in 1982 that Toyota Motor Corporation and Toyota Motor Sales of Japan merged into one entity again, the Toyota Motor Corporation.

As the company grew in the post-war era, exports became a major part of Toyota's business, thus leading to its venture into the U.S. in 1957 with the establishment of Toyota Motor Sales USA. In the meantime, in order to secure the local market, Chubu Nippon Drivers' School was established in 1957 as part of Toyota's marketing strategy, as it was very difficult to obtain driving licences in Japan (Toyota Motor Corporation, 1988). When more Japanese obtained their driving licences, there would be more demand from these new drivers for Toyota cars. It then also sponsored motorcar rallies and shows to enhance the reputation of its product as a durable and reliable car.

Corporate Culture

Toyota's corporate culture is deeply rooted in oriental philosophical values and beliefs. It stipulates a harmonious existence with the communities but, at the same time, is equally aggressive towards its competitors to gain higher market shares in the Japanese and global markets. Yet, corporate acquisitions and large takeovers are anathema. This culture is consistent with the Confucian values of harmony, order and serving others for the greater good of the society.

Management Style

Toyota is a traditional family-run business that emphasises its obligations towards its workers, customers and suppliers. Japan is a web society, where there is great interdependence between all members of a group and an abundance of moral and social obligations, both vertically and horizontally (Lewis, 1999). It has a masculine corporate culture with no female, foreign or outside directors on the nation's biggest company board, consisting of 58 members. It also sees very little need to listen to its shareholders, as 40% of the total shares in Toyota are held by Japanese banks and financial institutions, in which Toyota also has sizable holdings. Therefore, the top management of the company retains the key decision-making authority. The management of the company is strongly segmented on a functional basis, with managers having the responsibility for the major vertical operating functions. This causes serious problems, as every division works hard but is poorly coordinated, thus causing inefficiencies, unnecessary tensions and frustrations.

Toyota's Production System

Everyone works desperately, hoping that he is not a burden to others.

— Sachs, 1994, p. 102

Toyota sees the building of vehicles as a community project. There is an emphasis on the quality and the price of its products. Its success is linked to its process technology, the "just-in-time" production system, where all resources are minimised and constantly in use. This system has three components: *Kan-Ban*, *heijunka* and *jidoka*, which allow a functionally flexible workforce and products, customised production runs and shorter cycle times and quality control. *Kan-ban* is a process whereby material and components are supplied to the production assembly line just in time for production. This helps minimise waste and reduce the storage of unnecessary parts, thus reducing inventory cost. Secondly, the production system involves level production or *heijunka* and continuous flow production. Lastly, *jidoka* is incorporated too to monitor the automated production processes for abnormalities and strives to achieve zero defects (Basu, 1999).

However, there are certainly flaws to the just-in-time system, as it is vulnerable to delays and defects. There was an intensification of work, especially when the idle time of the workers in Toyota was reduced from 75 seconds to 45 seconds. There is also multi-tasking, including various unskilled tasks. This system works only when there is a cooperative relationship between trade unions and management. After the initial turmoil of the post-war years, the industrial trade unions in Japan have subordinated the interests of their workers to suit corporate goals, such as those of Toyota (Sach, 1994). There is strong peer pressure among the production workers in Toyota to keep up with the line, as all workers are forced to work overtime if the production quotas are not met and the production allowance risks being cut. It is set according to the amount of labour it takes a given team to reach its production quota. Quality circles[2] (QCs) and suggestion drives implemented by Toyota do not increase the autonomy of the workers, as the management still makes all the decisions and even sets the agenda for QCs. The main advantages of becoming a production worker at Toyota lay in the security of long-term employment, above average pay, the high bonuses, which could be up to 50% of the normal monthly pay, and corporate retirement pensions, which were lost in case the employer was changed.

Overseas Investment

Toyota used to be a very conservative company whose overseas ventures focused mainly on the search for export channels and local distributors for its products. Nonetheless, its approach changed

[2]A quality circle is a small group composed of employees who meet regularly to make suggestions on quality control and production rationalisation.

when faced with the impact of globalisation, protectionist pressures in the importing regions (U.S., EU, etc.) and the growing strength of its auto rivals. Toyota then reluctantly started to believe in localising its operations to provide customers with the products they need.

Investment in the U.S.

In 1981, voluntary restrictions on Japanese automobile exports to the U.S. were initiated (Toyota Motor Corporation, 1988). In response to the protectionist actions from the U.S. government, Toyota decided to enter into a 50-50 joint venture with General Motors to reduce the risk of establishing plants in the U.S. This cooperation would also allow Toyota to accumulate experience in local production in the U.S. This joint venture was marked with the official start of New United Motor Manufacturing, Inc. (NUMMI), capitalised at 200 million dollars at the Fremont plant in California (Toyota Motor Corporation, 1988). In starting the company, NUMMI emphasises teamwork and mutual trust between labour and management, by adopting an "open office" floor plan, the use of a single cafeteria for all employees and common parking facilities for everyone. The company also used a just-in-time production system for the body line. In January 1986, Toyota established Toyota Motor Manufacturing USA, Inc. (TMMU) and Toyota Motor Manufacturing Canada, Inc. (TMMC) for its operations in the U.S. and Canada, which subsequently set up four other plants in North America. In addition, Toyota introduced a luxury line in the U.S. — the Lexus — in 1989 to shed its cheaper-price and lower-quality image in the American market. Toyota's strategy in launching the Lexus division was to make a luxury car that demonstrates high technology and high quality and support it with the best service to gain high customer satisfaction (Basu, 1999). The consumer response towards the Lexus was overwhelming, with annual sales of more than 150,000 units in 1998, surpassing Honda, Nissan and BMW. Camry, another

U.S.-produced Toyota automobile, became the number one selling passenger car in the U.S. in 1997 and 1998 and remains one of the bestsellers of Toyota (*Business Week*, 7 April 1997).

Investment in Europe

The European market holds much potential for Toyota, and it demands only the finest products. Toyota is a latecomer in the European market, with plants set up in the U.K., Portugal, Turkey and the Central and Eastern Europe (CEE) regions.

Decision to Invest in the Czech Republic

Toyota expanded quickly only after 1999 into CEE to take advantage of the opportunities there. The Czech Republic offers low production costs and stable economic factors, and its European Union (EU) membership in 2004 provides access to EU markets. Kolin may not seem to be the best deal as Czech workers already earn more than three times compared to those in Romania, and their wages are still rising (*Business Week*, 15 November 2002). But the productivity of the Czech workforce is surely a compensating factor. The Czech Republic is home to the 100-year-old Skoda, which was acquired by Volkswagen (VW) in 1991. VW introduced Western quality controls and work habits to its Czech labour force and further built a network of Czech suppliers, who have since provided half its input by value. When Toyota decided on the location of its new plant, the Czech government granted generous investment packages to the new joint plant of Toyota and PSA. The plant would get public support worth 5–15% of its investment value, that is, €75–225 million (*CTK Business News Wire*, 7 January 2002). Likewise, the packages included a token fee of CKr 1 billion for the site and free infrastructure in line with EU competition legislation (*Global News Wire*, 7 January 2002). Job creation and training grants were also given, and Toyota was exempted from paying corporate tax for 10 years. All these government incentives were a significant pull factor drawing Toyota to invest in the country.

Strategy

Toyota entered into a joint venture with PSA Peugeot Citroen of France, the European champion of diesel cars, for the production of small cars at the $1.35 billion factory in Kolin in 2001. It was the largest single greenfield investment in the Czech industry ever. Starting in 2005, the plant assembled 300,000 minicars a year, all priced under $7,500, which was 50% less than Toyota's Yaris, its entry-level model for the European market (*Business Week*, 15 April 2002). This joint venture was seen as the best and most cost-effective way to obtain a substantial market share rapidly rather than acquisitions and takeovers of existing plants which remain anathema to Toyota. PSA and Toyota had split the investment costs and hoped to generate healthy margins by pooling their expertise in engine and emissions technology. In this joint venture, Toyota was responsible for the production, while PSA Peugeot was in charge of marketing. For Toyota, this investment was an important brand-building exercise to raise its then 4% share of the European market. Its strategy was to Europeanise design, production and marketing, so that Toyota was seen as a European car, like Opel (which is in fact American, being a GM subsidiary) or Volkswagen. The high quality of the diesel engines produced by the French company was able to command a better price for its diesel models, as PSA was the European champion of diesel cars, which contributed 49.5% of the carmakers' volume in 2001 (*Financial Times*, 9 July 2001).

Toyota's greenfield investment enables it to build its production system from scratch, thus allowing a full utilisation of its modern technology. Toyota's distinctive and highly efficient manufacturing technology of just-in-time systems leads to a horizontal spillover to the local workforce by improving their productivity and to a vertical spillover to the consumers with a rise in the product standards. PSA/Toyota's Kolin car plant also led the entry of other Japanese car component suppliers, such as TRCZ, Tris and Aoyama Seisakusho, into the region, thus providing new employment and training opportunities to the local workforce. The new Kolin-based plant created about 3,000 jobs and an increase in the number of indirect jobs. Toyota's investment venture in the Czech Republic will, in the long run, enhance the benefits for the workers in the automobile sector, also as a result of the entries of the international suppliers.

Toyota's Economic Involvement in Poland

The Czech project has prompted Toyota to raise investment in its engine and transmission plant in Walbrzych (Waldenburg), Poland, from €100 million to €400 million[3] (*Automotive News Europe*, 11 March 2002). It also built another 60-million-pound gearbox-and-engine plant in Poland to supply the Czech-based operation. The Walbrzych facility in Silesia became Toyota's largest auto components factory and should conclude the process of building the pillars of Toyota's production activities in Europe. The decision to supply car components from Poland resulted from the good infrastructure linking Poland to the Czech Republic, thus allowing for lower transportation cost of components. Furthermore, a 110-million-pound engine plant was set up in Wroclaw (Breslau), Poland, creating 350 jobs, which served the forecasted upturn in demand in Eastern Europe and supplied its plants in the U.K. and Turkey. These greenfield investments offered an opportunity to upgrade the quality of the domestic car component suppliers, as cooperation with Toyota stimulated horizontal spillovers

[3] This project added 300,000 engines and 50,000 transmissions to the 250,000 gearboxes already planned.

of technology. However, in the Polish case, spillover benefits are believed to be patchy due to the limitations of the local banking system. Bank loans are subjected to higher interest rates that hamper the development of local suppliers. Nonetheless, this project created new job opportunities in a country which was then troubled by high unemployment. Toyota has now localised the production of its European cars by also setting up component plants in Poland, but the positive contribution of such production continues to depend greatly on the policies of the government pertaining to upgrading human and technical capabilities of the local suppliers.

Investment in Asia

The first area chosen by Toyota to develop export channels and assembly operations was Southeast Asia due to its proximity to its headquarters in Japan and cheap labour costs. In the early 1990s, many of the Southeast Asian countries had requested Toyota to manufacture automobiles and trucks in their countries.

Toyota spent two years in discussions and negotiations with these countries. Finally, Toyota announced the ASEAN Complementary Program and set up four companies. Toyota decided to build the manufacturing plant for diesel engines in Thailand. The transmission business was given to the Philippines. The steering wheel system production went to Malaysia (Basu, 1999). Its strategy in Asia is to sell sturdy and simply designed cars to withstand the rigours of the local roads. In Singapore, Toyota cooperated with a distributor, Borneo Motors, and a new slogan was created, which stated, "Together, we must be the best". Gateway, one of its plants in Thailand, was rated as Toyota's best factory in the world. The factory employed about 1,800 people who bolted Toyota Camrys and Corollas together, alongside the new Vios. The production lines were capable of producing a complete car every two minutes, while parts shops stamped out enough bumpers and body panels for export as spares to Southeast Asia (*The Straits Times*, 18 January 2003).

Impact of Globalisation on Toyota

There was a major reorganisation and restructuring of the company by Okuda after he was appointed president of Toyota Motor Corporation. Toyota terrified its rivals by announcing the development of its recently launched Ipsum in record 15 months. The designers at Toyota have probably hit the human limit for product development (*Business Week*, 7 April 1997). The company has also created another breakthrough in making affordable hybrid engines that rely on both electric batteries and gasoline. In fact, product cycle speed-up is just one facet of Okuda's strategy to rekindle the killer instinct at Toyota. Other means include extending Toyota's edge in high speed, flexible car-making, shaking up the company's insular, consensus-driven culture and pursuing the most aggressive overseas expansion in automotive industry (*Business Week*, 7 April 1997). First, he reduced the size of its 58 board members, in order to improve management efficiency. Toyota also relocated its production from the home market to larger potential markets with cheaper labour costs, such as India, China, South America and Eastern Europe, where there are fewer cars on the roads. This decentralisation was necessary, as sales in Japan had saturated.

To the Japanese, the company is sacred. Once the employees are accepted, they show complete loyalty to the company, and this loyalty in theory and traditional post-war practice is rewarded with life-time employment and regular promotion to important positions, regardless of their effectiveness (Lewis, 1999). However, the impact of globalisation and Japan's structural crisis has forced an overhaul of the wage and promotion system. It is now increasingly linked to the performance of the employees rather than their seniority. Many older executives have been stripped of fancy titles and are given narrower responsibilities in order to create more opportunities for younger executives.

In order for Toyota to improve its profitability, there has to be more efficiency and productivity improvements in the decision-making process of Toyota executives. Evidence indicates that decisions still continue to be made mostly on a regional and divisional basis rather than on a global and company-wide basis. Therefore, a circle "I" team was created to tackle the significant issues beyond the prevailing divisional business units on a company-wide basis (Basu, 1999).

A business reform campaign was launched in 1993 after the plunge of Toyota's profitability, which targeted the productivity of white-collar workers by reducing the entire white-collar workforce in Japan by 20%. Toyota had been adding large numbers of top students graduating from prestigious Japanese universities. These people moved up the ranks by way of promotion based on seniority. These past practices have produced a glut of middle managers with little room to move up further (Basu, 1999). Therefore, in order to keep up with its rivals, Toyota reduced the number of new recruits and prepared attractive packages to entice early retirement. It limited the number of working hours and forced the employees to take their vacation entitlements. Operating budgets for most divisions were reduced by 5% per year. Thus, overtime work among white-collar workers was disallowed unless critically needed. Annual raises and bonuses were either severely reduced or cancelled.

Nonetheless, the decision to dismiss white-collar workers was not fully pursued, as it was in conflict with Toyota's responsibilities and social obligations as the industrial leader in Japanese society. It would have violated its long-practiced corporate values, such as family feeling and lifetime employment. Toyota's financial performance acts as a bellwether of the Japanese economy, and its performance affects confidence in the Japanese economy. The business reform proposal was a unique solution, as no one was fired, but redundant staff was deployed to Business Reform (BR) groups. These groups were assigned special tasks within the divisions, which included new business areas, new product areas and projects to consolidate the tasks of the divisions. Individuals from the BR groups were transferred to new markets such as China, Southeast Asia and Eastern Europe (Basu, 1999). This whole episode shows that Toyota still compromises profitability in view of its social obligations to its employees, while other Japanese companies such as Nissan, Mazda and Toshiba had laid off permanent employees in large numbers.

Toyota's Challenges of the 2000s

> *Toyota cannot control the wind, so it changes the position of its sail to catch the wind.*
>
> — Basu, 1999

Toyota will continue to be an influential global carmaker, after the successful restructuring of the company by Hiroshi Okuda. However, the benefits created by the restructuring process might be limited due to its social obligations to its employees and the Japanese society. Toyota has been flexible as an Asian company to adapt to the changes that are occurring now due to the impact of globalisation. One significant issue which remains unanswered is whether Toyota will change its focus in the near future from employee care to customer care under the severe pressures of the recession in Japan and the global competition.

Toyota faces the danger of being successful overseas while losing its top position in Japan. As most of the fat profits come almost entirely from the U.S., Japan, which accounts for 41% of vehicle sales, is contributing less to the bottom line. Honda, one-third of Toyota's size, has taken a big bite out of Toyota's sales in Japan with the successful launch of its Odyssey minivan and CR-V four-wheel-drive sports utility car (*Business Week*, 27 March 2002). That was bad news to Toyota, as it has long relied on robust Japanese earnings to finance its global expansion.

Its youth strategy is highly ineffective, as it took Toyota three years to launch a follow-up after it made a splash in Japan with the affordable Vitz subcompact. In the meantime, Honda and Nissan had grabbed significant market shares with their Fit and March, respectively, and were then leading the subcompact market (*Business Week*, 27 March 2002). Toyota also launched six sedans in Japan with the intention of stealing upwardly mobile customers from BMW and Honda, but it was a flop. Both Verossa and Will are only selling half of what they were targeted. Toyota failed because it has no real brand strategy in Japan, unlike its clearly defined Lexus and Toyota marques in the U.S.

Toyota has called for tough measures to reconquer its market share in Japan by selling minicars (made by affiliate Daihatsu Motors) in its showrooms to attract the younger generation and by offering cash rebates: $800 each to buyers of five flagging models, including the Verossa and Will (*Business Week*, 27 March 2002). To survive the competition, Toyota needs to be even more radical by streamlining its lineup and distribution networks and to come up with a new brand strategy by producing more new hits to cater to all age groups.

The Next Two Decades: Toyota as the World's Number One

After having completed his successful restructuring and innovation plans, Okada was replaced by Fujio Cho (1999–2005), under whose management Ford was bypassed in terms of the number of cars sold. His successor, Katsuyaki Watanabe (2005–2009), managed to do the same with General Motors, greatly aided by the latter's unfortunate model policy and management mistakes with 9 million cars sold in 2008. His deputy in 2005 became Akio Toyoda, then aged 48, who had successfully developed Toyota's difficult China business, foreshadowing that, in a few years, the world's largest car company would be led by a member of the founder family again. This duly happened in July 2009 with Toyota's first ever losses, following the Asian crisis of 2008, which, according to Toyoda, almost led to the collapse of the company.

Yet, his rescue plan worked. In 2020, Toyota became the world's largest car company again, this time ahead of Volkswagen with 9.3 million vehicles sold. They were produced in 12 factories in Japan plus in another 51 worldwide in 26 countries by a total of 377,000 staff (2022). Turnover by then reached €200 billion, with net profits aided by a weak yen amounting to some €25 billion, making Toyota easily the world's most valuable car company. This led Akio Toyoda in 2024 to complain that Toyota had become a money maker (known as "Zaitech" during the bubble years until 1990) and less a maker of cars.

Yet, it was not all smooth sailing. In 2010, there was a series of recalls: 4.1 million cars in the U.S. and Europe due to problems with the accelerator clutch. The U.S. National Highway Traffic Authority claimed that it had caused more than 200 accidents with 34 deaths. Yet there were none in Europe. In the end, Toyota was forced to pay $1.2 billion as indemnities. Soon after, it had to recall 440,000 Prius hybrid models in the U.S. People involved in accidents claimed that the brakes had not worked — nice try! Some of these driving geniuses seemed to have confused the throttle with the brake. In consequence, Toyota improved its quality management and promised quicker reactions to consumer complaints. In 2022, it became known that its subsidiary company, Daihatsu, a maker of small and compact cars, had faked safety and emission test results for years. Sales for a while were interrupted. Then, the same story emerged with truck-maker Hino and finally with the diesel engines of flagship Toyota itself. Root causes are the rigid hierarchies of a very traditional Japanese corporate giant, unremitting time and conformity pressures without adequate means to express criticism internally or report mistakes, plus the strong dependency of suppliers on Toyota. As Japanese customs require in such cases, Akio Toyoda bowed deeply to the public and his shareholders in atonement and promised repentance. But how he would do it remained very vague.

Toyota has always been a conglomerate of its own. Its core car business apart, inter alia, it also produces prefabricated houses and boats, offers financial services, runs driving schools, and runs Japan's second-largest mobile network. But on cars, it produces the full range, from mini cars to monster trucks. Let's take a look:

- ◊ Mini cars, like Toyota Aygo (since 2005).
- ◊ Small cars, like Toyota Yaris (since 1999).
- ◊ Compact cars, like best-selling Toyota Corolla (since 1966 in variations, including hybrid).
- ◊ Medium class cars, like Toyota Corona (since 1957) and Toyota Mirai (since 2014).
- ◊ Upper medium, like Toyota Camry (since 1980, also bestselling in the U.S.).
- ◊ Coupes, like Toyota GR 68 (since 2021).
- ◊ Sports cars and roadsters, like GR Supra (since 2019).
- ◊ SUVs and pick-ups, like Toyota Land Cruiser (since 1950) and Toyota Hilux (since 1968); being indestructible, it is well-liked by rebel and terrorist armies in West Asia and North Africa as "the poor man's cavalry".
- ◊ Compact vans, like the seven-seater Toyota Proace City (since 2020).
- ◊ Vans, like Toyota Hiace (since 1967).
- ◊ Finally, of course, its luxury brand Lexus (since 1989).

Two fully controlled, de facto subsidiaries with Toyota management are Daihatsu, a maker of small and compact cars, and Hino, the truck maker. Since October 2005, a cooperation agreement has existed with Fuji heavy Industries (trucks) and Subaru (medium cars), with a 16.5% capital participation from Toyota, and, since August 2017, a similar arrangement has existed with Mazda (compact and medium cars), with Toyota having 5.5% of its shares and Mazda 0.25% the other way round — just to show who is the master and who is not.

Toyota over the years has also built up a tightly controlled network with its primary suppliers, including capital tie-ups and management transfers, such as with Aichi Steel Works, Aisin Seiki, Denso and Toyo Tyre.

Toyota remains a major sponsor of rallies and motorsports following its successful slogan: "Nothing is impossible". It had its own formula one team in 2002, but exited in 2009, due to high costs and its own financial difficulties at the time.

During the COVID-19 crisis, like all other Japanese carmakers, Toyota faced temporary factory closures, also due to shortages of chips for engine management and driver assistance. Global sales went down by 5%, but recovered most quickly in China, with plus 30% and 2 million more cars sold than in 2020. Toyota in consequence also adjusted its celebrated just-in-time "Kanban" system for crucial chips. It now maintains stocks to last for at least four months!

On the e-mobility issue Toyota, like the rest of the Japanese car industry, remains agnostic (like most Japanese on religious subjects). On the one hand, they are pioneers, squeezed as they are between the Korean and Chinese competitions. Thus, Toyota, as early as in 1997, produced the first hybrid version of Prius (Volkswagen did so only in 2020). In 2021, it made the first hydrogen version of the Mirai and invested €15 billion in battery development. Already in 2020, Toyota (and Lexus) had sold 2.2 million electric cars worldwide. Yet, like the rest of the Japanese industry, it wisely remains open-minded for open-ended technological innovations and solutions — unlike Chinese and European political dogmatists on e-mobility — with e-fuels, hydrogen and hybrid. The current focus is on hybrids with small batteries and fuel-efficient motors, with drivers running about 60–80% electric. When in November 2021, at the World Climate Summit in Glasgow, carmakers GM, Ford, Daimler and (the Chinese-owned) Volvo solemnly announced that from 2040, they would no longer produce any fuel-driven cars, the Japanese — like a few others — wisely abstained. Not only is the CO_2 balance of e-car production and disposal highly problematic and so are their fire risks in tunnels, on ferries and during loading in garages. Most importantly, there will be a lasting shortage of loading stations and reliable electricity in much of the world outside the narrow confines of East Asia, Western Europe and North America. When Russian transportation officials were asked by their European Commission counterparts back in 2020 (when they were still talking), in the presence of this author whether they had loading facilities in great Russia for courageous e-drivers from Eastern Europe, the answer was: "Yes, of course. One in St. Petersburg, one in Moscow and one in Vladivostok". So much for Russian humour.

The individual mobility concepts of Japanese automakers however do not stop at cars. They already developed and publicly presented prototypes, such as that of electrical pilotless passenger drones, electrical walking aids, e-scooters, which cannot drop, and high-tech chairs climbing stairs, with Toyota being in the lead. So watch this space.

Bibliography

Basu, S. *Corporate Purpose: Why It Matters More than Strategy*. New York and London: Garland Publishing, Inc., 1999.

Kumon, H. "Overseas Production Activities of Toyota Motor", in Mirza, H. (ed.) *Global Competitive Strategies in the New World Economy: Multilaterism, Regionalisation and the Transitional Firm*. UK: Edward Elgar Publishing Ltd, 1998.

Lewis, D. R. *When Cultures Collide: Managing Successfully across Cultures*. London: Naperville, Ill., 1999.

Sachs, B. *Reorganising Work: The Evolution of Work Changes in the Japanese and Swedish Automobile Industries*. New York and London: Garland Publishing, Inc., 1994.

Toyota Motor Corporation. *Toyota: A History of the First 50 Years*. Japan: Toyota Motor Corporation, 1988.

New Literature, 2nd Edition

Finsterbusch, S. "Generationenwechsel bei Toyota", *Frankfurter Allgemeine*, 10 February 2005.

Finsterbusch, S. "Der Steuermann", *Frankfurter Allgemeine*, 11 May 2006.

Hubmann, D. "So erfindet sich Japans Autoindustrie neu", *Kleine Zeitung*, 31 October 2023.

Hübner, L. and Holzapfel, A. "Das Kanban-System bei Toyota", in: Rothacher, A. (ed.) *Die Rückkehr der Samurai. Japans Wirtschaft nach der Krise*. Heidelberg: Springer, 2007, pp. 86–94.

Kanning, T. "Toyodas kraftlose Ansage", *Frankfurter Allgemeine*, 8 February 2024.

Liker, J. K. *The Toyota Way*. New York: McGraw-Hill, 2004.

Lill, F. "Japans Autobauer gehen eigene Wege", *Die Presse*, 29 December 2021.

Rothacher, A. "The Rise and Fall of Labour-Management Consultations (Roshi Kyogisei) in Japan", in: Berger, S., Priess, L., Wanöffel, M. (eds.) *The Palgrave International Handbook on Workers' Participation*. London, 2018, pp. 419–436.

Sato, M. *The Toyota Leaders. An Executive Guide*. New York: Vertical, 2008.

"Toyota verkauft mehr als 2 Millionen Elektroautos", *Frankfurter Allgemeine*, 14 May 2021.

Völker, T. "Toyotas hybrider Weg: Das Schicksal der Dinosaurier vermeiden", *Die Presse am Sonntag*, 15 December 2021.

Woon, L. J. "Toyota: Weltkonzern wider Willen", in: Rothacher, A. (ed.) *Die Rückkehr der Samurai. Japans Wirtschaft nach der Krise*. Heidelberg: Springer, 2007, pp. 181–189.

Fiat: The Festa is Over

Fix It Again Tony.
— popular American pun on FIAT

In its heydays in the mid-1980s, FIAT produced close to 4 million cars, held a 60% share of the Italian car market, and as a group produced 5% of the GDP of Italy. With a 14% share of the EU's car market, it was Europe's largest car producer by volume, even ahead of Volkswagen. Its political influence until the early 1990s permitted import protection from Japanese and Korean competitors in the Italian market, the much delayed obligatory introduction of the catalytic converters and plenty of public subsidies, including scrapping funds introduced by the government of Romano Prodi in 1997 (then inducing customers to buy new Fiats with catalysts). Not by accident *La Stampa*, the Fiat-owned daily, had led the campaign to vote for Prodi's left-of-centre Ulivo list. When Giovanni Agnelli, Fiat's honorary chairman and *capo famigli* of the owning clan died in January 2003 at age 81, he was mourned in the streets of Turin by 200,000 people. Obituaries likened him to an "uncrowned King of Italy".

Yet, by the time of his death, Fiat Auto was haemorrhaging cash. Past policies to cut R&D had left the automaker without a competitive new model. The capital accumulated during good years had been spent on a diffuse diversification binge.

Sitting on €50 billion of loans downgraded to junk bond status, Fiat's friendly Italian bankers were turning less friendly. As General Motors, Fiat's minority shareholder, was unwilling to exercise its put option to purchase the car operator, Umberto Agnelli, Giovanni's younger brother, was forced to sell his group's most profitable assets to reduce the debt mountain. The turnaround of the Fiat group's core car operations, however, still remains to be seen.

Fiat started out in style. In 1899, eight bored rich young gentlemen decided in a trendy Turin café to set up a joint company to produce fashionable new automobiles. One of them was Giovanni Agnelli, the son of a large landlord, who was trained at a military academy. He had left the military at age 23 as a first lieutenant of the cavalry. He first set up a ball-bearing plant, RIV, which today is part of SKF.

The new company was called Fabbrica Italiana Automobili Torino (FIAT). It started by copying Mercedes engines. By 1901, 150 workers already manufactured 73 cars with a strength of 2 PS being able to speed up to 35 km/h. As one of Italy's then 30 car producers (including Alfa Romeo and Lancia, both today part of Fiat Auto), Fiat grew happily, allowing it to go public during 1906–1907. In a mysterious operation, its stock price crashed, allowing Agnelli, who acted also as chief executive officer, to buy out cheaply his erstwhile business partners. Later, the share values duly recovered.

When Turin's public prosecutor investigated the incidence, Giovanni Agnelli briefly resigned as CEO but later resumed his functions as an undisputed majority shareholder when no charges were filed.

Fiat built racing cars, running up to 100 km/h. More importantly, it supplied trucks for the Italian expeditionary forces, which, in 1911, moved into Libya against the Ottoman Empire. During the First World War, it benefited handsomely from military procurement, producing ship engines, trucks and other military vehicles. By 1917, Fiat had grown into Italy's third-largest industrial enterprise. During 1914–1918, the numbers of its workers, which stood at 4,000 at the start of the war, grew tenfold. Although Italy emerged on the winning side of the First World War, there was widespread social discontent, public disillusionment with the conduct of the war and criticism of war profiteering. Fiat was an obvious target. By 1920, Turin had become one of the focal points for post-war labour troubles. As part of the communist uprising in post-war Europe, following the October Revolution in Russia, armed Red Guards occupied the Fiat and Lancia car plants in Turin. Some 13,000 workers were involved. Violent fights with deaths ensued.

In 1922, Mussolini took power. His blackshirts had provided useful protection for the industrial plants and helped end civic strife. Although liberal minded as an industrial capitalist, Giovanni Agnelli had to coexist with Fascist rule to assure social stability and continued corporate growth. By 1929, Fiat had become Italy's largest industrial plant, producing 40,000 cars (60% of Italy's output) per year. As leader of a showcase modern industry, Agnelli was appointed senator for life. Aided by Italy's policies of autarchy, Fiat then diversified into steel manufacturing, aviation, shipbuilding and road construction. With Italy's attack on Ethiopia in 1935, armament orders came pouring in again. In 1936, Fiat designed its "Fiat 500", the "Topolino", as the people's car, of which until 1955, 510,000 vehicles would be built. Its new Mirafiori plants by 1939 represented state-of-the-art Taylorist modernism. Soon 22,000 of Fiat's total of 70,000 workers worked there. Mirafiori and the RIV ball-bearing factory were soon hit by Allied bombing raids. As the tide of war turned against the Axis powers, worker unrest began to spread. By March 1943, there were strikes for higher wages, better food supplies and the delivery of promised government aid for the victims of the bombings. In the confused and sometimes surreal agony of Fascist Italy, Giovanni Agnelli and his faithful administrator, Valesio Valleta, had walked a skilful tightrope act between the ruling Fascists, the German occupation army and the Communist underground, which had re-established its party cells in the Fiat works. After the war, in August 1945, Communist partisans were about to expropriate Fiat, yet U.S. occupation officers objected. In December 1945, Giovanni Agnelli died after having been acquitted of charges of collaborating with the Fascists. His only son, Eduardo, who had been married to a fairly non-conformist princess, had already been killed in a sea plane accident back in 1935.

Giovanni then had obtained the legal guardianship over his three grandchildren: Giovanni ("Gianni") (1921–2003); Susanna, in the mid-1990s serving as a Foreign Minister in Italy; and Umberto (1934–2004). Gianni was favoured by his grandfather as his successor. He was universally described as tough, intelligent and charming. After a gilded youth hobnobbing with Europe's interwar aristocracy and grand bourgeoisie, Gianni served as a lieutenant with Italy's expeditionary corps in Russia and North Africa before apparently defecting to the Partisans. After the war, he remained strongly disinclined to engage himself in business, which he left in the able hands of Valetta. He rather indulged himself into a well-publicised lifestyle of the new post-war jet-set, consorting with Hollywood stars such as Rita Haywood and Anita Ekberg. Corporate duties were limited to his presidency of the family-owned Juventus Turin football club (1946–1966). In 1953, he married a beautiful Neapolitan princess with expensive tastes. Compulsive partying with beautiful women and fast cars lasted until 1966, when at the relatively mature age of 45, he began to take his corporate and dynastic duties more seriously. Valleta, who had almost despaired about Gianni's lifestyle and business disinterest, had retired in 1964, aged 83, and died in 1967. After the Second World War, he had to weather a fair amount of labour troubles. In 1948, armed unionists locked him in his office for days. In 1950, a bomb exploded in the Mirafiori plant. In 1952, a senior Fiat manager was murdered. Many of the workers at Fiat and other Turin plants were migrants from Southern Italy. They lived in poor, overcrowded areas, were unwelcome by their Northern countrymen and flocked by the thousands to the communists and their militant trade unions, which had easy answers and promises to their despairing living conditions. Valletta reacted by offering Fiat's 140,000 employees a fair share of prosperity. He provided them with vacation homes, kindergartens, training courses and excursions to remote places such as Lourdes, a Catholic faith healing spa in the Pyrenees. Fiat was also known to pay better wages than other industries.

In 1955, the Fiat 600 was introduced, and in 1956, the Autostrada del Sole was opened. The new Fiat model (and the smaller Fiat 124) thus became the symbol of the new motorisation of Italy's young and working-class families as they moved from scooters to cars.

As Gianni reasserted family control, he introduced U.S.-style assembling and controlling operations in the late 1960s. By that time, there was trouble on the labour front again. The 1968 student rebellion in Italy spread to the working classes as well, part of which felt alienated from the PCI's then moderated Eurocommunist orientation. For militant students and anarchist workers in the late 1960s, Fiat with its autocratic leadership was easily public enemy number one. The militant labour fights starting in 1969 were no longer controlled by the PCI and its unions but by sympathisers of the Red Brigades and other violent communist sects. When Agnelli tried to fire 122 militant workers, he was forced to rehire them in a government-brokered peace plan. This was not to last. In 1973, the Mirafiori plants were occupied by armed workers, who held out for one week against the assaults of the carabinieri. Physical attacks on plants and managers multiplied. There was a need for continuous protection by bodyguards and the police for all Agnelli family members and senior management, affecting their way of life, with residences rebuilt into fortresses. In Italy, at least for them, *dolce vita* was no longer possible. Nonetheless, terrorists managed to kill four Fiat managers and wound 27 others, mostly by kneecapping.

In Agnelli's view, Fiat had become the victim of Italy's societal crisis, as political scandals eroded public confidence and public services deteriorated. Elected chairman of Confidustia, the association of Italy's employers, in 1974, Agnelli negotiated the (in)famous *scala mobile*, an agreement with inflation-indexed automatic wage increases: it staved off workers' unrest and bought time at best. As it also eroded Italy's competitiveness and the lira's value, it took a lot of political courage to rid the country off the *scala mobile* one decade later.

During the 1970s, a successful model, the Fiat 127, was on the market. Yet, when the oil crisis of 1974–1975 hit Italy and Fiat sales hard, Agnelli reacted in strange ways. He used Fiat's cash reserves for an ill-advised diversification into the production of buses and trains. In 1975, he also invited Carol De Benedetti (then owner of Olivetti) as a crisis manager in return for 5% of Fiat's shares. After three months, it became known that De Benedetti tried to purchase a relative majority of shares via strawmen. Then, Agnelli terminated the relationship, whereupon in 1976, another strange bedfellow entered as a major shareholder: none other than Libyan Colonel Gaddhafi purchased 9% of Fiat's shares for $415 million. It took a lot of U.S. pressure and the help of Deutsche Bank to buy out the Libyans for a multiple of their original investment at $3.1 billion one decade later.

In 1979, absenteeism rates at Fiat's workforce had increased to 20%. Labour troubles mounted again as 61 employees were fired due to alleged terrorist contacts. Reduced sales and increased debts forced Fiat in 1980 to dismiss 16,000 workers temporarily. The unions responded with a strike at Mirafiori. On its 55th day, they escalated by calling for a general strike. As Fiat was about to capitulate, a miracle happened. Following the call of a solitary Fiat engineer in October 1980 in what seems to have been a genuinely spontaneous demonstration, 40,000 Fiat workers took to the streets in Turin and called for an immediate resumption of work. The strike collapsed, and for the next two decades, there was to be peace at Fiat's chronically troubled labour front. In 1980, the new Panda was on the market, one of those once-in-a-decade strokes of genius, which, as a smart cheap car, saved Fiat from its recurrent financial predicaments. By 1983, Fiat was strongly profitable again. In 1984, the Fiat Uno, as the most produced Fiat models, enabled a Fiat market share of 60% in Italy and 15% in the EU. Both made the 1980s Fiat's most profitable decade.

In 1969, Lancia had been purchased, and in 1986, Alfa Romeo was bought as a defensive move against a threatened takeover by Ford. Alfa had always been a less-profitable upmarket competitor sponsored by the state-holding IRI, which for political reasons, financed the huge loss-making Alfasud plant near Naples in the South.

By 1980, Gianni Agnelli appointed himself chairman and delegated everyday management to the tough Cesare Romiti as CEO, whose role had been one of "bad cop" during the days of labour strife. Agnelli, however, retained ultimate control. Again, he insisted on a diversification drive, creating a conglomerate ranging from publishing to telecoms and pharmaceuticals, which were controlled by a pyramid structure of holdings (called IFI, IFIL, Exor, etc.) at the apex of which sat the Giovanni Agnelli & Co family trust. Most of these participations were highly profitable and gave the Agnellis a strong public voice in the daily printed press beyond its Turin paper *La Stampa* (owned since 1925), but they drained capital from the core car business.

As Europe's car business consolidated, Fiat stood out. Earlier attempts to take over Citroen in the 1960s had been vetoed by General de Gaulle. Now, it was Agnelli who blocked mergers with Daimler, BMW, Volkswagen and Ford for fear of losing control.

Finally, only a deal with General Motors (GM) materialised. GM had feared a German takeover of Fiat, which would have threatened its troubled European ("Opel") operations. GM and Fiat in 2000 swapped a 20% participation of GM in Fiat Auto (then worth $2.4 billion) with a 5% Fiat share in GM. GM was given a put (purchase) option to buy the remaining 80% shares in Fiat Auto by 2004. Both sides agreed on joint model development and joint production sites in Europe and Latin America to produce engines and gear boxes. Fiat may also have hoped to conquer the U.S. compact car market with the help of GM, from which it had withdrawn earlier.

By 2002, however, GM devalued its Fiat Auto share from $2.4 billion to $220 million (thus valuing the entire company at only $1.1 billion). GM's interest to exercise its put option in 2004 had grown decidedly cold. What would have been the consequences of a GM takeover? Alfa Romeo would have complemented GM's luxury brands (Cadillac and Saab). Fiat's Latin American operations would have been managed from Detroit. And for Fiat itself? Its cars in all likeliness would have become Opels with Fiat's logo stripes.

Independent of GM's capital participation, Fiat continued its boom-and -bust rollercoaster of an incorrigible one-model company: the "Tipo" of 1988 did well. But by 1993, there were again losses, following the attacks of Ford and the Japanese (allowed full access to the Italian market only after the creation of the EU's integrated internal market in 1992).

In addition, there were embarrassing inquiries by the Italian State prosecutors into donations paid by Fiat to smoothen political connections in Italian high politics. Cesare Rominti was interviewed by Milan public prosecutor Antonio Di Pietro of "*mani pulite*" fame. Apparently, up to 3% of Fiat's turnover was paid as contributions to the political system. Relations were particularly close to the DCI's reformist wing led by ex-PM Amitore Fanfani but also to centrist parties such as the Republicans, who, under PM Dini in 1995, made Gianni's sister, Susanna, foreign minister.

In 1996, the Agnelli's *La Stampa* successfully led the public drive to solicit votes for Romano Prodi's Ulivo centre-left alliance. The anti-corruption "mani puliti" campaign resulted in the arrest of a few lower-level Fiat managers, but no charges were raised against the top. Fiat is both the victim and the beneficiary of Italy's way of doing politics. It has had more than its usual share of social strife and labour troubles, but it also benefitted from generous public procurement, massive motorway construction, import protection and straight subsidisation (estimated by some experts to amount to €5 billion during 1992–2002).

So far, back in 1994, Fiat's last hurray was the Punto. In consequence, until 1997, Fiat Auto was profitable again. However, in 1996, Romiti was replaced by Paulo Fresco, a long-term disciple and deputy to Jack Welch at General Electric. His ambition was to create Fiat as "Europe's equivalent of GE" with the blessing of Gianni Agnelli. All profits and even more borrowed capital were ploughed into a massive diversification drive, while the core car business was starved of funds. Fresco's biggest acquisition was the $4.3 billion purchase of Case, a U.S. farm equipment marker, in 1999. Merged with Fiat's New Holland farm and construction machinery producer to form CNH, it made Fiat the world's second-largest operator after Canada's John Deere in the sector. Unfortunately, this coincided with a downturn in the global farm economy, and 17 plants of the newly merged company had to be closed, with 7,000 jobs lost.

While creating a diversified conglomerate, Fresco also attempted to globalise Fiat's operations with investments in Poland (for Eastern Europe) and Brazil. However, the Polish market was subsequently conquered by Daewoo (and the rest of East Europe by local products of Volkswagen/Skoda, Audi, Suzuki and Toyota), while the Brazilian market imploded in the crisis of 1998.

Having neglected R&D – expenditure had been cut by Fresco to $4.5 billion (1995–2001), equivalent to one-quarter of Volkswagen's expenditure — the Stilo saloon, which was to redress Fiat's fortune in the time-honoured fashion, however, duly flopped in 2001. After years of studious neglect, for once the magic failed to work. For the Agnellis now, (almost) all of their non-car operations were profitable, while only Fiat Auto was draining cash. Brother Umberto reportedly favoured disposing off the loss-making car operations altogether, while Gianni insisted on their continuation for reasons of familial piety and pride.

While Gianni became increasingly incapacitated in his battle against prostate cancer, it was the banks, which, in early 2002, forced the first attempts at restructuring. With debts at €28 billion as a result of Fresco's acquisition spree and group losses having escalated from €300 million (2000) to €1.8 billion (2001) and €2.1 billion (2002), there was little alternative. As the debt was mostly financed by friendly Italian banks, even their leniency came to an end once Fiat was rated to junk bond status, thus threatening their own standing, given that the exposure of Banca Intesa alone stood at €3 billion.

Milan's Mediobanca had wanted to force Fiat into bankruptcy and make creditor banks accept debt for equity swaps — all under lucrative Mediobanca control. The Italian government under PM Berlusconi — as an upstart capitalist himself no known friend of the aristocratic Agnellis — made his wish publicly known for an "Italian solution". The government would buy one-third of the shares of Italy's largest industrial conglomerate prior to recapitalising and floating the new "Italauto".

The 160-strong Agnelli clan, with their 80-year-old autocratic *capo famiglia* and *padrone* incapacitated, had a definite succession problem. Gianni's only son, Edouardo (1952–2000), had been a troubled soul, more interested in religion, Eastern philosophy, drugs and astrology than in automobile manufacturing. He died by his own hands in 2000. His cousin, Giovanino (1964–1997), Umberto's only son, was more balanced, a keen ambitious sportsman and groomed for succession, but died prematurely from cancer of the stomach. Finally, Gianni, in 2001, picked his grandson John Elkam, son of his daughter Margherita, in near despair. The 22-year-old American was an economics graduate with no practical business experience.

With Gianni's demise in January 2003, Umberto took over, fired Fresco and began a programme of divestment in order to reduce the mountain of debt. Fiat's GM share was sold for €1.2 billion, the aeroplane engine maker Fiat Avio for €1.6 billion, Toro Assicurazioni for €2.4 billion and Fraikin, a French long-term truck rental company for €800 million. It also sold one-third of Ferrari and raised €400 million by divesting its car-leasing business. All in all, sales generated €7 billion. Yet, the Agnellis did not become poor. Fiat Auto apart, their holdings still included controlling stakes in CNH, in the truck maker Iveco, in Ferrari, in SNIA–BDP an armament producer, in Magneti Marell, a components maker, and in Comau, a robotics producer, as well as in Juventus Turin, La Stampa newspaper, the Rizolli publishing group, the Chateau Margeaux winery near Bordeaux, and the sizable shares in Danone, a French dairy producer, Galbani, an Italian food producer, Accor Hotels, Club Med, etc., most of which remained highly profitable, thus putting the family's net worth at $5 billion (*Forbes*, 2000).

The objective of Umberto Agnelli as president and of his new CEO, Guiseppe Morchio, formerly with Pirelli Tyres, was to break even with a positive cash flow for the Fiat group by 2005 and for Fiat Auto in 2006. For the consolidated group's turnover of €50 billion, €22 billion would accrue from cars, €10 billion from CNH, €9 billion from Iveco trucks, €1 billion from Ferrari and the rest from construction and parts.

Cost cutting for Fiat Auto — 12,000 jobs were axed — will have had limited utility. The one-model company was in urgent need of rescue by a new model in order to revive its sagging sales. With the onslaught of Japanese and Korean competitors in the Italian home market, Fiat's image of a cute cheap car was no longer exclusive and good enough. Market shares had halved to 30% in Italy and to 7% in the EU. Capacities aimed at an annual output of 4 million units but produced less than 2 million. Previous cuts in R&D and investments had truly taken a heavy toll.

The Next Two Decades: Fiat Arrivederci – Benvenuto Stellantis

As described above, Fiat (as was Ferrari) was much a family-led company led with an iron fist by the charismatic and flamboyant patriarch Gianni Agnelli. The Turin clan was not only glamourous, powerful, stylish, rich and successful but also suffered its share of tragedy, death and intrigue. Since the monarchy was abolished in Italy in 1946, they almost acted like a substitute on the glamour pages and, not without reason, were named the Italian Kennedys. As Gianni's chosen heir, his nephew Giovanni Alberto Agnelli, died of stomach cancer aged only 33 in 1997, his grandson John Elkann was the anointed substitute. The son of Gianni's estranged daughter Margherita Agnelli hailed from her first marriage with a French writer with an Italo-Jewish background. John was born in New York, attended high school in Paris and later, when aged 22 he was already on the board of Fiat, received his BA in engineering management from the Politecnico di Torino with a thesis on e-commerce and online auctions. His grandfather groomed him by putting him on incognito traineeships at factories and offices at home and abroad, including at befriended companies such as General Electric. After the death of Gianni in 2003 and his grand uncle Umberto in 2004, John Elkann, the "great unknown", then aged 28, assumed the leadership of the clan, its holding company and Fiat and Ferrari themselves. This did not go undisputed. His own mother Margherita, Gianni's daughter, filed suits against him, his brother and sister from her first marriage and her own mother, as she felt shortchanged in her inheritance, to which she had renounced in an affidavit under Swiss law in exchange for the trifle amount of €1.2 billion. In a decade-long subsequent legal battle, she claimed that she had been misled about corporate values and disputed the legal basis of her renunciation.

Yet, at the time, Fiat was in dire straits, losing €2 million a day and had to be rescued from insolvency with baking loans of €3 billion. After Fiat had had four CEOs in three years (changing more frequently than the coaches of Juventus Turin), at the initiative of Gianni John Elkann had helped to install Sergio Marchionne (1952–2018), a no-nonsense Italo-Canadian, as CEO of both Fiat and Ferrari. He was not an auto engineer but rather acted like an investment banker, loved gruff informality and was soon both admired and feared for his emotional outbursts, straight talking and solitary decisions to which he stuck. He cut corporate bureaucracy, halved the development time for new models, stretched model cycles, closed factories and followed the strategy of less volume and more premium. After four years of losses, in 2005, he was able to show first profits in the car segment. He then decided to conquer Latin America, which had little car industry of its own, and then tried on the U.S. This broke the alliance with General Motors, which however could be persuaded to buy out Fiat for $2 billion.

At the time, Chrysler was in trouble again. After the 1998 Daimler–Chrysler divorce was finalised, following continued heavy Chrysler losses, in 2005, investment companies had taken major shares. Yet, in 2008, it was near collapse, from which government aid under President George W. Bush Jr. of $4 billion provided only temporary relief. In 2009, production stopped. In October 2009, Marchionne started by acquiring a strategic share of 20% in moribund Chrysler (not a merger of equals — see the following chapter! — to avoid misunderstandings), which later led to a full merger as Fiat Chrysler Automobiles (FCA) with a joint HQ in Amsterdam. He announced a five-year rescue plan: less models and gas guzzlers, more cooperation and fuel efficiency.

Joint global production platforms were used like one based on the Dodge. From it, in 2011, the Fiat Freemont emerged, and in 2013, the Dodge Dart in the U.S. His concepts worked so well that he later had to publicly regret that demand for the Grand Cherokees and Wranglers (off-roaders of the Jeep brand) had outstripped supply. One of his memorable sayings was on the newly developed Fiat 500e e-car: "I hope nobody buys it, since I am losing $14,000 on each one of them". As a Ferrari president, he also forcefully put its troubled Formula One team in order. Shortly before his death in 2018, probably from lung cancer, the chain-smoking disciplinarian, though mortally sick, could still proudly announce that FCA was now finally debt-free. While having gradually moved production out of high-cost Italy without the unions screaming, the "general without fear" (*Detroit Free Press*, 2012) had managed to rescue not only one but two venerable global carmakers from extinction.

John Elkann had mostly taken care of the family business and left Marchionne a free hand. Earlier merger talks of Fiat with Ford and Daimler had failed because Gianni Agnelli had insisted on continued full control. With John Elkann, minority shareholdings were fine, provided the new global operator was viable and profitable. In 2009, he merged the two family holding companies IFI and IFIL to create Exor and became its chairman. In 2010, he also became chairman of Fiat and in 2017 of Ferrari, which was subsequently listed on Wall Street. But he could also be tough. When Juventus Turin was hit by a match-rigging scandal, he fired the management. Juventus was relegated to the second division from which it has since reemerged. Exor's portfolio roughly consists of one quarter each of FCA, Ferrari and CNH Industrial shares, plus investments in other groups such as Iveco trucks, controlling stakes in the GEDI publishing group, which owns La Stampa, a centrist paper in Turin, the leftist La Repubblica in Rome and The Economist group in London, as well as of course Juventus Turin. In 2023, Exor also bought a 15% stake in Philips for €2.6 billion, by now a maker of medical appliances.

The reinsurance company PartnerRe had been bought by Elkann in 2017 for $6.9 billion and was resold three years later for $9 billion after having supplied $660 million in dividends. Such are the joys of a cash-rich investor having done due diligence.

Perhaps as a just reward, Elkann, who according to Forbes in 2024 was considered worth $2.6 billion, could marry a veritable Italian princess with a lavish reception at her family's island in Lago Maggiore in truly lavish Agnelli style, with the bon chic bon genre of Italian and international society, from Henry Kissinger (an old family friend) to Silvio Berlusconi in attendance.

With Marchionne's successor as CEO of FCA, Mike Manley, the British former head of Jeep at Chrysler, Elkann started their €50 billion merger talks on a 50:50 share basis with the Peugeot group (PSA), which in 2017 had bought Opel (Germany) and Vauxhall (U.K.) from General Motors for $1.3 billion. After a few twists and turns, the merger was agreed in 2019, blessed by 80% of Fiat's shareholders, thus creating the world's fourth-largest original equipment manufacturer in automobiles. The new giant valued at $53 billion at market value, in which Exor has a share of 14%, was to be named Stellantis. In this Franco-Italo-American "menage a trois", the old Agnelli heritage with its firm and almost exclusive manufacturing, cultural and political roots in Italy had become very distant, as had probably always been the intention of the cosmopolitan John Elkann. Subsequently, relations with the Italian government, especially under Prime Minister Georgia Meloni of the Fratelli d'Italia, suffered perceptively, a development unthinkable under Gianni.

Stellantis now offers 14 brands (Abarth, Alfa Romeo, Chrysler, Citroen, Dodge, DS Automobiles, Fiat, Jeep, Lancia, Maserati, Opel, Peugeot, RAM and Vauxhall), has production sites in 29 countries and 400,000 employees and is present in 130 markets. Fiat is still the bestselling company within Stellantis, which in Latin America has a leading share of 14% (2023), especially in Brazil (20.4%). In Italy (with Fiat Panda) and Turkey (with Fiat Tipo), the share stands at 12.3% each, and in Algeria, thanks to Fiat Doblo, it stands at a mighty 68.3%. All of these success markets are emerging economies with very little inclination to go for e-cars. Yet in Europe, the Fiat managers of Stellantis proclaim there would soon be only models like the Fiat 500e, Fiat 600e, Fiat 500 Hybrid and Fiat Grande Panda — both electric and hybrid — on offer. Their secret of success would be Italian design (for which they have recruited none other than star designer Georgio Armani), global platforms and local adaptations, as evident in their few key leading markets.

In 2023, Stellantis enjoyed a record profit margin of 13% and a net gain of €13 billion, more than any other European carmaker. Yet, one year later, due to Chinese competition and fall in demand, the profit margin is expected to be cut by half.

The CEO of Fiat is now Olivier Francois, who started his career with Citroen. As head of Citroen Italia, he was recruited by Marchionne as the CEO of Lancia, later to be appointed as chief of Chrysler as its leading marketing executive for all Chrysler brands. As such, he had moved a lot between Turin and Auburn Hills, the Detroit suburb in Southern Michigan, where Chrysler is headquartered.

Chairman of Stellantis' Board of Directors is John Elkann, his vice chair is Robert Peugeot, and the CEO of Stellantis since 2021 has been the Portuguese Carlos Tavares, who, after five years with Nissan in the U.S., spent 32 years in Renault's management and, since 2014, had been CEO of the Groupe PSA. While their professional international qualifications certainly look impressive, the jury is obviously still out on how this daring intercultural merger will work out.

Bibliography

Avantario, V. *Die Agnellis*. Frankfurt/Main: Campus Verlag, 2002.

Betts, P. "Italy's firm family ties", *Financial Times*, 24 March 2003.

Betts, P. and Simonean, H. "Obituary Giovanni Agnelli", *Financial Times*, 25 January 2003.

Edmondson, C. "More smoke is pouring from Fiat's engine", *Business Week*, 23 December 2002.

"Fiat. Under Siege", *The Economist*, 19 October 2002.

"Fiat after Gianni Agnelli, The party's over", *The Economist*, 1 February 2003.

"Fiat's running out of gas", *Bloomberg*, 31 July 2003.

"In Search of Fiat's Soul", *The Economist*, 3 June 2000.

Kapner, F. "Fiat drama produces cast with a past", *Financial Times*, 14 January 2003.

Kapner, F. "Fiat's day of reckoning", *Financial Times*, 24 January 2003.

Piller, T. "Die Automisere von Fiat", *Frankfurter Allgemeine*, 1 June 2002.

Piller, T. "Der schwierige Neuanfang von Fiat", *Frankfurter Allgemeine*, 23 June 2003.

Piller, T. "Fiat will bis 2005 wieder die Gewinnschwelle erreichen", *Frankfurter Allgemeine*, 27 June 2003.

Schlamp, H-J. "Clan auf Crash-Kurs", *Der Spiegel*, 29 July 2002.

New Literature, 2nd Edition

"Autohersteller fürchten um ihre Gewinne", *Die Presse*, 1 October 2024.

Bernet, L. "Die Liebe der Italiener zur Fiat Dynastie ist erkaltet", *Neue Zürcher Zeitung*, 26 February 2024.

Betts, P. "Man in the News: John Elkann", *Financial Times*, 23 October 2010.

Bläske, G. "Die Geldvermehrungsmaschine der Fiat-Erben", *Neue Zürcher Zeitung*, 4 March 2020.

"Carlos Tavares, the Peugeot petrol head steering Fiat Chrysler deal", *Financial Times*, 1 November 2019.

Eckl-Dorna, W. "Warum sich der neue Fiat Chrysler Chef sofort bewähren muß", *Manager Magazin*, 24 July 2018.

"Fiat Chrysler and Peugeot agree to merge in giant auto deal", *Financial Times*, 18 December 2019.

"Fiat suitor Great wall hits road bumps as bid prospects fail", *Financial Times*, 23 August 2017.

"Great Wall states ambition to buy Fiat Chrysler", *Financial Times*, 21 August 2017.

"How a survivalist mentality has helped Stellantis eclipse VW", *Financial Times*, 12 March 2024.

"Project Newton: How Fiat Chrysler solved the Renault merger puzzle", *Financial Times*, 25 July 2019.

"PSA and Fiat Chrysler overhaul terms of € 50 bn merger", *Financial Times*, 14 September 2020.

Schlamp, H. J. "Der General kommt nicht zurück", *Der Spiegel*, 25 July 2018.

"Sergio Machionne. Fiat's fearless saviour, 1952–2018", *Financial Times*, 25 July 2019.

"The 20-year inheritance feud dividing the Fiat dynasty", *Financial Times*, 2 March 2024.

"The long and winded road to the marriage of Fiat and Peugeot", *Financial Times*, 30 October 2019.

"The threat to the Italian heritage of car manufacturing", *Financial Times*, 28 February 2024.

"Why Georgia Meloni is picking a fight with Stellantis John Elkann", *Financial Times*, 27 January 2024.

Corporate Mergers, Merged Brands in Trouble: DaimlerChrysler and BMW–Rover

DaimlerChrysler and BMW–Rover are two of the largest takeovers of the late 1990s. There are many parallels between the two cases: both were originally applauded as brilliantly executed merger operations, and both went badly wrong after two years of German *laissez-faire* management. Both were the consequences of discarded management fads and the product of a new one. In the 1980s, diversification was the craze among most management gurus. It was claimed to liberate companies from the cyclical downswings of product cycles, allowing new synergies and limitless prospects of growth. When these visions turned sour, strained management resources and persistent losses began to threaten core business operations. In 1995, British Aerospace put Rover up for sale, which was promptly snapped up by BMW. Daimler's new chief, Jürgen Schrempp, had begun to sell off or close down his predecessor's dream of a diversified high-tech conglomerate. The aerospace and defence interests, purchased and operated together with troublesome minority shareholders, such as DASA (consisting of MTU, Dornier, MBB and Fokker), the electrical engineering (AEG), software and service (Debis) branches were either scaled down or closed down altogether. The new fad of the mid-1990s was to refocus on one's core business. In order to survive as an independent company producing cars, one was supposed to become a multi-brand, full-range vehicle producer with global reach and enjoy lower per-unit costs, with an annual output of between 2 and 4 million units at least. BMW and Mercedes, as leading up-market high-margin producers, had neither of them, but they had a well-filled war chest (with Daimler, as a result of restructuring, having become profitable again since 1996) and the ambition to join the global top four players.

For Daimler, the new deal meant utilising Chrysler's dominance in the growing U.S. segment of mini vans and sports utility vehicles — as well as a regional complementarity in utilising Chrysler's marketing network in the U.S. For BMW, it meant acquiring Rover's four-wheel drive technology and a range of small- to medium-sized mass-produced cars.

The logic and the execution of both takeovers were praised as brilliant and faultless by analysts and the business press at the time, creating high expectations, although the seeds for the future managerial and financial disasters were sown at that time already. Both Daimler and BMW undertook great efforts to accommodate perceived political sensitivities, also in order to protect the precious reputation of their cash-generating main premium brands.

Given the "latent hostility to things German at senior levels of the British establishment" (Brady & Lorenz, 2002, p. 179), BMW chief Piechetsrieder announced a policy of no redundancies for Rover's over-manned and outdated operations and left an underperforming British management team in place, which, in the view of the authors, was "tantamount to negligence" (Brady & Lorenz, 2002, p. 69).

In the case of Chrysler, which, as the third-largest U.S. car manufacturer, was historically particularly prone to the up-and-down swings of car demand in the U.S. market and had been bailed out at American taxpayers' expense following its last crisis in 1981, both sides publicly insisted on a myth that it was a friendly merger of equals, though in reality, it was a friendly takeover. Daimler, in fact, paid a premium over Chrysler's then current share price (Waller, 2001, p. 191). The results were oversized management boards, sweet and expensive compromises, resistance to change in Chrysler with encouraged score-keeping and a two-year "power vacuum" at the top of Chrysler (Waller, 2001, p. 266), as its U.S. managers began their mental divorces from the company and ultimately left in large numbers. Suddenly enriched with generous options packages, they were left with little incentives to work.

Both Daimler and BMW allowed *laissez-faire* with mounting losses to rule for two years. Then, under public pressure due to continuing losses and depressed share prices, they suddenly shifted into reverse gear. Daimler managers replaced Chrysler's top staff, ending the expensive illusion of a merger. After Piechetsrieder's dismissal, hundreds of BMW engineers were flown in to Rover to rescue the British operations with micro- management. This was as insensitive with its "sledgehammer approach" (Brady & Lorenz, 2002, p. 197) as to amount to a "human relations disaster" (Brady & Lorenz, 2002, p. 142).

Brady and Lorenz conclude that a more rational, hard-headed and honest approach, such as the one Volkswagen adopted with Skoda (Brady & Lorenz, 2002, p. 53), would have been preferable to shifting between two undesirable extremes. In retrospect, it appears that only the British workers, their union, the TGWU and their industrial negotiator, Tony Woodley, recognised early enough that BMW was Rover's only hope for survival and that this required thorough, tough restructuring from the start, not the *laissez-faire* injection of funds into a company suffering from 20 years of under-investment by British Leyland, with endemic quality problems and a seriously damaged brand.

The intercultural differences between the merged companies could not be removed by extensive and expensive get-to-know sessions and funny seminars organised by intercultural communicators.

To the Germans, British management appeared as intransigent, arrogant, grasping and egoistic, with an aversion to risk (Brady & Lorenz, 2002, p. 62). In the U.S., they were shocked at the Americans' insistence on hierarchy and multiple earnings for top management, their humourless political correctness in racial, sexual and no drinking/no smoking codes and their refusal to socialise after work (Waller, 2001, pp. 251/4).

In return, the Anglo-Saxons were annoyed by the Germanic habit of decision-making at formal meetings in a memo-based corporate bureaucracy.

In the end, after billions of losses, Chrysler ended up as the U.S. sports utility and four-wheel drive subsidiary of Daimler, and after having swallowed an investment of £2.5 billion, Rover, in early 2000, was sold for £10 million to the capital-starved Alchemy Syndicate, whose ambition was to allow Britain's last independent car production to survive on the basis of a positive cash flow alone.

In all fairness, there were other contributing factors which conspired to these spectacular merger failures in the global car industry in the late 1990s. In Rover's case, they are as follows: the appreciation of the pound Sterling to levels of DM3.10 — far above the levels of the price competitiveness of the British export industry; the hesitant and delayed delivery of the U.K. government aid for Rover; aggressive pricing by Rover's competitors; and waning demand for its products. Chrysler was mainly hit by the contraction of the U.S. car market in the late 1990s, which once again affected Chrysler most dramatically.

All in all, these are two sorry tales of well-intentioned cross-national mergers gone wrong. They went wrong due to cultural reasons, for which most cross-national mergers and takeovers — from Swissair to Vivendi — usually fail: the unhappy mixture of managerial hubris, faddish wishful thinking and persistently incompatible national business cultures. Perhaps a growing realisation of the importance of the latter could not only save capital and human resources but also be helpful for much needed, more differentiated corporate approaches to globalisation.

Six years later, Daimler is still struggling with its Chrysler subsidiary. It still has cost problems with U.S. made steel, as well as labour and pension obligations. Worse, despite strong cuts in purchasing costs, GM and Ford had started an aggressive price discount war to fight back the recurring Japanese competition. After losing sales, Chrysler responded with financial incentives, cash back schemes and a free seven-year engine warranty. With a squeeze on margins and declining sales, even further cost cutting could not prevent further losses. As a result, DaimlerChrysler shares traded at €29 by April 2003, down 70% from their €96 levels a few years earlier. The value destroyed represented more than the $36 billion which Daimler had paid for Chrysler. It is now valued at nil by the stock market.

In the meantime, German managers had taken over key functions at Chrysler. When David Eaton retired as CEO in 1980, Dieter Zetsche succeeded him. Yet, it took three years to use joint components between Daimler and Chrysler models — things which are usually cited as the key advantage of corporate mergers and their fabulous synergies.

By 2003, Chrysler put two new major models on the market:

◊ a two-seater rear-wheel-drive sports car called "Crossfire" (which finally had 39% of its components produced by Daimler); and
◊ a blend of a mini-van and a sports utility car named "Pacifica".

Both are positioned as newly invented "premium brands", below the luxury level and above the mass market. So far, nobody in the U.S. had been aware of this market segment (which is very much in existence in Europe with its sizable upper-middle class).

It remains to be seen whether Chrysler, with its fading mass market appeal, will manage its "upgrade" with crossbreeds. If successful, it would be the most surprising stroke of genius in the world's best researched car market. If the strategy flopped, a sizable divestment would probably be in order before long.

In contrast, BMW seems to live happily ever after following its costly divorce from Rover. Rather, it was Ford who eventually acquired the loss maker and continued to struggle with Rover's problems, which BMW left behind.

According to Helmut Panke, BMW's CEO (2002–2006), BMW has learnt its lesson not to venture into the mass market again. With its 11 different series, it rather aims at the top segment of each vehicle type. This not only applies to sports cars and off-roaders but also to Minis, the only successful brand retained from the Rover adventure.

Although their margins have become smaller than in BMW's traditional luxury segment, demand growth has been particularly strong in Asia and the U.S., especially for the more expensive elaborate versions. Production at its Spartanburg plant (South Carolina) had to be increased to 150,000 units p.a. (accounting for 15% of BMW's total production). BMW also went top market with its Rolls Royce production at its new plant in Goodwood on the English south coast.

Originally, BMW had lost a bidding war for Rolls Royce and Bentley manufacturing against a £470 million bid from Volkswagen back in 1998. Once it acquired the overpriced works from Vickers, VW then discovered that the Rolls Royce name was owned by Rolls Royce Aerospace, which sold it to BMW for £40 million. It was probably the largest amount ever paid for a trade name but still a bargain compared to Volkswagen's purchasing price for the decrepit Crewe (North England) plants, which needed another £600 million from VW for an upgrade.

BMW and VW then agreed to split operations, with VW producing 7,000 Bentleys p.a. in modernised Crewe facilities and with BMW assembling its new RR01 in the south of England. There, its German-produced body, 460PS strong engine and gear boxes are put together, painted and the extensive trimming done by craftsmen, who earlier built luxury boats along the coast. BMW's new Rolls Royce starts with an asking price of £208,000. An annual production of 1,000 units is envisaged.

The lesson of the two costly mergers is pretty straightforward: mergers don't create synergies for brands. They rather pose mortal threats by diffused images and inconsistent qualities and pricing. BMW rescued itself with a clear refocus on its traditional brand strength and a carefully expanded up-market scope.

DaimlerChrysler, however, continued to struggle. Its national and segmental brand identities were more diffuse than ever. As success remained persistently elusive, even Daimler's highly profitable core brand could ultimately be threatened.

The Next Two Decades: After the Dual Divorce

In 2000, after billions of losses, as described above, BMW pulled the plug and sold MG Rover, which by then had no resources and no new models, for the symbolic amount of £10 to Phoenix Consortium, which subsequently however seemed to be more interested in milking the company dry, leaving Rover in 2005 indebted at the order of more than £1 billion. After takeover talks with a Chinese investor failed, Rover went into receivership; 5,000 of the last 6,000 remaining workers were dismissed instantly and operations ceased. This was the sad end of almost 110 years of a once glorious industrial venture which had started in Longbridge, Birmingham, in 1896.

BMW however had kept as a souvenir the Mini. Rover and previous owners back to British Leyland had developed the Mini models from various British producers, such as Austin, Morris, Wolseley or Riley, into a proper brand of its own as a small compact car with a distinctive, attractive exterior and interior design, which continued to be produced in the old Morris works in

Cowley near Oxford. With new designs now developed in Munich, the Mini turned out to become a highly successful brand, typically used as a secondary urban car. In 2017, 370,000 units were sold worldwide, including versions as hatchbacks, roadsters and SUVs as Countryman and Aceman while still somehow trying to imitate the classical designs.

Into this almost partial happy ending of an industrial tragedy, Brexit intervened cruelly: Britain's disastrous exit from the EU, against which both sides — neither London nor Brussels — undertook serious efforts to avoid it. With sudden customs barriers between the U.K. and continental Europe, with the lousy Brexit "deal" agreed between both sides, responsible of which were a series of clearly dysfunctional Tory governments and on the other side a rigid and punitive Commission and EU member state majority bilateral trade was seriously disturbed. This meant that, from February 2020, a 10% import tariff was imposed on British-made cars imported to the continent, plus the added disadvantage of hundreds of supply trucks for components per week from the continent having to cross the channel to reach the works in Cowley, including tons of unproductive documented paperwork for customs, which the U.K. was uniquely unprepared and undeequipped for the job, thus creating huge delays and costs. To the credit of BMW management, it must be said that they had loudly and clearly warned against these risks and wisely demanded a free trade agreement between the U.K. and the EU. However, given Tory anti-EU populism and the political and bureaucratic rigidity on the other side in Brussels and other EU capitals, it was, unfortunately, to no avail.

For the successful Mini brand, the writing is now on the wall. As some are already produced by Nedcar in the Netherlands or by Magna in Austria, the rest could be shifted to Leipzig in Germany. There is also a joint BMW — Great Wall venture for electro-Minis made in China, for the time being only for the Chinese market but ultimately also for export. What future is then there for the workers at the Cowley plant as victims of Brexit?

Hence, this sequel to a failed merger policy has also become a case of a tragic policy failure created by increasingly dysfunctional European political elites on both sides of the Channel.

As mentioned above, after mounting losses, the value of Chrysler had declined by €35 billion and that of DaimlerChrysler in total by €50 billion. In 2007, Dieter Zetsche (2006–2019), Daimler's CEO and successor to Jürgen Schrempp (1995–2005), pulled the plug on this disastrously managed venture. In May 2007, 80.1% of Chrysler shares were sold to the U.S. investment fund Cerberus. Daimler's remaining share of 19.9% was sold in 2009. Apart from the financial losses of this mesalliance, originally praised by its unlucky architect Schrempp as a "marriage made in heaven", a major reputational damage to the Daimler brand had to be repaired, as quality problems — intolerable for premium cars — had emerged after successive rounds of cost cuttings and savings. Also, the strict U.S. SEC began to investigate charges that DaimlerChrysler had used bribes (luxury cars or cash) to get public procurement orders in 22 countries, including Russia, China, Indonesia, Thailand, Turkmenistan, Iraq, Turkey, Egypt, Nigeria, Liberia and Serbia, where this seems an incurable national habit, yet outlawed in the U.S. as an effective means of export promotion. After a confession, a declaration of atonement and a payment of $185 million to the U.S. Department of Justice (not a bribe!) by Daimler, the charges were dropped in April 2020 and 45 culprits fired, though senior management should have been perfectly aware of this frequent practice.

The divorce from Chrysler did not spell the end of Daimler's international cooperative ambitions. In 2005, with Hyundai and Mitsubishi Motors, a joint venture called "Global Engine Manufacturers Alliance" (GEMA) was set up, although in November 2005, Daimler already sold its 12.4% holding in Mitsubishi Motors and the "alliance" was subsequently discreetly dissolved. In 2007, it agreed to cooperate with Fiat on the joint supply of engines for trucks, vans and other utility vehicles, starting with Daimler's Japanese subsidiary Mitsubishi Fuso. In 2010, Daimler also joined an "alliance" with Renault-Nissan. It also has a strong foreign shareholder base. Its largest (2019) are the Beijing Automotive Group, BAIC (10%), Li Shufu, the owner of Geely (9,7%) and the Kuwait Investment Authority (5,6%).

After having regained the world leadership in premium cars, surpassing its arch-rival BMW in 2020, the new CEO, Ola Källenius (2019–), a Swedish national, decided to split off the trucks and buses division as Daimler Trucks AG and its financial services and fleet management units as Daimler Mobility AG, with Mercedes Benz AG focusing on the core car business with 166,000 employees and a turnover of €153 billion (2023). In Daimler Trucks, Mercedes would continue to hold a 35% share. Daimler Trucks employs 100,000 and sells about 500,000 trucks and buses worldwide, with a turnover of €45 billion and brands such as Bharat Benz, Freightliner, Fuso, Mercedes Benz, Setra, Thomas Built Buses and Western Star. All three nominally independent joint-stock companies form part of a Mercedes-Benz Group.

Thus, Daimler Benz in a roller coaster went full circle, from a widely acquired diffuse high-tech conglomerate in the late 1980s under Edzard Reuter as CEO (1987–1995), followed by the "Welt AG" of DaimlerChrysler and Mitsubishi Motors under Jürgen Schrempp (1995–2005), to its consolidation to the core car business thereafter and its segmentation since 2022.

In both cases, BMW and Daimler, one could argue that if the top management of cash-rich corporations have too much money to play around, delusions of grandeur — which in politics is known as "Caesarean madness" — would sooner or later inevitably set in, for whose megalomanic errors and misjudgements in the end shareholders and staff are footing the bill.

Bibliography

Brady, C. and Lorenz, A. *End of the Road. BMW and Rover — A Brand Too Far*. Harlow: Pearson Education, 2002.

"DaimlerChrysler learns to share, 5 years later", *International Herald Tribune*, 25 March 2003.

Fockenbrock, D. "Daimler und Chrysler. Ein Stern auf der Erde", *Tagesspiegel*, 7 May 2003.

Grant, J. "Chrysler chief faces twists and turns on road to rebranding", *Financial Times*, 16 June 2003.

Grant, J. "The heat is on for DaimlerChrysler costs", *Financial Times*, 3 September 2003.

Griffiths, J. "Bavaria tries to make a British marque", *Financial Times*, 4 January 2003.

Harnischfeger, U. "Daimler profit target looks a long way away", *Financial Times*, 10 April 2003.

Waller, D. *Wheels on Fire. The Amazing Inside Story of the Daimler-Chrysler Merger*. London: Hodder and Stoughton, 2001.

New Literature, 2nd Edition

"BMW erwägt mehr Produktion und höhere Preise in Amerika", *Frankfurter Allgemeine*, 26 May 2003.

Burt, T. "Profile Helmut Panke, BMW", *Financial Times*, 13 May 2002.

"Daimler kauft sich für 185 Millionen Dollar frei", *Der Spiegel*, 1 April 2020.

"Daimler teilt sich auf", *Omnibus News*, 3 February 2021.

Fasse, M. "No-Deal-Brexit: BMW könnte die Mini-Produktion verlagern", *Handelsblatt*, 16 December 2020.

Harnischfeger, U. "BMW in drive to maintain goals", *Financial Times*, 9 May 2003.

Meier, L. "Wie Bernd Pischetsrieder die Rover Übernahme versemmelte", *Capital*, 5 March 2020.

Rothacher, A. "Global alliances, production changes and mature markets: Japanese FDI in the European car industry and their implications for bilateral trade relations", *Asia Europa Journal* 13, 2015, pp. 163–174.

"Suche nach den BMW Milliarden", *Stern*, 17 April 2005.

The Lego Universe of Building Bricks

All of Denmark is basically a small Legoland.
— Frits Brendal

In 2003, Lego was active in 33 countries with 10,000 employees, achieving a turnover of €600 million per year with production sites in Denmark, Switzerland, the U.S., Brazil and Korea. Lego aimed to become the world market leader for construction toys, preschool and school materials, family parks and lifestyle and media products in its target group of families with children of up to 16 years of age. In some of these segments, this third-generation owned and managed company was quite close to its declared objective.

It all started when in the poor farming village of Billund, located in Central Jylland, a pious carpenter and cabinet-maker named Ole Kirk Christiansen ran out of orders during the world economic crisis of 1929, which hit Denmark and its farm sector hard, as it depended on livestock exports.

Rather than firing his redundant craftsmen and apprentices, Christiansen reacted by diversifying his artisanal production and offering a wider product range to his rural clientele, such as ladders and wooden farm implements. When orders did not pick up, they produced toys from scrap wood like walking ducks, fire engine cars and furniture for puppet homes. His son Godtfred, a trained carpenter with only elementary school education, proved to be a gifted salesman as well.

Through commission sales in village Kobmands stores all over Denmark, he assured the survival of his father's workshop. They also used the short-lived yoyo craze in the mid-1930s well. During this time, the fledgling company shortened its slogan "Leg godt" (play well) memorably to "Lego" as its future trademark.

In 1942, a fire destroyed the wood workshop in Billund. It was soon replaced by a then modern toy factory, where 40 workers began to produce foremost wooden animals, coloured toy cars and railway carriages.

During the Second World War, plastics saw a quick and dramatic development. Hence, in 1947, Ole fatefully decided to purchase a plastic injection moulding machine — for experimental purposes. In 1949, the original Lego stone was invented and patented as an "automatic building brick". Although packaged in bright colourful boxes, the toy trade was slow to accept the new product. After Denmark, the West German market was targeted in the 1950s. The rest of Western Europe followed.

In a toy factory in Rudolfstadt/Thuringia, during the pre-war years itself, a similar toy brick had been invented. As Rudolfstadt became part of Soviet-occupied East Germany, Communist state management held the poor plastic brick in neglect and poor quality and thus left the field to Lego. (This author had both types in his toy collection and definitely preferred the Danish variant, which, unlike the East German product, never lost its shape and hold.) In 1958, Ole's son, Godtfred Kirk Christiansen, took over.

He had been the inventor of the improved combination technique of the adhesive bricks and defined the timeless principles of the "Lego System": unlimited possibilities to play, be attractive to both boys and girls, all juvenile age groups, invite healthy and quiet play, develop fantasy and creativity with new elements easy to add on, those add- ons to enhance the play and, finally, to insist on perfect quality.

In 1960, a fire once again helpfully destroyed the wood-processing facilities. Godtfred decided to discontinue the wooden toy lines. His older brothers, who disagreed, were bought out, and they went on to set up their own companies.

Given the Lego system, there was a permanent need for new product ideas to complement the staple brick. Initially, ideas originated from Godtfred's hobby cellar. But in 1959, a development department ("Lego Futura") with five employees was set up. Forty years later, this unit employs 300 creative people in three continents at various locations, including Boston, Tokyo, Milan and London, apart from Billund. The plastics used were improved to be ever safer, more indestructible and to maintain their brighter colours (1963). Duplo bricks were developed for the little hands of two- to six-year-olds (1969). Plastic tools for kids were invented.

The first Legoland Park was opened in Billund (1968). At its origin was the nuisance value of an ever-increasing stream of visitors, who began to obstruct smooth work operations. Special permanent exhibits were set up for them, which, with continued attractivity, were expanded into a well-designed mini-world of Lego-build world sites, castles, harbours, fairy-tale landscapes, jungle paths, Western towns, pirate hideouts, Indian camps, goldmines, Lego ships, cruises, rafts and Lego cars. Originally designed for parents with children aged 3–12, it was soon found that one-third of the 1.4 million annual visitors in Billund were unaccompanied adults, attracted by the notion of the big wide world turned into small format, a Gulliver's perspective, which lends an illusion of power and oversight.

Following Billund's success, in 1996, in Windsor, U.K., a derelict safari park was turned into another Legoland, with plenty of British themes, such as replicas of the Tower, Scottish castles and Welsh mines, thus providing edifying features for compulsory school excursions. Soon afterwards, in the course of a sustained market penetration effort in the U.S., on an abandoned tomato plantation in Carlsbad, California, Legoland No. 3 was opened. Two more openings followed: in Makuhari on reclaimed land near Tokyo for Japan's captive parents and in Günzburg, Swabia, on an abandoned U.S. army base located in between Munich and Stuttgart in May 2002.

Half a century of growth left its traces on corporate culture. But its unique pietist origins are still visible in pronounced intentions of good corporate citizenship and worthy educational aspirations.

Founder Ole was a devout Protestant, whose poor childhood years were followed by an apprenticeship in Norway and Germany. His son, Godtfred, engineered the 1960s boom but still insisted on egalitarian structures. He dispensed paternalist goodwill and accepted subordinates' mistakes while insisting on tight, frugal cost management. Up to the 1960s, each working day would still start with a voluntary common prayer session for all staff in Billund.

The village was gradually transformed into a corporate small town. In the 1940s, Lego financed the sidewalks, piped water and sewage systems and a crafts school. In 1964, Lego initiated the establishment of a regional airport in Billund. Located in central Jylland, today it is Denmark's second-largest after Copenhagen. Contemporary Billund has 8,500 inhabitants, out of whom 1,200 work full-time for Lego and some 700 work as seasonal helpers (March/October) in Legoland.

Observers such as Margaret Uhle have noted the strong nexus between the Lego designs and the country of Denmark itself: both are clean, well-ordered and functioning smoothly with small homes, small towns and neat roads, as well as lots of traffic lights, trees and respectable people on bicycles and in small cars — about as exciting as a real-sized Legoland. At the same time, Danes are reputed to be gifted craftsmen and creative tinkers who love their children. This amounts to a corporate identity well matched with national culture.

As a well-intentioned pragmatic Danish company, Lego has so far also provided for smooth generational transition. Successors were well groomed in due time. The old generation faded away in due course. Family control remains completely assured. For once in Scandinavia, transparency is thought dispensable. Balance sheets remain confidential.

In 1979, grandson Kjeld Kirk Christensen took over. He inherited the need to improve management and streamline production. Lego had adhered to the laudable principle of "few chiefs and many Indians", with strong roles of senior Indians such as foremen and industrial craftsmen, with weekly planning sessions of senior management as a relatively feeble link to arrive at and communicate management direction to the ground troops.

With a staff of 2,300 in 1980, Kjeld felt that time had come to introduce proper middle management to take care of the increasing complexity of decisions. It was also clear that there were too many Lego products on the market. Even for Lego staff, it had become difficult to keep track.

Output was then streamlined into three product lines:

◊ Lego Duplo for small children;
◊ Lego construction toys for the basic boxes and thematic programmes, such as City, Castle, Space, Railways, and Technic;
◊ XYZ: other quality toys.

Two-thousand elements were sorted along basic, decorative, functional and figurative lines.

Lego research found that its products were rather boys' favourites. They liked to build massive structures, preferably towers, which could be dramatically crashed, or set up street crossings, where masses of cars could wonderfully crash as well. Girls also did play with Lego, but usually lost interest after ages 5–6. They preferred to work with wide-open structures: to furnish homes and populate streets, coffeehouses and beach sites. In order to service the quiet social games which girls prefer (different from the boys' explorative action games), Lego provided rounder, softer figurines with a bit of glamour for the girls' preferred role plays. Dream houses and assorted decoration, including flowers, were designed for this purpose.

Faced with shrinking markets for educational toys in Europe and in the U.S. in the 1990s, under license from Disney, figures like Winnie the Pooh were produced as Duplo figurines, with others to follow. This was a significant departure from Lego's doctrine away from educational toys.

As early as 1983, in cooperation with McDonald's, small Lego sets began to be included in Junior packs ordered at their fast-food outlets. This spread basic Lego bricks all over the U.S. and generated the demand for follow-up purchases. This strategy worked well in most other countries except Germany, where McDonald's is met with poor parental acceptance. In fact, it is seen not as a family restaurant but rather as a sub-standard junk food provider and hangout for delinquent, mostly immigrant, kids. This led Lego to the correct conclusion that an association with McDonald's would hurt its very positive brand image in Germany.

Starting out with its Lego figurines (1974), its Legoland features (1978), which allowed whole townships to be built and settled, Lego went on to successfully produce Duplo zoo animals and thematic figures as casts for Robin Hood scenes, castles and pirates.

Faced with computer toys in the mid-1990s in core European markets, Lego sales began to shrink. Lego responded by producing Lego Robots and Technic computers, which could be used as educational toys for school use. Efforts were undertaken to design digital bricks, which could be programmed by children — and hence thought to be more exciting than the pre-programmed Tamagochi blurbs. Yet, the "programmable brick", which in 1998 was put on the market, has remained too expensive for mass marketing so far. Also, with many of the complicated Lego Technic toys, it was frankly getting too difficult to recognise the basic guiding Lego principle: never to produce a "ready" finished product for children and to make it easy for assembly, disassembly and recombination, allowing them to develop their own new toys.

These slow and painful departures from corporate philosophy were triggered by mounting heavy losses, which started in 1998. In 1999, 1,000 employees had to be laid off. In 2002, 200 more were fired. Growth in the 1980s had been brought about by achieving global reach. By then, 300 million children had played with Lego bricks. Yet, the lives of middle-class children were about to change. Their days became programmed with extracurricular activities. Toys had to compete with electronic games and instant media access. The sad truth was that there was simply no time left to play the slow-paced games which Lego offered. With licensed toys — from Star Wars Legos to Winnie the Pooh and Harry Potter — there is a definite departure by Lego from the ideal of open-ended self-guided play. As Charles Fishman rightly observed, this may be trendy, but it is not a sign of leadership, which Lego had exercised 30 years earlier.

Lego remains very adept at the right PR: by stimulating the highest Lego tower construction (currently at 35 meters) and other highly visual Guinness Records; by having the UNHCR in a celebrated poster and free advert campaign pose 40 Duplo figures of all colours, occupations and ages, and ask "Who is the refugee?"; by organising civic-minded sponsoring for the reconstruction of Frauenkirche, Dresden's largest landmark baroque church, which was destroyed during Allied bombing in February 1945; by popular model competitions; and, last but not least, by having the Danish mail issue a Lego postage stamp.

A fair amount of merchandising has started, with Lego toothbrushes and kids wear: true to Lego style, they are colourful, solid and highly priced.

Marketing was done increasingly through "Lego shops in shops" in department stores or at special counters in toy shops or duty-free shops, where pricing and display were under control. Yet at the same time, there was also a fair amount of Lego discount sales by larger retailers. Perhaps the company became resigned to this, as there was a major market entirely out of its corporate reach: Lego, indestructible as they are, formed a staple of flea markets across the globe, as children sold the bricks which they had outgrown. It should come as a comfort to the good people in Billund that even second-hand Legos regularly fetched good prices. And in clinching the deal, the Lego box did one last pedagogical service to the budding 14-year-old salesman: his entrepreneurial spirits had been encouraged. No small feat for a bunch of coloured plastic bricks.

The Next Two Decades

Around the turn of the millennium, Lego, in trying to diversify widely from clothing to bicycles, had lost its way and abandoned parts of its core business, such as the Duplo stones for small children. The fashionable Star Wars and Harry Potter figurines also did not fit its profile. Annual losses of €160–180 million brought it close to bankruptcy. By 2005, Niels Christiansen as the new CEO and Kjeld Kirk Kristiansen as his deputy and major shareholder returned to its classic designs — Duplo and simplified but highly complex building sets with fewer parts — and thus brought about a turnaround. Lego's offer is now well structured according to age group: 1.5 years, 4 years, 6 years, 9 years, 13 years and 18 years plus. About 78,000 parts are offered in up to 98 colours, in sets with either prescribed building plans or for free imagination. These may contain up to 11,700 parts and are priced up to €700 per box, including for those — probably adults with too much time on their hands — wishing to recreate the Eiffel Tower or a Millennium Falcon. Bestselling thematic series include Lego City, Lego Castles, pirates, locomotives and trains, Technic, the lone ranger, Lego Star Wars and other space themes, historical buildings, the skylines of prominent metropolises (once built, usually kept on display shelves), video games and Lego Mindstorms with programmable robots, a useful educational toy for schoolchildren. With a total staff of 26,000, Lego produces its toys mainly in the Czech Republic and, since 2024, Vietnam, but also in Denmark, Hungary, Mexico, Virginia and Jiaxing (China). With annual sales of €8.6 billion (2023), it is clearly the world's largest toy maker, ahead of Mattel (€4.9 billion) and Hasbro (€4.5 billion), with a brand value estimated at €7.4 billion and profits at €1.3 billion.

As a popular toy maker, Lego has not escaped the usual controversies, such as over copyright, marketing, patent and trademark issues, but also charges that its figurines allegedly perpetuated female stereotypes or displayed violent characters. The use of plastics was reproached, as were its partnerships with Shell and the Daily Mail, which were duly discontinued.

Bibliography

Note: Any links to online sources were valid as of the publication of the first edition, in October 2004. Many of the pages have since been taken down.

Fishman, C. "Why Can't Lego Click?", *Fast Company* 50, September 2001, p. 144.

"Lego company information". http://www.lego.com/info

Uhle, M. *Die Lego Story. Der Stein der Weisen*. Reinbek/Hamburg: Rowohlt, 2000.

Wiencek, H. *The World of Lego Toys*. New York: Harry N. Abrams, 1987.

New Literature, 2nd Edition

Danzer, A. "Lego in der Plastikfalle", *Der Standard*, 26 June 2022.
"Marketing mit Rollenbildern", *Handelsblatt*, 4 December 2016.
"Wie der Krieg ins Kinderzimmer kam", *Bayrischer Rundfunk*, 29 January 2013.

The Magic of Disney

There is little doubt that the magic behind Disney lies with the man himself. Indisputably, the driving force and direction of the company stem from Walt Disney's creative X-factor and his abiding influence. The "Disney Image" is one emanating the realisation of dreams, the perpetual state of childhood and the enchanting lure of escape into a fantastic and happy world of childhood innocence. Behind this surreal world of magical dreams lies the history of a company that is not unlike other successful companies of today. The struggling start experienced by its creator(s) in the early years, the internal disputes that weighed the company down time and time again and the takeovers and financial battles that took place — these were all present throughout the formation of what is now greatly loved and widely known as The Walt Disney Company.

The Beginnings of Magic

Before Walt Disney became the man who opened the creative door to popular, accessible children's entertainment and made it, as such, globally appealing, it is said that he first received such creative inspiration as an ambulance driver during the First World War, often coming across great castles in Europe (Grover, 1997, p. 1). In the years to come, the fruit of such inspiration would present itself as the magnificent imitation castles that one finds in Disneyland these days. Before the internationally renowned icon Mickey Mouse (who curiously enough nearly became Mortimer Mouse[1]) came to dominate the hearts of many, it must be mentioned that Walt started off dealing with a rabbit instead — Oswald the Lucky Rabbit to be exact. Drawing crude cartoon strips for local theatres and sketching advertisements for a barbershop, together with the Oswald and Alice Comedies projects he involved himself with in the early 1920s, comprised Walt's first business ventures, which ultimately failed. However, on hindsight, they served as important stepping stones in the grand scheme of things.

Walt and his older brother, Roy Disney, later became partners and started the Disney Brothers Cartoon Studio in 1923. Here, the starkly different characters came out strongly in the often unsmooth working relationship. Walt was decidedly the more creative, let's-give-it-all-we've-got person, while Roy seemed to provide the business expertise his brother lacked. Roy was in charge of persuading the bankers and investors to lend Walt money but, at the same time, often dissuading Walt from spending money the company managed to receive. Having prudence and extravagance working alongside each other, it was little wonder friction arose between the two brothers. However, it seemed that Walt was the one who called the shots, as the studio later changed its name to Walt Disney Studios in 1926 and later Walt Disney Productions in 1929. Given that, clearly much good came out of this partnership, and the link

[1] Walt Disney had initially wanted to name this 1928 creation "Mortimer". It was his wife who suggested the (more appealing and appropriate) name "Mickey" instead (Grover, 1997, p. 2).

between the two brothers would set the pace for many other alliances that would develop in the future.

> *Partnerships were obviously an integral part of Walt Disney's business strategy … and agreements between Disney and the likes of Exxon, AT&T and General Motors … still contribute thousands annually to the Disney coffers.*
>
> — Grover, 1997, p. 110

The examples in later sections will demonstrate the prowess of partnerships and how they can truly rake in the cash.

The Disney Service Culture

Orlando Disney is an example which the Manchester Business School, University of Manchester, has chosen as a model for emulation. In the school's opinion, "Walt Disney World has achieved an enviable reputation for outstanding service that has made it the premier entertainment centre in the World". Working closely with the Disney Institute, tailored programmes are made available for companies who wish to come and pick up essential business skills. Delegates are promised an in-depth experience on how Disney's service strategy actually functions. The institute provides extensive training in the following areas: quality service, leadership excellence, people management, loyalty, organisational creativity and value chain management.

According to the school,

Leadership Excellence + Cast Excellence
+ Service Excellence = Future Success.

Disney defines its excellence in the ability to accurately empathise with customers as "guestology". This means "to identify their customers through a compass model that focuses on needs, wants, stereotypes and emotions". Both in theory and in practice, the importance of a "service philosophy" is greatly stressed upon. As such, the legacy of Walt and his detailed attention to customer experience lives on even after his death in 1966. Each customer is treated exactly the way Walt would have treated them himself. This is the key to Disney's lasting, enduring appeal. People feel like they are important, apart from the fact that they are simply out there having a good fun, worry-free time.

There is indeed little wonder as to why "the Walt Disney Company is repeatedly hailed as a superior service provider, perhaps the best in the world" (Capodagli and Jackson, 1998, p. 59). Essentially, Walt Disney recognised and had great understanding of his customer base. An example given in Tom Connellan's *Inside the Magic Kingdom: Seven Keys to Disney's Success* demonstrates how successful the company is in understanding and subsequently meeting the needs of potential guests. It is widely known that Disney sees people more as guests and less as customers per se. On the day Disneyland opened, Walt Disney announced the theme park's motto: "At Disneyland, the visitors are our guests." Connellan tells in his book of how a couple at Epcot could not afford to go to France or Italy for their vacation at that time and so, as an almost equally appealing alternative, replaced such an experience with a more inexpensive trip to the Epcot's (The Experimental Prototype Community of Tomorrow) French Pavilion. Of course, they knew it was not the real thing, but as Connellan explained, the experience and illusion of it all provided a sense of real magic that was quite wonderful altogether.

An illustration of how Disney's attention to detail is in fact twofold, i.e., for the park visitor and the employee, is seen in the imprinting of names on the second-storey windows on Main Street of people who contributed to the design, implementation and running of Disneyland. One of the most recently added names is Charles Boyers, who is noted for his famous Disneyland artwork. Not only are Disney's employees appreciated and honoured, but the customer also receives a sense of family warmth and aesthetic value from it all. Another example of Walt Disney's attention to customer satisfaction is demonstrated in the fact that he was adamant that designers take the perspective of young children into account when designing the park. Walt would frequently stoop down while looking at a partially constructed building to consider how smaller people would see things.

The employees at Disney are also trained in team commitment. Besides the not-to-be-taken-for-granted mission statement comprising the company's mission and goals that guide employee vision, it is known that Disney often groups similar people when working on various projects. For example, on a certain movie project, the teammates are all staff who have worked together before. Thus, a solid sense of rapport and effective group dynamics are fostered amongst the teams.

The company also recognises the pointlessness of having a mismanaged, ineffective and rigid hierarchical organisation. As such, "top Disney executives go out of their way to solicit advice from staff members ... frontline people who hear guests' comments and see their reactions". Efforts are thus made to go beyond the strict hierarchical chains of information and, instead, to get direct, and ultimately advantageous, information for those who really need to receive feedback and for those who, in effect, have the powers to make the necessary changes. One sees that the lower-rung staff works together with those higher up in the corporate ladder.

Also, Disney works by a process called "co-locating", where the emphasis is on bringing teams together to work in a central location. At Disney, these "planning centres" have proven to be highly successful, especially when they facilitate brainstorming sessions amongst the staff.

We have seen how Disney's success is strongly factored in by the company's painstaking efforts at providing excellent customer, or rather guest, service. Quite simply, the success of Disney has to do with two chief factors: firstly, a tapping into and a sound understanding of the psyches of people — that, ultimately, everyone wants to have a good time; secondly, utilising the above knowledge to its fullest potential to extend it in an all-encompassing reach to all the possible markets, as we will see in later sections. In effect, it attempts to meet the demands and wishes of the people in every way: physically (thrill rides), emotionally (happy feelings and a sense of return to normal irretrievable childhood innocence and memories) and socially (family unit and strengthened ties, as well as friendships).

More Than Just Child's Play

The Disney Company is certainly more than just a happy place for people to visit. Behind the wondrous experiences, which the company offers via its various resort lands, the Disney Company is primarily a place of business. The people behind the company are foremost there to see that profits are made and business is booming. The company, unlike what most of its customers are inclined to assume, represents more than Saturday morning cartoons and the Disneyland theme parks. To say the least, takeovers and acquisitions are not the kind of things that make up a happy state of affairs (at any rate, surely not for those who are at the losing end of the deal). Michael Eisner, who took over the leadership of the company in 1984 until 2005, continued in a different manner from Walt Disney by maintaining that an effective partnership requires "… nurturing, hand-holding, head-cracking, and once-in-a-while arm-twisting".

Besides the already established four destination resorts in the U.S., Japan and France, a fifth addition to the group of successful resorts is Hong Kong Disneyland, which, "subject to the Government's completion of reclamation and infrastructure by specified target dates", opened in late 2005. However, the company's business is reaching ever further, and it has diversified into many other profitable organisations since.

Anaheim Sports, Inc., operates the Walt Disney Company's two professional sports franchises, Major League Baseball's Anaheim Angels and the National Hockey League's Mighty Ducks of Anaheim. The Walt Disney Internet Group (WDIG) provides a platform where Disney operates some of the more highly visited internet properties, including ABCNEWS.com, Disney.com and ESPN.com. Through Disney Auctions, the Internet Group, in partnership with eBay, offers consumers the opportunity to purchase authentic Disney memorabilia sourced directly from business units of the Company. Disney is also working hand-in-hand with MSN to provide comparable internet services at affordable prices to the entire family, with unlimited dial-up service, Disney Games, smart junk-mail filters and powerful parental controls. All of this is, of course, in line with Disney's wholesome family-oriented image.

The Disney Mobile and Phone Center, working jointly with Motorola, has come up with a range of themed phones and thus entered competitively into the profitable handphone market with its own unique brand of Disney character graphics, ringtones, logos, animations and games. There is now even a Disney Visa Card from Bank One, where members are provided full Visa platinum benefits and no annual fee. A scheme was also put in place allowing a customer to earn one Disney Dream Reward Dollar^{SM} for every hundred dollars in net purchases, up to a maximum of 750 Disney Dream Reward Dollars^{SM} on \$75,000 in net purchases in a calendar year. Linking this with their own Disney Cruise Line® and Disney Vacations, one also pays zero interest for six months on cruise packages or ticket-inclusive Disney vacation packages when booking through the Walt Disney Travel Company and charging the package to the Visa card prior to arrival.

Disney's Studio Entertainment arm comprises the following: Walt Disney Feature Animation, Walt Disney Television Animation,

Walt Disney Pictures, Touchstone Pictures, Miramax, Giant Screen, Buena Vista Theatrical Group, Buena Vista International, Buena Vista Home Entertainment — Domestic/International and the Buena Vista Music Group. It would surely be striking to many "lay persons" not in the media loop to realise that the company has dealings with movies such as *The Rookie*, *The Sixth Sense*, *In the Bedroom* and *Gangs of New York*, apart from the obvious Disney productions such as *Lilo & Stitch* and *Treasure Planet*, via all the above groups involved.

Disney's longstanding relationship with the media conglomerate American Broadcasting Corporation (ABC) is, however, well known. In the early years, ABC invested $500,000 outright and guaranteed a $4.5 million loan in order to purchase 34.5% of Disneyland (opened 17 July 1955) and a commitment from Walt to produce a regular TV show. The power relations reversed later when, in the mid-1990s, Disney acquired Capital Cities/ABC for $19 billion. With ABC News, ABC Sports, ABC Daytime, ABC Kids and ABC Radio underpinning the media network as such, Disney's overall stand in the media industry strengthened further. Notably, "Disney is the #2 media conglomerate in the world", only behind AOL Time Warner. Competition is tough though, with the likes of AOL Time Warner, Viacom and NBC being the top competitors in the field.

The hugely popular EPSN — together with ESPN2 (sporting events and news), ESPN Classic (historical sports footage) and ESPNEWS (24-hour news and information) — that reach more than 87 million U.S. homes and also another 119 million homes worldwide with its ESPN International unit — is clear evidence of what some might call the Disney Phenomenon, that Disney has truly diversified from funny cartoons with its mounting stakes over various entertainment groups. In addition, ESPN creates content for TV and radio and operates one of the most popular sports sites on the internet. ESPN has also lent its name to a magazine and a chain of eight sports-themed restaurants. Disney's 80% stake in ESPN is indeed strengthening its financial standing.

Equally important to note is that Disney manages an extensive range of consumer products as well. Disney Licensing consists of Disney Toys, Disney Softlines (apparel and accessories) and Disney Hardlines (packaged goods, stationery, home furnishings and consumer electronics). The popular products comprise Disney juices developed with the Minute Maid division of The Coca-Cola Company, cereals, two-way radios and 2.4 GHz cordless telephones manufactured and distributed by Motorola, Inc, all of which have varying levels of success upon their entries into the North America, Latin America, Mexico, U.K. and Japanese markets. Under the direct-to-retail model, Disney Consumer Products licenses its characters and brands to select retailers globally, rather than to third-party manufacturers and distributors. Retailers will source and manufacture products directly, for sale exclusively through all channels of their retail outlets. This, in turn, leads us to Disney's entrance into the European market. Characteristically, German and U.K. operations were driven by merchandise licensing while French and Italian operations by book and magazine licensing (Bartlett and Ghoshal, 2000). In Europe, Disney's direct-to-retail agreement with Carrefour, the largest retailer in Europe, resulted in the launch of an exclusive line of children's clothing and accessories at Carrefour stores in 30 countries. Agreements with major retailers, including H&M, C&A and Tesco, also resulted in the placement of exclusive Disney product lines in key European markets. Disney Publishing, the world's largest children's publisher with books and magazines, sells 345 million copies annually. Publishing is also responsible for the highly successful publications like Eoin Colfer's hit *Artemis Fowl: The Arctic Incident* — the sequel to the best-selling children's thriller *Artemis Fowl*, and *W.i.t.c.h.*, a monthly comic magazine developed in Milan, Italy, which claims to be the no. 1 children's magazine title in Germany, France, Italy, Benelux and the Nordic markets.

The above shows the impressive range of services provided by Disney. On the other hand, unlike in any one of Disney's own fairytales, not everything is perfect. There is increasing discontent and less agreement amongst shareholders within the Disney Group. Of late, ABC has suffered from weak ratings, and its theme parks have been receiving fewer international visitors. Michael Eisner, the man who took over at the helms of the company in 1984 and who pretty much sees himself as a populist communicator to be regarded as the rightful heir to Uncle Walt, ascribes the flounder, as do operators, to mainly external factors beyond the group's control: 11 September 2001, attacks that hit tourist traffic; ABC suffering from global advertising downturn; and the emergence of a host of rival studios in the animation business. DreamWorks, Warner Bros and Nickelodeon serve as tough competition to Disney, portioning off terrain once previously exclusive to Disney. The Disney theme parks also face the rivals of Legoland, Magic Mountain and Knotts Berry Farm. As one media insider succinctly and accurately put it, "They [Disney] no longer own the kids demographic". Juxtaposing all the above factors against the lack of confidence by U.S. consumers and security concerns of travellers effectively puts Disney in an unfavourable position as such.

Against professional opinion, Eisner, according to one board member, maintains that the purchase of ABC and the integration of ESPN sports businesses have always been the right strategic move, despite disappointing downturns. There is confidence in the management, despite economic downturns, with people having less disposable income during times of recession, that ultimately, "America and Americans always bounce back" and that "people hardly ever actually cancel their Disney vacations ... they only defer them until the time is right". There is great belief amongst the Disney management in the lasting attractivity and enduring power of the Disney brand. Recent laws passed also strengthen the safeguards with which the company holds to protect her ageing brand name and products by upholding "lengthier copyrights protecting the profits of songs, books and cartoon characters". Michael Eisner wrote, "Frankly, with the Disney brand and the great assets of our company, it isn't easy to fail. It's much easier to succeed. And we will". Shareholders' main concern, however, is not so much the potential earnings capacity of Disney's assets as whether it has been, as promised, managed effectively to deliver growth and shareholder value. Facing increasingly intense competition in the areas of media networks and theme parks, the Disney Company indeed has much to live up to. Maintaining its unrivalled position as a service provider, therefore, is one of the key areas that, if continued excellence is pursued, will ensure that The Disney Company remains a magic kingdom.

The Next Two Decades: Times of War and Peace in the Magic Kingdom

Unfortunately, the management stories of Hollywood studios are one of outsized egos, abuse, greed, unending intrigues and well-publicised conflicts. The House of the Mouse is no exception to the rule. Michael Eisner (1984–2005), who originally as CEO had been celebrated as the saviour of Disney, later picked public fights with his erstwhile friend Jeffrey Katzenberg, the head of Disney's animation, and Steve Jobs, who ran the Pixar animation studio. For a company like Disney, successful animation was and remains the engine driving merchandising and theme park attendance. Eisner, who apparently perceived Katzenberg as a rival, had him fired just after the success of "Lion King". His successor, Michael Opitz, did not fare better and was dismissed after only 14 months. Opitz sued and received a severance pay of $140 million. Katzenberg, with $280 million, obtained twice the amount, which allowed him to set up his own "Dream Works Animation", which turned out to become Disney's toughest competitor. Roy E. Disney, then aged 73, son and nephew of the two founders, then tried to get rid of

Eisner and, in a memo titled "Save Disney", blamed him for underperforming theme parks, the brain drain of talent, the squandering of Disney's assets through reckless spending on Euro-Disney near Paris, overprized forays into the internet and the acquisition of Fox Family cable networks, costing the company $1 billion each, his refusal to plan his succession and having turned Disney into a soul-less conglomerate chasing a fast buck. It was "time for new blood" concluded Disney. But since he held only 1% of shares, it was he who lost his position, as Eisner managed to manipulate his board skilfully and purge potential rivals in time. In the end, after a few box office flops, he was made to resign in September 2005, and he had the headquarters building, the House of the Mouse, in Burbank named after him.

His successor and previous deputy, Robert Iger, steered Disney into steadier waters. Iger had bought Steve Jobs graphics shop and animation studio Pixar for Disney. In 2007, he purchased "Image Movers" and in 2012 "Maker Studios" for $500 million. In 2009, he bought the comics publisher Marvel for $4.3 billion, and in 2012 the movie maker Lucasfilm for $4.05 billion. In 2019, he followed them up with the major acquisition of 21st Century Fox for $71.3 billion — without however Fox Broadcasting Network, including Fox News. Although there were subscriber losses in the TV industry in general, ABC remained stable, while the Disney streaming services, including Disney itself, the videos of Hulu LLC and the sports channel ESPN+ with 221 million subscribers, had bypassed Netflix.

Charges of politically correct censorship of Disney productions emerged after 2011, when Laurene Powell Jobs inherited her late husband's Steve Jobs Disney shares (acquired when selling his Pixar studios in 2006 to Disney), which made her Disney's largest individual shareholder by far — a position which she used to push her left-wing cultural and political agenda, including LGBTQ issues, thus turning Walt Disney into "Woke Disney", quite at variance with its erstwhile traditional family and capitalistic values. Massive losses of subscribers to Disney+ and its streaming offers and box office flops followed.

The COVID-19 pandemic hit Disney hard in 2020: theme parks had to be closed, films were held back for the lack of cinema audiences, and Disney Cruise Lines had to stop; 32,000 staffers — mostly part-timers in resorts, in animation parks and on the ships — were dismissed out of a total of 220,000. Except for the year 2020, Iger produced a steady growth of turnover, from $27 billion (2003) to $83 billion (2023), and profits, from $1.3 billion (2003) to $12.2 billion (2023). After 15 years at the helm of Disney, Iger retired from the Magic Kingdom and made way for his successor, Bob Chapek. Chapek, however, survived in the job only for 11 months until November 2022, when he was fired for poor performance and unfortunate decisions. Thus, Robert Iger was recalled from retirement as the new-old CEO to general relief.

Bibliography

Bartlett, C. A. and Ghoshal, S. *Transnational Management: Text, Cases, and Readings in Cross-border Management*. 3rd ed. Boston: Irwin/McGraw-Hill, 2000.

Capodagli, B. and Jackson, L. *The Disney Way: Harnessing the Magic of Disney in your Organization*. New York: McGraw-Hill, 1998.

Connellan, T. *Inside the Magic Kingdom: Seven Keys to Disney's Success*. Austin, Texas: Bard Press, 1997.

Grover, R. *The Disney Touch: Disney, ABC & the Quest for the World's Greatest Media Empire*. Revised ed. New York: McGraw-Hill, 1997.

Parkes, C., Grimes, C. and Burt, T. "The Fairytale may end in tears as Eisner's Magic Kingdom shows signs of crumbling", *Financial Times*, 24 September 2002.

New Literature, 2nd Edition

Bohas, A. *The Political Economy of Disney. The Cultural Capitalism of Hollywood*. London: Palgrave Macmillan, 2018.

Eisner, M. D. *Work in Progress. Risking Failure, Surviving Success*. New York: Random House, 1998.

Eisner, M. D. *Working Together. Why Great Partnerships Succeed*. New York: Harper, 2010.

"How to do CEO succession planning right and how to do it wrong. Starbucks learnt from a big mistake, but it seems Disney hasn't", *Bloomberg News*, 30 March 2017.

Iger, R. *The Ride of a Lifetime. Lessons Learnt From 15 Years as CEO of the Walt Disney Company*. New York: Random House, 2019.

Klug, L. "Who said Jews run Hollywood?", *The Times of Israel*, 23 June 2016.

Masters, K. "The Epic Disney Blowup of 1994: Eisner, Katzenberg and Opitz 20 Years Later", *The Hollywood Reporter*, 9 April 2014.

McCarthy, M. "War of Words Erupts at Disney", *USA Today*, 12 February 2003.

"Michael Eisner on Former Disney Colleagues, Rivals and Bob Iger's Successor", *The Hollywood Reporter*, 27 July 2016.

Stewart, J. B. *Disney War*. New York: Simon & Schuster, 2005.

Stewart, J. B. "Behind the Scenes at Disney as it Purged a Favorite son", *The New York Times*, 7 April 2016.

von Storch, B. "Weltherrschaft made by Disney", *Junge Freiheit*, 6 September 2024.

www.ingramcontent.com/pod-product-compliance
Lightning Source LLC
Chambersburg PA
CBHW061235220326
41599CB00028B/5434